AI's Take on Money, Volume I

AI's Take on Money, Volume 1

Sandy Y. Greenleaf

Published by Sandy Y. Greenleaf, 2024.

While every precaution has been taken in the preparation of this book, the publisher assumes no responsibility for errors or omissions, or for damages resulting from the use of the information contained herein.

AI'S TAKE ON MONEY, VOLUME I

First edition. March 29, 2024.

Copyright © 2024 Sandy Y. Greenleaf.

ISBN: 979-8224773114

Written by Sandy Y. Greenleaf.

Also by Sandy Y. Greenleaf

AI's Take on Money
AI's Take on Money, Volume I

Standalone
AI's Take on Personal Growth
AI's Take on Relationships

Table of Contents

Preface

Welcome to "AI's Take on Money," a groundbreaking book that explores the complex world of personal finance through the unique lens of artificial intelligence. As you embark on this journey, prepare to challenge your assumptions, expand your knowledge, and gain valuable insights that will empower you to make informed financial decisions.

In today's rapidly evolving world, money plays a crucial role in shaping our lives and securing our futures. However, navigating the labyrinth of financial concepts, strategies, and tools can be overwhelming, especially for those without a background in finance. This book aims to bridge that gap by presenting a comprehensive, yet accessible guide to understanding and managing money in the modern era.

What sets this book apart is its unique perspective, as the majority of the content has been generated by a sophisticated AI system. By leveraging the vast knowledge and analytical capabilities of AI, we can explore financial topics with unprecedented depth and clarity, uncovering insights that may have been overlooked by traditional approaches.

It is important to note that while AI offers a powerful tool for understanding and analyzing financial concepts, it is not infallible. Like any technology, AI has its limitations and may be subject to biases or errors. Throughout the book, I have made a concerted effort to curate the AI-generated content, asking the right questions and providing human oversight to ensure accuracy and relevance. However, as with any information source, readers should approach the content with a critical eye and seek additional guidance when making significant financial decisions.

As the author and curator of this book, my role has been to guide the AI's exploration of financial topics, shaping the narrative and ensuring that the content remains accessible and engaging for a general audience. My mission statement, "Democratizing knowledge for the betterment of human lives," has been the driving force behind this project. By harnessing the power of AI to demystify complex financial concepts, I hope to empower readers from all walks of life to take control of their financial futures.

Throughout the book, you will find a wealth of information covering various aspects of personal finance, from the fundamentals of money management to more advanced topics like investing and retirement planning. Each chapter builds upon the previous ones, creating a logical flow that will guide you through the essential concepts and strategies you need to know.

Whether you are just starting your financial journey or looking to refine your existing knowledge, "AI's Take on Money" offers a fresh perspective and practical insights that will help you navigate the ever-changing landscape of personal finance. So, let's dive in and explore the exciting world of money through the eyes of AI, together.

Chapter 1: Understanding the Fundamentals of Money

Money is a concept that permeates every aspect of our lives, from the day-to-day transactions we make to the long-term financial goals we set for ourselves. It is a powerful tool that shapes our society, influences our decisions, and determines our quality of life. Yet, despite its ubiquity, many people struggle to grasp the fundamental principles that govern money and its role in the economy.

In this chapter, we will embark on a journey to explore the basics of money, delving into its history, evolution, and the various forms it has taken over time. We will examine how money emerged from ancient barter systems and trace its development through the rise of precious metals, the introduction of paper currency, and the advent of digital transactions.

As we unravel the mysteries of money, we will discover the key functions it serves in our economy, acting as a medium of exchange, a unit of account, and a store of value. We will explore the characteristics that make money an effective tool for facilitating trade and enabling economic growth, such as its divisibility, portability, and durability.

Furthermore, we will investigate the complex relationship between money and society, examining how it shapes human behavior, influences power dynamics, and contributes to economic inequality. By understanding the psychological and social aspects of money, we can gain valuable insights into our own financial habits and make more informed decisions about how we earn, save, and spend our resources.

Throughout this chapter, we will lay the groundwork for the rest of the book, establishing a solid foundation of knowledge that will empower you to navigate the complex world of personal finance with confidence and clarity. Whether you are a student, a working professional, or a retiree, understanding the fundamentals of money is an essential step towards achieving your financial goals and securing a brighter future for yourself and your loved ones.

So, let us embark on this exciting journey together, as we uncover the secrets of money and learn how to harness its power to create a life of abundance, security, and prosperity.

Section 1: The History and Evolution of Money

Imagine a world without money. How would you buy your daily essentials, like food and clothes? How would you pay for a place to live or travel from one place to another? In today's world, it's hard to picture life without this essential tool that we often take for granted. But have you ever wondered how money came to be and how it has evolved over time?

The history of money is a fascinating journey that spans thousands of years, from ancient civilizations to the modern digital age. It's a story of innovation, adaptation, and the ever-changing needs of human societies. Money has taken many forms throughout history, from cowrie shells and cattle to gold coins and paper currency, each reflecting the values and challenges of its time.

In this section, we'll embark on a captivating exploration of the origins and development of money. We'll trace its roots back to the early days of barter and trade, and discover how the limitations of these systems gave rise to the first forms of currency. As we journey through time, we'll witness the birth of the gold standard and its eventual replacement by government-backed fiat currencies. We'll also examine the transformative impact of technology on money, from the rise of digital payments to the emergence of cryptocurrencies.

But the story of money is more than just a historical account; it's a reflection of human ingenuity, power struggles, and the constant pursuit of efficiency and convenience. By understanding the evolution of money, we gain a deeper appreciation for its role in shaping our economies, societies, and individual lives.

So, let's dive into the rich tapestry of monetary history and uncover the fascinating story behind the coins in your pocket and the numbers in your bank account. Get ready to discover how money has evolved from ancient times to the present day, and how it continues to shape our world in ways we may not even realize.

Subsection 1.1: Barter Systems and the Emergence of Currency

In the early days of human civilization, long before the concept of money as we know it today, people relied on barter to exchange goods and services. Barter is a system of direct exchange, where individuals trade one item or service for another without the use of a common medium of exchange. For example, a farmer who had a surplus of wheat might trade some of it with a fisherman in exchange for a portion of their catch.

While barter systems allowed for the exchange of goods and services, they had several inherent limitations. One of the primary drawbacks was the need for a "double coincidence of wants," meaning that both parties in the exchange had to have something the other desired. If the farmer needed tools but the blacksmith didn't need wheat, the trade could not take place. This limitation made it difficult to find suitable trading partners and hindered the efficiency of trade.

Another challenge with barter systems was the lack of a common measure of value. It was difficult to determine the relative worth of different goods and services, leading to complex negotiations and subjective valuations. For instance, how many bushels of wheat should be traded for a cow? The absence of a standardized unit of account made it challenging to compare the value of dissimilar items and establish fair exchange rates.

As societies grew and trade expanded beyond local communities, the limitations of barter became increasingly apparent. The need for a more efficient and convenient means of exchange led to the emergence of early forms of currency. One of the first examples of primitive money was the use of commodities, such as livestock, shells, beads, or salt, which had intrinsic value and were widely accepted as a medium of exchange.

Over time, these commodity currencies evolved into more standardized forms, such as metal coins. The use of precious metals, like gold and silver, as currency offered several advantages over barter and commodity money. Metals were durable, portable, and could be divided into smaller units, making them suitable for a wide range of transactions. The intrinsic value of these metals also provided a relatively stable store of value, allowing individuals to accumulate wealth and facilitating long-distance trade.

The emergence of currency marked a significant milestone in the history of money, overcoming the limitations of barter and paving the way for more complex economic systems. As societies continued to evolve, so did the forms and functions of money, adapting to the changing needs and challenges of human civilization.

Subsection 1.2: The Gold Standard and the Shift to Fiat Currency

As early forms of currency evolved, precious metals like gold and silver emerged as the preferred medium of exchange due to their inherent value, durability, and portability. The gold standard, a monetary system in which the value of a country's currency is directly linked to a fixed quantity of gold, became the dominant financial framework in the late 19th and early 20th centuries.

Under the gold standard, governments guaranteed the conversion of paper money into a predetermined amount of gold. This system provided stability and confidence in the value of currency, as it was backed by a tangible and scarce resource. The gold standard also facilitated international trade by establishing a common currency that could be used across borders, reducing the need for complex exchange rate calculations.

However, the gold standard had its limitations. The supply of gold was finite, and the discovery of new gold reserves could lead to inflation. Conversely, a shortage of gold could result in deflation and economic stagnation. Governments found it increasingly difficult to maintain the gold standard during times of economic crisis or war, as they needed more flexibility in monetary policy to stimulate growth and finance military expenses.

The Great Depression of the 1930s exposed the weaknesses of the gold standard, as countries struggled to maintain the convertibility of their currencies while facing mounting economic challenges. Many nations abandoned the gold standard to regain control over their monetary policy and stimulate their economies through increased government spending and lower interest rates.

The shift away from the gold standard paved the way for the rise of fiat currency, which is not backed by a physical commodity but rather by the trust and credibility of the issuing government. Fiat money derives its value from the stability and strength of the issuing country's economy and the faith that people have in its currency.

The transition to fiat currency gave governments greater flexibility in managing their economies, as they could now control the money supply and interest rates to promote growth and stability. However, this flexibility also came with the risk of inflation if governments printed too much money or failed to manage their economies responsibly.

The shift from the gold standard to fiat currency marked a significant milestone in the history of money, reflecting the changing needs and challenges of modern economies. While the gold standard provided stability and confidence, the move to fiat currency offered greater flexibility and control over monetary policy, enabling governments to respond more effectively to economic crises and promote growth in an increasingly complex and interconnected world.

Subsection 1.3: The Digital Age and the Future of Money

The advent of the digital age has brought about a profound transformation in the way we perceive, use, and interact with money. The rapid advancement of technology has not only altered the form and function of money but has also paved the way for innovative financial services and payment systems that have revolutionized the global economy.

One of the most significant developments in the digital age has been the rise of electronic payment systems. The proliferation of credit cards, debit cards, and online payment platforms has made it easier and more convenient for people to conduct transactions without the need for physical cash. The growth of e-commerce has further accelerated this trend, with millions of people around the world using digital payment methods to purchase goods and services online.

The emergence of mobile technology has also had a profound impact on the way we use money. The widespread adoption of smartphones has given rise to mobile banking and payment apps, allowing people to manage their finances and make transactions on the go. Mobile payment systems, such as Apple Pay and Google Wallet, have made it possible for people to make purchases using their smartphones, eliminating the need for cash or cards.

In recent years, the rise of cryptocurrencies has further pushed the boundaries of digital money. Cryptocurrencies, such as Bitcoin and Ethereum, are decentralized digital currencies that operate independently of traditional financial institutions. These currencies use complex cryptographic algorithms to secure transactions and prevent fraud, offering a new level of security and privacy in the digital age.

The growth of cryptocurrencies has sparked a global debate about the future of money and the role of traditional financial institutions. Some experts believe that cryptocurrencies have the potential to revolutionize the global financial system, providing a more efficient, secure, and accessible way to store and transfer value. Others, however, have raised concerns about the volatility and lack of regulation in the cryptocurrency market.

Looking to the future, it is clear that technology will continue to shape the evolution of money. The rise of blockchain technology, which underlies cryptocurrencies, has the potential to transform the way we record and verify transactions, creating a more transparent and secure financial system.

The growth of artificial intelligence and machine learning could also lead to the development of more sophisticated financial services and tools, such as personalized investment advice and automated trading systems.

As the digital age continues to unfold, it is likely that we will see even more innovative and disruptive technologies emerge in the world of money. From mobile payments to cryptocurrencies and beyond, the future of money is likely to be shaped by the rapid pace of technological change and the evolving needs of a global, digital economy. As individuals and societies, it is important that we stay informed and adaptable, embracing the opportunities and challenges that the digital age presents while also being mindful of the potential risks and unintended consequences.

Summary: The Enduring Legacy of Money's Evolution

Throughout history, money has undergone a remarkable transformation, adapting to the changing needs and complexities of human societies. From the early days of barter to the rise of digital currencies, the evolution of money reflects the ingenuity, challenges, and aspirations of civilizations across time.

The limitations of barter systems, such as the need for a double coincidence of wants and the lack of a common measure of value, paved the way for the emergence of early forms of currency. Commodities like shells and beads, and later, precious metals, served as a more efficient and standardized means of exchange, facilitating trade and economic growth.

The gold standard, which linked the value of currencies to a fixed quantity of gold, provided stability and confidence in the monetary system for a time. However, the inherent limitations of the gold standard, combined with the economic challenges of the 20th century, led to its eventual abandonment in favor of fiat currencies, which derive their value from the trust and credibility of the issuing government.

In recent decades, the digital age has brought about a profound transformation in the way we perceive and use money. The rise of electronic payment systems, mobile banking, and cryptocurrencies has revolutionized the financial landscape, offering new levels of convenience, security, and accessibility.

As we look to the future, it is clear that the evolution of money is far from over. The rapid pace of technological change, coupled with the evolving needs of a global economy, will undoubtedly shape the future of money in ways we can only begin to imagine. From blockchain technology to artificial intelligence, the possibilities are endless, and the implications for individuals, businesses, and societies are profound.

The history of money is a testament to human resilience, adaptability, and the enduring quest for progress. By understanding the past and embracing the present, we can better navigate the challenges and opportunities that lie ahead, and continue to shape the future of money in a way that benefits all of humanity. As we move forward, let us remember the lessons of history and strive to create a financial system that is more inclusive, transparent, and equitable for all.

Section 2: The Functions and Characteristics of Money

Imagine a world without money. How would you buy your daily necessities, save for the future, or measure the value of goods and services? Money plays a crucial role in our lives and the economy as a whole, serving as the lifeblood that keeps the financial system functioning smoothly. But have you ever stopped to think about what money really is and how it works?

In this section, we'll dive deep into the fundamental functions and characteristics of money, exploring its multifaceted nature and the ways in which it shapes our economic interactions. We'll uncover the secrets behind money's ability to facilitate transactions, store value, and provide a common measure of worth. By understanding these essential aspects of money, you'll gain a deeper appreciation for its importance and the ways in which it impacts your daily life and financial decisions.

As we embark on this journey, we'll discover that money is more than just a piece of paper or a number in your bank account. It's a powerful tool that has evolved over time to meet the changing needs of societies and economies. From ancient barter systems to modern digital currencies, money has undergone a remarkable transformation, adapting to the ever-shifting landscape of human exchange.

So, whether you're a seasoned financial expert or simply curious about the inner workings of the economy, this section will provide you with a comprehensive understanding of the functions and characteristics of money. Get ready to unravel the mysteries of this essential component of our lives and discover how it shapes the world around us. Let's dive in and explore the fascinating world of money together!

Subsection 2.1: Money as a Medium of Exchange

Picture a world without money, where people trade goods and services directly with one another. In this world, if you're a baker who needs a new pair of shoes, you'd have to find a shoemaker who happens to want bread in exchange. This is the essence of a barter system, where individuals trade their goods or services directly for other goods or services.

While bartering may work on a small scale, it quickly becomes impractical in a complex economy. The baker might spend hours or even days searching for a shoemaker who wants bread, and even then, they'd need to negotiate how many loaves of bread are worth a pair of shoes. This is where money comes in as a game-changer.

Money serves as a medium of exchange, a universally accepted item that can be used to purchase goods and services. Instead of directly trading bread for shoes, the baker can sell their bread to anyone who wants it and receive money in return. They can then use that money to buy shoes from the shoemaker, who in turn can use the money to purchase whatever they need.

This simple concept revolutionizes the way we trade. Money eliminates the need for a coincidence of wants, where both parties must have exactly what the other desires. It allows for specialization, as people can focus on producing what they're best at and then use the money they earn to buy everything else they need.

Moreover, money makes transactions much more efficient. Instead of haggling over the value of goods in a barter system, prices can be set in terms of the monetary unit, making it easy to compare the relative value of different items. This price system allows for quick and straightforward transactions, reducing the time and effort required to trade.

In essence, money acts as a lubricant for the economy, facilitating the exchange of goods and services and enabling a more complex and efficient system of trade. It's no wonder that money has been a central part of human civilization for thousands of years, evolving from shells and beads to coins, paper currency, and now digital transactions.

As we delve deeper into the world of personal finance, understanding money's role as a medium of exchange is crucial. It underpins the very foundation of our economic interactions and shapes the way we earn, spend, and save. By grasping this fundamental concept, you'll be better equipped to navigate the complexities of money management and make informed financial decisions.

Subsection 2.2: Money as a Unit of Account

Imagine you're at a local market, browsing through the various stalls and shops. You come across a vendor selling handcrafted pottery, with prices listed next to each item. One beautiful vase catches your eye, and you see that it's priced at $50. Instantly, you understand the value of the vase in relation to other goods and services available in the market and beyond.

This is the power of money as a unit of account. In addition to serving as a medium of exchange, money also functions as a standard measure of value, allowing us to assign prices to goods and services and compare their worth in a consistent and easily understandable way.

Before the advent of money, determining the value of goods and services was a much more complex and subjective process. In a barter system, the value of an item would depend on the specific needs and desires of the trading parties. For example, a farmer might consider a sack of potatoes to be more valuable than a woven basket, while a weaver might have the opposite perspective. This subjectivity made it difficult to establish a clear and consistent sense of value across a society.

With the introduction of money, however, a common unit of measurement emerged. By assigning a monetary value to each good or service, it became possible to compare their worth objectively. This is because money acts as a numeraire, a basic standard by which the value of all other goods and services can be measured.

Having a standardized unit of account brings numerous benefits to an economy. It allows for the easy comparison of prices, helping consumers make informed decisions about where to allocate their resources. It also enables businesses to set prices for their products and services, track their financial performance, and make strategic decisions based on a clear understanding of their revenues and expenses.

Moreover, a common unit of account facilitates economic analysis and planning on a larger scale. Governments, policymakers, and economists rely on monetary measures to assess the health and growth of an economy, set fiscal and monetary policies, and make projections about future economic trends.

In the realm of personal finance, understanding money's role as a unit of account is crucial for making sound financial decisions. By recognizing the value of goods and services in monetary terms, you can create a budget, track your spending, and make informed choices about how to allocate your income. This awareness also helps you evaluate the costs and benefits of different financial options, such as loans, investments, and purchases, enabling you to make decisions that align with your goals and values.

As you navigate your financial journey, keep in mind that money's function as a unit of account is a fundamental pillar of the modern economy. By embracing this concept and using it to guide your financial choices, you'll be better equipped to make informed decisions, set clear goals, and achieve long-term financial success.

Subsection 2.3: Money as a Store of Value

Imagine you've been working hard for months, diligently saving a portion of your income. As you watch your bank account grow, you're not just accumulating numbers on a screen – you're storing value for the future. This is one of the key functions of money: its ability to serve as a store of value, allowing you to preserve your wealth over time.

In the past, people used various items as stores of value, such as precious metals, gems, or even livestock. However, these physical assets had limitations. They could be difficult to transport, divide, or protect from theft or damage. The introduction of money as a store of value revolutionized the way people could save and accumulate wealth.

When you hold money, whether in the form of cash or in a savings account, you're essentially storing purchasing power for later use. This means that you can defer consumption, choosing to save your money now and spend it at a later date. This ability to store value is crucial for financial planning, as it allows you to save for short-term goals like a vacation or long-term objectives like retirement.

One of the key advantages of money as a store of value is its liquidity. Unlike physical assets that may take time to sell or convert into cash, money can be easily exchanged for goods and services whenever you need it. This liquidity makes money a convenient and reliable store of value, as you can access your wealth quickly and easily.

However, it's important to note that the value of money can fluctuate over time due to inflation. Inflation is the gradual increase in the prices of goods and services, which erodes the purchasing power of money. For example, if you save $100 today and the annual inflation rate is 2%, that same $100 will buy fewer goods and services a year from now. To combat inflation, it's essential to consider investment strategies that can help your money grow and maintain its value over time.

Despite the challenges posed by inflation, money remains an essential store of value in the modern economy. It allows individuals to save, plan for the future, and make informed financial decisions. Understanding how money functions as a store of value is crucial for effective money management and long-term financial success.

As you navigate your personal finance journey, remember that saving money is not just about accumulating wealth – it's about storing value for the future. By making smart financial choices and using money effectively as a store of value, you can build a strong foundation for your financial well-being and achieve your long-term goals.

Subsection 2.4: The Importance of Money's Divisibility, Portability, and Durability

Imagine you're at a store, ready to make a purchase. You reach into your wallet and pull out a crisp, clean bill. You hand it to the cashier, who swiftly provides you with change. The transaction is smooth, efficient, and hassle-free. Have you ever stopped to consider what makes this process so seamless? It's the essential characteristics of money: divisibility, portability, and durability.

Divisibility is a crucial feature of money that allows it to be easily divided into smaller units. This characteristic enables transactions of various sizes and facilitates the exchange of goods and services. Without divisibility, making change or purchasing items of different values would be a daunting task. Imagine trying to buy a candy bar with a gold bar – it would be impractical and inefficient. Money, on the other hand, can be divided into smaller denominations, such as coins or bills, making it convenient for everyday transactions.

Portability is another essential characteristic of money. It refers to the ease with which money can be carried and transported. In the past, people used various items as currency, such as livestock or heavy metals, which were often cumbersome and difficult to move around. The development of lighter, more compact forms of money, such as paper currency and coins, revolutionized trade and commerce. Today, with the advent of digital transactions and mobile payments, money has become even more portable, allowing individuals to carry and transfer large sums of money with just a few clicks on their smartphones.

Durability is the third essential characteristic of money. For money to function effectively as a medium of exchange and a store of value, it must be able to withstand the wear and tear of daily use. Imagine if your bills disintegrated after a few transactions or your coins crumbled in your pocket. The durability of modern currency, achieved through the use of high-quality materials and advanced printing techniques, ensures that money can be used repeatedly without losing its value or functionality. This durability also contributes to money's ability to serve as a reliable store of value over time.

The combination of divisibility, portability, and durability makes money a practical and functional tool for economic transactions. These characteristics have evolved throughout history, from the use of shells and beads to the development of paper money and digital currencies. As society continues to advance, the forms and characteristics of money may change, but the importance of these essential attributes will remain.

Understanding the significance of money's divisibility, portability, and durability is crucial for navigating the world of personal finance. By recognizing these characteristics, you can make informed decisions about how to manage your money effectively. Whether you're making everyday purchases, saving for the future, or investing in assets, the practical features of money play a vital role in facilitating your financial transactions and ensuring the stability of your wealth over time.

As you continue to explore the fascinating world of money and its role in your life, keep in mind the importance of these essential characteristics. Embrace the convenience and flexibility that divisibility, portability, and durability provide, and use this knowledge to make smart financial choices that support your goals and aspirations.

Summary: Embracing Money's Multifaceted Nature for Financial Success

Throughout this section, we've explored the fundamental functions and characteristics of money, uncovering its multifaceted nature and the crucial roles it plays in our lives and the economy as a whole. We've seen how money serves as a medium of exchange, facilitating transactions and enabling the smooth flow of goods and services. As a unit of account, money provides a common measure of value, allowing us to compare the worth of different items and make informed financial decisions. Moreover, money acts as a store of value, preserving our purchasing power over time and providing a means to save and accumulate wealth.

Beyond these core functions, we've also examined the essential characteristics that make money practical and functional. Divisibility allows money to be easily divided into smaller units, facilitating transactions of various sizes. Portability enables money to be carried and transported with ease, making it convenient for everyday use. Durability ensures that money can withstand the wear and tear of circulation, maintaining its value and functionality over time.

As you reflect on the insights gained from this section, remember that understanding money's functions and characteristics is not just an academic exercise – it's a powerful tool for navigating your financial journey. By recognizing the ways in which money facilitates exchange, measures value, and stores wealth, you can make more informed decisions about earning, spending, saving, and investing. Embrace money's multifaceted nature and use this knowledge to build a strong financial foundation, set clear goals, and work towards long-term prosperity.

As we move forward in our exploration of personal finance, keep these fundamental concepts in mind. They will serve as a guiding light, illuminating the path to financial success and empowering you to make wise choices that align with your values and aspirations. With a deep understanding of money's functions and characteristics, you'll be better equipped to navigate the complexities of the modern economy, seize opportunities, and create a brighter financial future for yourself and your loved ones.

So, take a moment to internalize these lessons, and let them shape your perspective on money and its role in your life. Embrace the power of money as a tool for growth, security, and fulfillment, and approach your financial journey with confidence, purpose, and a steadfast commitment to success. The world of personal finance awaits, and with the knowledge gained from this section, you're ready to embark on a transformative journey towards financial mastery.

Section 3: The Role of Money in the Economy

Money is the lifeblood of any economy, flowing through its veins and enabling the exchange of goods and services, the creation of wealth, and the pursuit of economic growth. Just as the human body relies on a healthy circulatory system to function properly, an economy depends on a well-functioning monetary system to thrive. In this section, we will embark on a fascinating journey to uncover the profound impact of money on economic activity and growth.

Imagine a world without money: a place where people must resort to bartering, trading one good or service directly for another. In such a world, transactions would be cumbersome, time-consuming, and inefficient. Money, in its various forms, has evolved to grease the wheels of commerce, facilitating smooth exchanges and enabling individuals, businesses, and governments to make decisions with greater ease and confidence.

As we delve into the intricacies of money's role in the economy, we will explore how central banks, through monetary policy, influence the money supply and shape economic conditions. We will examine the delicate balance between money, inflation, and purchasing power, and how these factors interact to determine the value of currency over time. Furthermore, we will investigate the ways in which money can promote or hinder economic stability and growth, depending on how it is managed and utilized.

By understanding the fundamental role of money in the economy, we can gain valuable insights into the forces that drive economic decision-making, shape financial markets, and ultimately impact our daily lives. Whether you are an individual seeking to make informed financial choices, a business owner navigating the economic landscape, or a policymaker tasked with steering the economy towards prosperity, this section will provide you with the knowledge and tools necessary to comprehend and harness the power of money in the modern world.

Subsection 3.1: Money Supply and Monetary Policy

At the heart of every modern economy lies the central bank, a powerful institution tasked with the crucial role of managing the money supply and implementing monetary policy. These actions have far-reaching effects on economic conditions, influencing interest rates, inflation, and overall economic growth. To understand the role of money in the economy, it is essential to grasp how central banks control the money supply and the tools they employ to achieve their objectives.

The money supply refers to the total amount of money circulating in an economy, including cash and various forms of bank deposits. Central banks, such as the Federal Reserve in the United States, have the authority to control the money supply through several key mechanisms. One primary tool is open market operations, which involve buying or selling government securities in the open market. When the central bank buys securities, it injects money into the economy, increasing the money supply. Conversely, when it sells securities, it reduces the money supply by removing money from circulation.

Another important tool in the central bank's arsenal is the setting of interest rates. By adjusting the federal funds rate, which is the rate at which banks lend money to one another overnight, the central bank can influence the cost of borrowing throughout the economy. Lower interest rates encourage borrowing and spending, stimulating economic growth, while higher rates tend to slow down economic activity by making borrowing more expensive.

The central bank also has the power to adjust reserve requirements, which determine the amount of money banks must hold in reserve against their deposits. By changing these requirements, the central bank can impact the amount of money banks can lend out, thus influencing the money supply and economic conditions.

Monetary policy decisions are typically guided by the central bank's mandate, which often includes maintaining price stability and promoting full employment. In pursuit of these goals, central banks closely monitor economic indicators such as inflation, unemployment rates, and gross domestic product (GDP) growth. Based on their assessment of the economy's performance and potential risks, central banks make decisions to either stimulate or slow down economic activity by adjusting the money supply and interest rates.

It is important to note that the relationship between money supply and economic conditions is complex and subject to various factors, including market expectations, consumer and business confidence, and external economic shocks. Effective monetary policy requires careful consideration of these factors and a balanced approach to achieve the desired outcomes.

In conclusion, understanding how central banks control the money supply and implement monetary policy is crucial to grasping the role of money in the economy. Through tools such as open market operations, interest rate adjustments, and reserve requirements, central banks wield significant influence over economic conditions, aiming to maintain stability and promote growth. As we continue to explore the intricacies of money and its impact on our lives, recognizing the power of monetary policy will provide a solid foundation for making informed financial decisions and navigating the ever-changing economic landscape.

Subsection 3.2: Money, Inflation, and Purchasing Power

The value of money is not static; it evolves over time, influenced by a complex interplay of economic forces. One of the most significant factors affecting the value of currency is inflation, a sustained increase in the general price level of goods and services. As prices rise, the purchasing power of money—the amount of goods and services that can be bought with a unit of currency—declines. This relationship between money, inflation, and purchasing power is crucial to understanding how the economy functions and how individuals and businesses make financial decisions.

Imagine a scenario where you have a fixed amount of money in your wallet. Over time, you notice that the prices of your favorite products and services are gradually increasing. A cup of coffee that once cost $2 now costs $2.50, and a movie ticket that used to be $10 is now $12. This increase in prices across the economy is a result of inflation. As inflation occurs, the same amount of money in your wallet can buy fewer goods and services than it could before, effectively reducing your purchasing power.

The rate of inflation is typically measured by the percentage change in the Consumer Price Index (CPI), which tracks the prices of a basket of commonly purchased goods and services. Central banks around the world closely monitor inflation rates and use monetary policy tools to keep inflation within a target range, often around 2% per year. When inflation rises above this target, central banks may take action to curb it by raising interest rates or reducing the money supply, as discussed in the previous subsection.

The impact of inflation on purchasing power can be significant over time, especially for those on fixed incomes or with long-term savings. For example, if you have $10,000 in a savings account earning 1% interest annually, but inflation is running at 2% per year, the real value of your savings is actually decreasing. After 10 years, your $10,000 would have grown to $11,046 with compound interest, but its purchasing power would be equivalent to only $9,044 in today's dollars, assuming a constant 2% inflation rate.

To combat the erosion of purchasing power, individuals and businesses often seek investments that offer returns higher than the inflation rate. This is where the concept of "real" returns comes into play. Real returns are the returns on an investment after accounting for inflation. For instance, if an investment yields a 5% nominal return, but inflation is 2%, the real return is approximately 3% (5% - 2%). By focusing on real returns, investors can ensure that their wealth grows faster than the rate of inflation, preserving and enhancing their purchasing power over time.

Governments and central banks also play a crucial role in managing inflation and its impact on the economy. Inflation that is too high can lead to economic instability, as people lose confidence in the value of money and the economy suffers from reduced investment and consumption. On the other hand, inflation that is too low or negative (deflation) can also be problematic, as it may discourage spending and investment, leading to economic stagnation. Striking the right balance is a delicate task that requires careful monitoring and adjustment of monetary policy.

In conclusion, understanding the relationship between money, inflation, and purchasing power is essential for making informed financial decisions and navigating the economic landscape. By recognizing how inflation affects the value of currency over time, individuals and businesses can take steps to protect and grow their wealth, while policymakers work to maintain economic stability by managing inflation. In the following subsection, we will explore how money and its management contribute to overall economic stability and growth.

Subsection 3.3: Money and Economic Stability

The stability of an economy is a delicate balance, influenced by a myriad of factors that work together to create an environment conducive to growth and prosperity. At the heart of this intricate web lies money, a powerful force that can either promote or hinder economic stability. In this subsection, we will explore the role of money in maintaining economic equilibrium and fostering sustainable growth.

Money, in its various forms, acts as a lubricant for the gears of the economy, facilitating the smooth exchange of goods and services. When the money supply is well-managed and aligned with the needs of the economy, it provides a stable foundation for economic activity. Businesses can make informed decisions, consumers can confidently spend and save, and investors can allocate resources effectively. This stability is crucial for long-term economic growth, as it allows for the efficient allocation of resources and encourages innovation and entrepreneurship.

However, when the delicate balance of money and the economy is disrupted, the consequences can be severe. Inflation, as discussed in the previous subsection, is one such disruptive force. When inflation runs rampant, it erodes the purchasing power of money, creating uncertainty and instability in the economy. People may lose confidence in the value of their currency, leading to reduced spending and investment. Businesses may struggle to plan for the future, as the cost of goods and services becomes unpredictable. In extreme cases, hyperinflation can occur, where prices rise at an exponential rate, rendering money practically worthless and causing economic chaos.

On the other hand, deflation, a sustained decrease in the general price level, can also be problematic for economic stability. While falling prices may seem beneficial to consumers in the short term, persistent deflation can lead to a vicious cycle of reduced spending and investment. People may delay purchases in anticipation of even lower prices, leading to a decrease in demand and a slowdown in economic activity. Businesses may struggle to maintain profitability, leading to layoffs and further economic contraction. Deflation can also increase the real burden of debt, as the value of money increases relative to the original borrowing, making it harder for individuals and businesses to repay their obligations.

To promote economic stability, central banks and governments employ various monetary policy tools, as discussed in Subsection 3.1. By carefully managing the money supply and interest rates, they aim to keep inflation and deflation in check, maintaining a balance that fosters sustainable growth. When the economy is facing a downturn, central banks may lower interest rates and increase the money supply to stimulate borrowing, spending, and investment. Conversely, when the economy is overheating and inflation risks are high, central banks may raise interest rates and reduce the money supply to cool down economic activity and maintain price stability.

However, monetary policy alone is not a panacea for economic stability. Fiscal policy, which involves government spending and taxation, also plays a crucial role in promoting stability and growth. Governments can use fiscal policy to stimulate the economy during downturns by increasing spending on infrastructure, social programs, and other initiatives that create jobs and boost demand. During periods of economic expansion, governments can use fiscal policy to manage inflationary pressures by reducing spending or increasing taxes to prevent the economy from overheating.

The interplay between monetary and fiscal policy is crucial for maintaining economic stability. When these policies are well-coordinated and aligned with the needs of the economy, they can create a virtuous cycle of sustainable growth and stability. However, when monetary and fiscal policies are misaligned or poorly managed, they can exacerbate economic imbalances and contribute to instability.

In conclusion, money plays a vital role in promoting or hindering economic stability and growth. By understanding the complex relationship between money, inflation, deflation, and economic activity, individuals, businesses, and policymakers can make informed decisions that contribute to the overall health and stability of the economy. Through the careful management of monetary and fiscal policy, central banks and governments can work together to create an environment that fosters sustainable growth and prosperity for all. In the following section, we will explore the social and psychological aspects of money, delving into how it influences human behavior, shapes power dynamics, and reflects personal values.

Summary: Navigating the Economic Landscape with Money as Your Compass

In this section, we have embarked on a captivating journey to uncover the profound role of money in shaping the economic landscape. From the intricate workings of monetary policy to the delicate balance between inflation and purchasing power, we have seen how money acts as a catalyst for economic activity and growth. The lessons learned here serve as a compass, guiding us through the complexities of the modern economy and empowering us to make informed decisions.

Central banks, the guardians of monetary stability, wield immense power in steering the economy through the manipulation of money supply and interest rates. By understanding how these institutions operate and the tools at their disposal, we can better anticipate and adapt to the ever-changing economic conditions. The intricate dance between money, inflation, and purchasing power has revealed the importance of preserving the value of our currency over time, encouraging us to seek investments that outpace inflation and secure our financial future.

Moreover, we have witnessed the crucial role of money in promoting economic stability and fostering sustainable growth. The delicate balance between monetary and fiscal policies, when executed in harmony, can create an environment conducive to prosperity and opportunity. However, we have also seen the perils of economic instability, from the erosive effects of hyperinflation to the stagnating consequences of deflation, underlining the need for prudent management of our monetary system.

As we reflect on the knowledge gained in this section, let us remember that money is not merely a means to an end, but a powerful tool that shapes the very fabric of our society. By understanding its role in the economy and making informed decisions, we can harness its potential to create a brighter, more prosperous future for ourselves and generations to come. With this newfound wisdom, we stand ready to navigate the economic landscape with confidence, armed with the knowledge and tools necessary to thrive in an ever-changing world.

In the following section, we will delve into the social and psychological dimensions of money, exploring how it influences human behavior, shapes power dynamics, and reflects our deepest values and aspirations. As we continue on this enlightening journey, let us carry forward the insights gained here, leveraging the power of money to build a more equitable, sustainable, and fulfilling economic reality for all.

Section 4: Money and Society

Money, often seen as a mere medium of exchange, holds a much deeper significance in our lives and society. It is not just a tool for transactions but a powerful force that shapes our behaviors, relationships, and social structures. In this section, we will delve into the complex interplay between money and the human psyche, exploring how it influences our decisions, motivations, and overall well-being.

From the way we prioritize our spending to the way we perceive success and happiness, money plays a central role in shaping our values and goals. We will examine the psychological effects of wealth and scarcity, and how they impact our mental health and life satisfaction. By understanding the emotional and cognitive biases that often cloud our financial judgment, we can develop a healthier relationship with money and make more informed decisions.

Moreover, money is not just a personal matter; it is a social construct that reflects and reinforces power dynamics, inequality, and social norms. We will investigate how the distribution of wealth affects social cohesion, mobility, and overall societal well-being. By recognizing the systemic factors that perpetuate financial disparities, we can work towards creating a more equitable and inclusive society.

Throughout this section, we will draw upon the latest research in psychology, sociology, and behavioral economics to provide a comprehensive understanding of the social and psychological dimensions of money. By gaining insight into these often-overlooked aspects, readers will be better equipped to navigate the complex landscape of personal finance and make choices that align with their values and contribute to a better society.

Subsection 4.1: Money and Human Behavior

Money, a concept that has evolved over centuries, has become an integral part of our lives, shaping our behaviors, decisions, and even our sense of well-being. It is fascinating to explore how this intangible construct can wield such a profound influence on the human psyche. In this subsection, we will delve into the complex relationship between money and human behavior, examining how financial factors impact our motivation, decision-making processes, and overall happiness.

One of the most striking ways in which money affects human behavior is through motivation. The prospect of financial gain or loss can be a powerful motivator, driving individuals to work harder, take risks, and pursue their goals with greater intensity. This phenomenon is evident in various aspects of life, from the competitive world of business to the realm of personal finance. Studies have shown that financial incentives can significantly increase productivity and performance, highlighting the motivational power of money.

However, the influence of money on motivation is not always straightforward. While financial rewards can encourage positive behaviors, they can also have unintended consequences. For instance, extrinsic motivators, such as monetary incentives, can sometimes undermine intrinsic motivation, which is the inherent desire to engage in an activity for its own sake. When people focus too heavily on financial gains, they may lose sight of the inherent value and enjoyment of their work, leading to decreased job satisfaction and creativity.

Money also plays a crucial role in decision-making processes. When faced with financial choices, individuals often rely on a complex interplay of rational and emotional factors. On one hand, people strive to make logical decisions based on cost-benefit analyses and long-term financial goals. They may carefully consider factors such as interest rates, investment returns, and budgetary constraints when making financial decisions. On the other hand, emotions and cognitive biases can significantly influence financial behavior.

For example, the fear of loss can lead to risk aversion, while the desire for immediate gratification can result in impulsive spending.

Behavioral economists have identified several cognitive biases that can impact financial decision-making. One such bias is the sunk cost fallacy, where individuals continue to invest time, money, or effort into a project or investment that is no longer viable, simply because they have already invested resources into it. Another bias is the herd mentality, where people tend to follow the financial behaviors of others, even if those behaviors may not be optimal for their own circumstances. Understanding these biases and learning to recognize them can help individuals make more rational and informed financial decisions.

Beyond motivation and decision-making, money also has a significant impact on our overall well-being and happiness. While it is true that money cannot buy happiness in a literal sense, financial security and stability can contribute to a greater sense of life satisfaction. When individuals have enough money to meet their basic needs and pursue their goals, they tend to experience less stress and anxiety related to financial matters. This, in turn, can lead to improved mental health and a more positive outlook on life.

However, the relationship between money and happiness is not linear. Research has shown that beyond a certain threshold, additional income does not necessarily translate into increased happiness. This phenomenon, known as the hedonic treadmill, suggests that as people's incomes rise, their expectations and desires also increase, leading to a constant pursuit of more wealth without a corresponding increase in happiness. Therefore, it is important to recognize that while money can contribute to well-being, it is not the sole determinant of happiness.

In conclusion, money is a powerful force that shapes human behavior in profound ways. It influences our motivation, decision-making processes, and overall sense of well-being. By understanding the psychological and emotional factors that drive financial behavior, individuals can develop a healthier relationship with money and make more informed choices.

Ultimately, the key to financial well-being lies in finding a balance between the pursuit of financial goals and the cultivation of intrinsic values and happiness.

Subsection 4.2: Money, Power, and Inequality

Money, beyond its role as a medium of exchange, is a powerful force that shapes social structures and influences the distribution of resources within a society. The unequal distribution of wealth has far-reaching implications, affecting not only individual lives but also the fabric of communities and the overall well-being of nations. In this subsection, we will examine the complex relationship between money, power, and inequality, exploring how financial disparities impact social dynamics and perpetuate systemic challenges.

One of the most visible manifestations of money's influence on society is the concentration of wealth in the hands of a few. The growing gap between the rich and the poor has become a defining feature of many modern economies, with a small percentage of the population holding a disproportionate share of financial resources. This concentration of wealth translates into a concentration of power, as those with greater financial means often have more influence over political decisions, economic policies, and social norms.

The consequences of wealth inequality extend far beyond individual bank accounts. It can lead to disparities in access to education, healthcare, and opportunities, creating a cycle of disadvantage that is difficult to break. Children born into low-income families often face significant barriers to upward mobility, as they may lack the resources and support necessary to pursue higher education or secure well-paying jobs. This perpetuates a system where financial success is often determined by one's starting point in life, rather than individual merit or effort.

Moreover, the concentration of wealth can have a corrosive effect on social cohesion and trust. When the gap between the rich and the poor becomes too wide, it can breed resentment, frustration, and a sense of injustice among those who feel left behind. This can lead to social unrest, political polarization, and a breakdown of the social contract that binds communities together. In extreme cases, it can even contribute to the rise of populist movements and the erosion of democratic institutions.

To address the challenges posed by wealth inequality, it is essential to recognize the systemic factors that contribute to the unequal distribution of resources. This includes examining the role of tax policies, labor laws, and financial regulations in shaping economic outcomes. By understanding how these systems can either perpetuate or mitigate inequality, we can work towards creating a more equitable and inclusive society.

One approach to reducing wealth inequality is through progressive taxation, where higher earners pay a larger share of their income in taxes. This can help redistribute wealth and fund social programs that provide support and opportunities for those in need. Additionally, policies that promote access to education, healthcare, and affordable housing can help level the playing field and give individuals from all backgrounds a chance to succeed.

However, addressing wealth inequality is not just a matter of government policies. It also requires a shift in social attitudes and values. By recognizing the inherent worth and dignity of all individuals, regardless of their financial status, we can create a more compassionate and inclusive society. This means challenging stereotypes and biases that associate wealth with merit and poverty with personal failings. It means fostering a culture of empathy, where we see the struggles of others as our own and work together to create a more just and equitable world.

In conclusion, the relationship between money, power, and inequality is a complex and multifaceted one. While the unequal distribution of wealth can have significant social implications, it is important to recognize that these challenges are not insurmountable. By understanding the systemic factors that contribute to inequality and working towards creating a more equitable and inclusive society, we can harness the power of money as a force for positive change. Ultimately, the key to building a better future lies in recognizing our shared humanity and working together to create a world where everyone has the opportunity to thrive.

Subsection 4.3: Money and Personal Values

Money, while often viewed as a neutral medium of exchange, is deeply intertwined with our personal values, goals, and priorities. The way we earn, spend, save, and invest our money reflects our underlying beliefs and attitudes about what matters most in life. In this subsection, we will explore the complex relationship between money and personal values, examining how our financial choices are shaped by our individual priorities and how we can align our money management with our deepest held convictions.

At the core of the relationship between money and personal values lies the concept of intentionality. When we are intentional about our financial decisions, we are able to use money as a tool to support our values and achieve our goals. This means taking the time to reflect on what truly matters to us, whether it's family, community, personal growth, or social responsibility, and then making financial choices that are in alignment with those priorities.

One way to cultivate intentionality in our financial lives is through the practice of values-based budgeting. This approach involves allocating our financial resources in a way that reflects our personal values and priorities. For example, if we value experiences over material possessions, we may choose to allocate a larger portion of our budget to travel, learning opportunities, or cultural events. Similarly, if we prioritize giving back to our community, we may set aside a specific percentage of our income for charitable donations or volunteer work.

However, aligning our money management with our personal values is not always easy. In a society that often equates financial success with personal worth, it can be challenging to resist the pressure to prioritize wealth accumulation over other important aspects of life. Moreover, our financial choices are not made in a vacuum, but are influenced by a complex web of social, cultural, and economic factors.

To navigate these challenges, it is essential to cultivate financial self-awareness and to be honest with ourselves about our true priorities and motivations. This may involve examining our spending patterns, reflecting on the emotions and beliefs that drive our financial decisions, and seeking out the support and guidance of trusted mentors or financial professionals.

Another key aspect of aligning our money management with our personal values is the concept of conscious consumption. This means being mindful of the social and environmental impact of our purchasing decisions and choosing to support businesses and products that align with our values. For example, if we value sustainability and environmental responsibility, we may choose to invest in companies with strong environmental track records or to prioritize purchases from local, ethical, and eco-friendly businesses.

Ultimately, the relationship between money and personal values is a deeply personal one, shaped by our unique experiences, beliefs, and aspirations. By being intentional about our financial choices, cultivating self-awareness, and aligning our money management with our deepest held convictions, we can use money as a powerful tool for creating a life that is truly meaningful and fulfilling.

In conclusion, money is not just a practical necessity, but a reflection of our personal values, goals, and priorities. By examining the complex relationship between money and our individual beliefs, we can develop a more intentional and values-driven approach to financial management. Through practices such as values-based budgeting, conscious consumption, and financial self-awareness, we can align our money choices with our deepest held convictions and use our financial resources to support the things that matter most to us. Ultimately, by putting our money where our values are, we can create a life that is not only financially secure, but also personally meaningful and fulfilling.

Summary: Money's Profound Impact on Society and the Individual

In conclusion, money is not merely a neutral medium of exchange but a powerful force that shapes our behaviors, relationships, and social structures. By delving into the complex interplay between money and the human psyche, we gain a deeper understanding of how financial factors influence our decisions, motivations, and overall well-being. Recognizing the emotional and cognitive biases that often cloud our financial judgment empowers us to develop a healthier relationship with money and make more informed choices.

Moreover, money's influence extends beyond the individual, reflecting and reinforcing power dynamics, inequality, and social norms. The unequal distribution of wealth has far-reaching consequences, affecting access to education, healthcare, and opportunities, and perpetuating cycles of disadvantage. Addressing these systemic challenges requires a multifaceted approach, including progressive policies, social support systems, and a collective shift in attitudes and values.

At the heart of the relationship between money and personal values lies the concept of intentionality. By aligning our financial choices with our deepest held convictions and using money as a tool to support our goals and priorities, we can create a life that is both financially secure and personally fulfilling. Through practices such as values-based budgeting, conscious consumption, and financial self-awareness, we can harness the power of money to effect positive change in our lives and the world around us.

As we navigate the complex landscape of money and society, it is essential to approach financial matters with empathy, compassion, and a commitment to building a more equitable and inclusive world. By recognizing our shared humanity and working together to address the challenges posed by wealth inequality, we can create a future where everyone has the opportunity to thrive, both financially and personally. Ultimately, by understanding the profound impact of money on our lives and society, we gain the knowledge and tools necessary to make informed, values-driven financial decisions and contribute to a better, more just world for all.

Chapter Summary: Mastering the Basics of Money

In this chapter, we have explored the fundamental concepts of money, tracing its evolution from ancient barter systems to the digital currencies of today. By understanding the history and characteristics of money, we can better appreciate its crucial role in our lives and the global economy.

Money serves as a medium of exchange, a unit of account, and a store of value, facilitating transactions and enabling economic growth. The shift from commodity-based currencies to fiat money has been a significant milestone in monetary history, and the rise of digital currencies hints at a future where money may take on new forms and functions.

However, money is more than just an economic tool; it has profound social and psychological implications. Our attitudes towards money, and how we choose to earn, spend, and save it, are influenced by a complex interplay of personal values, cultural norms, and societal expectations.

By gaining a deeper understanding of the nature and role of money, we can make more informed decisions about our finances and work towards building a more stable and equitable economic future. In the following chapters, we will explore practical strategies for earning, saving, investing, and managing money effectively, empowering you to take control of your financial well-being and achieve your goals.

As we delve further into the world of personal finance, remember that mastering money is not just about accumulating wealth, but about using it as a tool to live a fulfilling and purposeful life. With the knowledge and skills you will gain from this book, you will be well-equipped to navigate the complex landscape of money and create a brighter financial future for yourself and those around you.

Chapter 2: Setting Financial Goals and Creating a Plan

Imagine yourself five, ten, or even twenty years from now. What does your ideal financial future look like? Do you envision owning a home, starting a business, or retiring comfortably? Whatever your aspirations may be, the key to turning those dreams into reality lies in setting clear financial goals and developing a comprehensive plan to achieve them.

In this chapter, we will embark on a journey of self-discovery and strategic planning. We'll explore the importance of defining your financial priorities, distinguishing between short-term and long-term objectives, and utilizing proven frameworks to set effective goals. By taking a deep dive into your current financial situation, you'll gain a better understanding of your starting point and identify areas for improvement.

Armed with this knowledge, we'll guide you through the process of creating a tailored financial plan that aligns with your unique goals and circumstances. You'll learn how to break down your objectives into manageable milestones, establish realistic timelines, and allocate your resources accordingly. We'll discuss strategies for staying on track, overcoming potential obstacles, and adapting your plan as your life evolves.

But a plan is only as good as its execution. That's why we'll also focus on the critical aspect of implementation. From automating your finances to building a support network, we'll provide you with practical tips and tools to help you stay motivated and accountable. Along the way, we'll celebrate your progress and explore the power of rewarding yourself for reaching key milestones.

By the end of this chapter, you'll have a clear vision of your financial future and a roadmap to guide you there. Whether you're just starting out on your financial journey or looking to refine your existing goals, the principles and strategies outlined here will empower you to take control of your financial destiny. So let's dive in and start turning your dreams into actionable plans!

Section 1: Understanding the Importance of Financial Goal Setting

Imagine yourself standing at a crossroads, with countless paths stretching out before you. Each path represents a potential financial future, filled with opportunities, challenges, and unknowns. Without a clear sense of direction, it's easy to feel overwhelmed and lost, unsure of which way to turn. This is where the power of financial goal setting comes into play.

Setting clear financial goals is like having a compass in your pocket, guiding you towards the future you envision for yourself. It's a way to take control of your financial destiny, rather than letting life's twists and turns dictate your path. By defining your objectives and creating a roadmap to achieve them, you give yourself the gift of clarity, focus, and purpose.

But the benefits of financial goal setting extend far beyond simply knowing where you're headed. When you have a target to aim for, you're more likely to make conscious, intentional choices about how you spend, save, and invest your money. You'll find yourself motivated to seek out opportunities for growth, whether that means pursuing a promotion at work, starting a side hustle, or investing in your education.

Moreover, financial goal setting is a powerful tool for building long-term success. By breaking down your larger aspirations into smaller, achievable milestones, you create a sense of momentum and progress. Each step you take brings you closer to your ultimate destination, whether that's buying your first home, starting your own business, or retiring comfortably.

Of course, the journey towards your financial goals won't always be smooth sailing. There will be obstacles to overcome, setbacks to navigate, and tough decisions to make along the way. But with a clear sense of purpose and a well-defined plan, you'll have the resilience and adaptability to weather any storm.

In the following subsections, we'll dive deeper into the art and science of financial goal setting. We'll explore how to identify and prioritize your objectives, create a comprehensive plan to achieve them, and stay motivated and accountable along the way. By the end of this section, you'll have the tools and knowledge you need to take control of your financial future and start turning your dreams into reality.

Subsection 1.1: Defining Your Financial Priorities

Before embarking on your financial journey, it's crucial to take a step back and reflect on what truly matters to you. Defining your financial priorities is the foundation upon which you can build a meaningful and fulfilling financial plan. It's about understanding your values, dreams, and aspirations, and translating them into concrete financial objectives.

To begin, ask yourself: What do I want my life to look like in the short-term, medium-term, and long-term? What experiences do I want to have? What milestones do I want to achieve? Your answers to these questions will help you identify your financial priorities.

For some, financial freedom may be the ultimate goal – the ability to live life on your own terms without worrying about money. For others, building a legacy for future generations or making a positive impact on the world through philanthropy may be the driving force behind their financial decisions.

Your financial priorities might include buying a home, starting a family, traveling the world, launching a business, or retiring comfortably. They could also encompass more intangible objectives, such as achieving a sense of security, maintaining a certain lifestyle, or having the flexibility to pursue your passions.

Once you have a clear picture of your financial priorities, it's essential to rank them based on their importance to you. This process of prioritization helps you make informed decisions when allocating your limited resources, such as time and money.

One effective way to prioritize your financial objectives is to use the Eisenhower Matrix, a tool that helps you categorize tasks based on their urgency and importance. By placing your financial priorities into the matrix's four quadrants – urgent and important, important but not urgent, urgent but not important, and neither urgent nor important – you can gain clarity on where to focus your efforts.

For example, if buying a home is both urgent and important to you, it would fall into the first quadrant and require immediate attention and action. On the other hand, if traveling the world is important to you but not urgent, it would fall into the second quadrant, requiring careful planning and consistent effort over time.

It's worth noting that your financial priorities may evolve as your life circumstances change. What matters most to you in your 20s may be different from what matters most in your 40s or 60s. Regularly reassessing and adjusting your financial priorities ensures that your financial plan remains aligned with your values and goals.

In summary, defining your financial priorities is a deeply personal process that requires introspection, self-awareness, and honesty. By identifying what matters most to you and ranking your objectives based on their importance, you lay the groundwork for creating a financial plan that is meaningful, motivating, and uniquely tailored to your life's vision.

Subsection 1.2: Short-Term vs. Long-Term Financial Goals

When it comes to setting financial goals, it's essential to distinguish between short-term and long-term objectives. Each type of goal plays a crucial role in your overall financial plan, and understanding the difference between the two can help you prioritize your efforts and allocate your resources effectively.

Short-term financial goals are typically defined as objectives you aim to achieve within a year or less. These goals are often more immediate and focused on your current financial needs and wants. Examples of short-term financial goals might include saving for a vacation, paying off a credit card balance, or building an emergency fund to cover unexpected expenses.

One of the key benefits of setting short-term financial goals is that they provide a sense of accomplishment and momentum. By achieving these smaller milestones, you build confidence in your ability to manage money and make progress towards your larger financial aspirations. Short-term goals also help you develop healthy financial habits, such as budgeting, saving regularly, and avoiding unnecessary debt.

On the other hand, long-term financial goals are those that take more than a year to achieve, often spanning several years or even decades. These goals are typically more significant and complex, requiring careful planning, consistent effort, and a long-term perspective. Examples of long-term financial goals might include saving for retirement, buying a home, starting a business, or funding your children's education.

Long-term financial goals are crucial for building lasting financial security and achieving your life's vision. By setting your sights on these larger objectives, you give yourself a clear direction and purpose for your financial decisions. Long-term goals also require you to think strategically about your money, considering factors such as investment returns, inflation, and risk management.

One effective way to balance short-term and long-term financial goals is to use a "bucket" approach. This involves dividing your financial resources into separate "buckets" or accounts, each dedicated to a specific goal or time horizon. For example, you might have a short-term bucket for emergency savings and a long-term bucket for retirement investments. By compartmentalizing your money in this way, you can ensure that you're making progress on both your immediate and future financial objectives.

It's important to note that short-term and long-term financial goals are not mutually exclusive. In fact, they often work together in a complementary fashion. For instance, achieving a short-term goal of paying off high-interest debt can free up more money to contribute towards your long-term goal of saving for retirement. Similarly, the financial discipline and habits you develop while pursuing short-term goals can serve you well as you work towards your larger, long-term aspirations.

Ultimately, the key to success in setting and achieving financial goals, whether short-term or long-term, is to have a clear plan and stay committed to it. By breaking down your objectives into manageable steps, tracking your progress regularly, and adjusting your approach as needed, you can turn your financial dreams into reality, one goal at a time.

Subsection 1.3: SMART Goal Setting Framework

In the world of personal finance, setting goals is essential for achieving success. However, not all goals are created equal. To increase your chances of turning your financial aspirations into reality, it's crucial to set goals that are well-defined, purposeful, and actionable. This is where the SMART goal setting framework comes into play.

SMART is an acronym that stands for Specific, Measurable, Achievable, Relevant, and Time-bound. By applying these five criteria to your financial goals, you can transform vague desires into concrete, attainable objectives. Let's explore each component of the SMART framework in more detail.

Specific: A specific goal is one that is clear, focused, and unambiguous. Instead of setting a general goal like "save more money," a specific goal would be "save $10,000 for a down payment on a house." By being specific, you give yourself a clear target to aim for and a sense of direction for your financial efforts.

Measurable: A measurable goal is one that can be quantified and tracked. In the example above, the goal of saving $10,000 is measurable because you can easily monitor your progress by tracking your savings account balance. Measurable goals allow you to assess whether you're on track to achieve your objectives and make adjustments as needed.

Achievable: An achievable goal is one that is realistic and attainable given your current resources and constraints. While it's important to dream big, setting goals that are too far out of reach can be demotivating. When setting financial goals, consider your income, expenses, and other financial obligations to ensure that your targets are feasible.

Relevant: A relevant goal is one that aligns with your values, priorities, and long-term financial vision. Ask yourself whether the goal you're setting is truly important to you and whether it contributes to your overall financial well-being. By setting relevant goals, you ensure that you're directing your energy and resources towards the things that matter most to you.

Time-bound: A time-bound goal is one that has a specific deadline or time frame attached to it. In the example above, you might set a deadline of saving $10,000 within the next two years. By setting a time limit, you create a sense of urgency and accountability for your financial actions. Time-bound goals also help you break down larger objectives into smaller, manageable milestones.

To illustrate the SMART goal setting framework in action, let's consider a real-life example. Imagine that you're a 30-year-old professional who wants to start saving for retirement. A SMART retirement savings goal might look like this:

"I will save $500 per month in a Roth IRA account for the next 35 years to accumulate a retirement nest egg of $1 million by age 65."

This goal is specific (saving $500 per month in a Roth IRA), measurable (tracking monthly contributions and account balance), achievable (based on your current income and expenses), relevant (aligning with your long-term financial security), and time-bound (set deadline of age 65).

By breaking down this larger goal into smaller, monthly contributions, you can make steady progress towards your retirement savings objective. The SMART framework provides a roadmap for turning your financial dreams into actionable steps.

It's worth noting that setting SMART financial goals is an ongoing process. As your life circumstances change, your financial priorities may shift as well. Regularly revisiting and adjusting your goals ensures that they remain aligned with your values and aspirations.

In conclusion, the SMART goal setting framework is a powerful tool for creating effective, purposeful financial goals. By setting goals that are specific, measurable, achievable, relevant, and time-bound, you give yourself the best chance of achieving financial success. Whether you're saving for a down payment, paying off debt, or planning for retirement, the SMART approach can help you turn your financial dreams into reality, one goal at a time.

Summary: Charting Your Course to Financial Success

Setting clear financial goals is the foundation upon which you can build a prosperous and fulfilling future. By taking the time to define your priorities, distinguish between short-term and long-term objectives, and employ the SMART goal setting framework, you arm yourself with the tools and mindset necessary to navigate the complex landscape of personal finance with confidence and purpose.

Just as a sailor charts a course before setting sail, defining your financial goals provides direction and focus, guiding your decisions and actions towards the life you envision for yourself. Whether your aspirations involve achieving financial freedom, building a legacy, or simply enjoying a comfortable retirement, having well-defined targets to aim for is essential.

Remember, your financial journey is unique, shaped by your values, circumstances, and dreams. What matters most is that you take control of your financial destiny, rather than letting life's currents dictate your path. By regularly reassessing your priorities, breaking down your goals into manageable milestones, and staying committed to your plan, you can weather any storm and emerge victorious.

As you embark on this transformative journey, embrace the power of goal setting as your compass, guiding you towards the financial success and personal fulfillment you deserve. With clarity of purpose, determination, and the right tools at your disposal, there are no limits to what you can achieve.

In the coming sections, we will delve deeper into the practical strategies and techniques that will help you translate your goals into reality. From budgeting and saving to investing and risk management, each step of the way will bring you closer to the financial future you envision. So, let us set sail together, charting a course towards the life of your dreams, one goal at a time.

Section 2: Assessing Your Current Financial Situation

Picture this: you're about to embark on a life-changing journey to financial freedom, but before you can take that first step, you need to know exactly where you stand. Assessing your current financial situation is like creating a roadmap for your money – it helps you understand where you are today and what you need to do to reach your destination.

In this section, we'll dive deep into the process of analyzing your financial standing, giving you the tools and knowledge you need to create a solid foundation for your financial goals. We'll explore how to calculate your net worth, track your income and expenses, and conduct a thorough financial health checkup.

But why is this so important? Think of it this way: if you were planning a cross-country road trip, you wouldn't just hop in your car and start driving without knowing how much fuel you have, what route to take, or how much money you have for gas and accommodations. The same principle applies to your financial journey.

By taking stock of your current financial situation, you'll gain a clear understanding of your starting point. You'll be able to identify your strengths, such as a steady income or a robust savings account, as well as areas that need improvement, like high credit card debt or a lack of emergency funds.

Armed with this knowledge, you'll be empowered to make informed decisions about your money and create a realistic, achievable plan to reach your financial goals. Whether you're saving for a down payment on a house, planning for retirement, or simply trying to get a handle on your day-to-day finances, assessing your current situation is the critical first step.

So, let's roll up our sleeves and get started on this exciting journey to financial self-discovery. By the end of this section, you'll have a clear picture of where you stand financially and be ready to take control of your money like never before.

Subsection 2.1: Calculating Your Net Worth

Your net worth is a snapshot of your financial health, providing a clear picture of where you stand at a given point in time. It's the foundation upon which you can build your financial goals and plan for the future. But how do you calculate your net worth?

At its core, your net worth is the difference between what you own (your assets) and what you owe (your liabilities). Assets include everything from the cash in your bank account to the value of your home, investments, and personal possessions. Liabilities, on the other hand, encompass all of your debts, such as credit card balances, student loans, and mortgages.

To calculate your net worth, start by making a list of all your assets and their corresponding values. Be thorough and honest, including items such as:

- Cash and savings accounts

- Checking accounts

- Retirement accounts (e.g., 401(k), IRA)

- Investment accounts (e.g., stocks, bonds, mutual funds)

- Real estate (e.g., primary residence, rental properties)

- Vehicles (e.g., cars, motorcycles, boats)

- Personal possessions (e.g., jewelry, art, collectibles)

Next, make a list of all your liabilities and their outstanding balances, including:

- Credit card balances

- Student loans

- Mortgages

- Auto loans

- Personal loans

- Any other debts or obligations

Once you have your lists, add up the total value of your assets and the total amount of your liabilities. Then, subtract your total liabilities from your total assets. The resulting figure is your net worth.

Mathematically, the formula for calculating your net worth can be expressed as:

$$\text{Net Worth} = \text{Total Assets} - \text{Total Liabilities}$$

For example, let's say your assets include a home valued at $300,000, a retirement account with a balance of $100,000, and a savings account with $10,000. Your liabilities consist of a mortgage with a remaining balance of $200,000 and a student loan of $20,000. Your net worth would be calculated as follows:

$$\text{Assets} = \$300,000 + \$100,000 + \$10,000 = \$410,000$$
$$\text{Liabilities} = \$200,000 + \$20,000 = \$220,000$$
$$\text{Net Worth} = \$410,000 - \$220,000 = \$190,000$$

In this scenario, your net worth would be $190,000.

Keep in mind that your net worth is a dynamic figure that will fluctuate over time as your assets and liabilities change. Regularly updating your net worth calculation, such as annually or quarterly, can help you track your progress and make informed decisions about your financial future.

Calculating your net worth is an essential first step in assessing your financial situation and setting meaningful goals. By understanding where you stand today, you can create a roadmap to guide you toward a more secure and prosperous tomorrow.

Subsection 2.2: Tracking Your Income and Expenses

Imagine you're the captain of a ship, navigating the vast ocean of your financial life. To reach your desired destination, you need a clear understanding of two critical elements: the wind in your sails (your income) and the currents that may slow you down (your expenses). This is where tracking your income and expenses comes into play.

Tracking your income and expenses is the process of regularly monitoring and recording the money that comes in and goes out of your life. It's a simple yet powerful habit that can provide you with invaluable insights into your financial situation and help you make informed decisions about your money.

Let's start with your income. Your income is the foundation of your financial well-being, the fuel that powers your ability to save, invest, and achieve your goals. By keeping a close eye on your income sources, such as your salary, freelance earnings, or investment returns, you can ensure that you have a steady flow of money coming in and identify opportunities to increase your income over time.

On the other hand, your expenses are the silent killers of your financial dreams. Every dollar you spend is a dollar that could have been saved, invested, or used to pay down debt. By tracking your expenses, you can identify areas where you may be overspending and make adjustments to align your spending with your priorities and goals.

To start tracking your income and expenses, you can use a simple spreadsheet or a budgeting app. Begin by listing all of your income sources and their corresponding amounts. Then, categorize your expenses into different buckets, such as housing, transportation, food, entertainment, and so on. Record every transaction, no matter how small, to get a complete picture of your spending habits.

As you track your cash flow over time, you'll start to notice patterns and trends. You may discover that you're spending more than you realized on dining out or that your monthly subscription services are adding up. By identifying these areas for improvement, you can make conscious decisions to cut back on unnecessary expenses and redirect that money towards your financial goals.

But tracking your income and expenses isn't just about cutting back. It's also about optimizing your spending to align with your values and priorities. By understanding where your money is going, you can ensure that you're allocating your resources in a way that brings you joy and fulfillment, whether that means investing in experiences, supporting causes you care about, or saving for a long-term goal.

In addition to providing clarity and control over your finances, tracking your income and expenses can also help you build better financial habits. By regularly reviewing your cash flow, you'll become more mindful of your spending decisions and more proactive about finding ways to save and invest. Over time, these small habits can compound into significant financial progress, bringing you closer to your dreams of financial freedom and security.

In the words of financial expert and author, Dave Ramsey, "You must gain control over your money or the lack of it will forever control you." By tracking your income and expenses, you're taking the first step towards gaining that control and charting a course towards a brighter financial future.

So, start today. Grab a spreadsheet or download a budgeting app, and begin the journey of tracking your income and expenses. It may seem daunting at first, but with each passing day, you'll gain a clearer understanding of your financial situation and the power to make meaningful changes. And as you watch your savings grow and your goals come within reach, you'll realize that the effort was well worth it.

Subsection 2.3: Conducting a Financial Health Checkup

Just like your physical health, your financial well-being requires regular checkups to ensure that you're on track and to identify any potential issues before they become major problems. Conducting a financial health checkup is a crucial step in assessing your current financial situation and determining areas where you may need to make changes or improvements.

Think of a financial health checkup as a comprehensive evaluation of your financial vital signs. It's an opportunity to take a step back and look at the big picture of your money management, from your income and expenses to your savings and investments, and everything in between.

One of the primary goals of a financial health checkup is to identify any potential risks or gaps in your current financial plan. This could include things like inadequate insurance coverage, lack of emergency savings, or high levels of debt. By identifying these issues early on, you can take proactive steps to address them before they become more serious problems down the road.

To conduct a thorough financial health checkup, start by gathering all of your financial documents and information in one place. This may include bank statements, credit card bills, investment account statements, insurance policies, and tax returns. Having everything organized and easily accessible will make the process much smoother and more efficient.

Next, take a close look at your income and expenses. Are you bringing in enough money to cover your basic needs and save for the future? Are there any areas where you could cut back on spending or find ways to increase your income? Analyzing your cash flow is a critical component of assessing your overall financial health.

Another important aspect of a financial health checkup is evaluating your debt situation. Are you carrying high levels of credit card debt or struggling to make your student loan payments? Developing a plan to pay down debt and improve your credit score can have a significant impact on your long-term financial well-being.

In addition to looking at your current financial situation, a comprehensive health checkup should also consider your future goals and needs. Are you saving enough for retirement? Do you have a plan in place to pay for your children's education? Have you considered the potential impact of long-term care expenses on your financial plan? By identifying these future needs and developing a strategy to address them, you can help ensure that you're prepared for whatever life may bring.

One helpful tool for conducting a financial health checkup is the use of financial ratios. These ratios can provide valuable insights into your financial situation and help you identify areas where you may need to make changes. For example, the debt-to-income ratio compares your monthly debt payments to your monthly income, providing a clear picture of how much of your income is going towards debt repayment. Another important ratio is the savings rate, which measures the percentage of your income that you're saving for the future.

To calculate your debt-to-income ratio, use the following formula:

$$\text{Debt-to-Income Ratio} = \frac{\text{Total Monthly Debt Payments}}{\text{Gross Monthly Income}}$$

For example, if your total monthly debt payments are \$1,500 and your gross monthly income is \$5,000, your debt-to-income ratio would be:

$$\text{Debt-to-Income Ratio} = \frac{\$1,500}{\$5,000} = 0.30 \text{ or } 30\%$$

A debt-to-income ratio of 30% or less is generally considered healthy, while a ratio above 40% may indicate that you're carrying too much debt relative to your income.

To calculate your savings rate, use this formula:

$$\text{Savings Rate} = \frac{\text{Total Monthly Savings}}{\text{Gross Monthly Income}}$$

For instance, if you're saving $500 per month and your gross monthly income is $5,000, your savings rate would be:

$$\text{Savings Rate} = \frac{\$500}{\$5,000} = 0.10 \text{ or } 10\%$$

Financial experts often recommend aiming for a savings rate of at least 10-15% of your income, depending on your age and retirement goals.

Conducting a financial health checkup may seem overwhelming at first, but it's a critical step in taking control of your financial future. By regularly assessing your financial situation and making adjustments as needed, you can help ensure that you're on track to achieve your short-term and long-term financial goals.

Remember, just like with physical health, prevention is often the best medicine when it comes to financial well-being. By identifying potential problems early on and taking proactive steps to address them, you can avoid more serious issues down the road and set yourself up for a lifetime of financial success.

So, take the time to conduct a thorough financial health checkup on a regular basis. Your future self will thank you for it.

Summary: Laying the Foundation for Your Financial Future

Assessing your current financial situation is a critical step in setting the stage for a successful financial journey. By taking the time to calculate your net worth, track your income and expenses, and conduct a thorough financial health checkup, you've gained a clear understanding of where you stand today.

Your net worth provides a snapshot of your financial position, helping you understand the resources available to you as you work towards your goals. Tracking your income and expenses has given you valuable insights into your spending patterns and opportunities for improvement, empowering you to make informed decisions about your money.

Through conducting a financial health checkup, you've identified potential risks, gaps, and areas for growth in your financial plan. By addressing these issues proactively, you're setting yourself up for long-term success and minimizing the likelihood of future financial setbacks.

Remember, assessing your financial situation is not a one-time event, but rather an ongoing process. As your life circumstances change and your goals evolve, it's essential to regularly revisit your financial standing and make adjustments as needed. By staying attuned to your financial health, you can navigate challenges with confidence and seize opportunities for growth.

As you move forward in your financial journey, the knowledge and insights you've gained from this self-assessment will serve as a solid foundation. You're now equipped with the tools and awareness necessary to set meaningful goals, create a comprehensive financial plan, and take control of your financial destiny.

In the next section, we'll dive into the process of setting financial goals and creating a roadmap for achieving them. With a clear understanding of your starting point, you'll be well-positioned to define your aspirations and chart a course towards financial success.

So, take a moment to celebrate the progress you've made and the commitment you've shown to your financial well-being. The journey ahead may have its challenges, but armed with self-awareness, knowledge, and determination, you're ready to face them head-on and emerge stronger, wiser, and more financially secure.

Section 3: Developing a Comprehensive Financial Plan

Imagine embarking on a journey without a map or a clear destination in mind. You might stumble upon some interesting sights along the way, but you're likely to get lost, waste time, and miss out on the most rewarding experiences. The same holds true for your financial life. Without a well-defined plan, you may find yourself drifting aimlessly, unable to achieve your dreams and aspirations.

Developing a comprehensive financial plan is like creating a roadmap for your money. It's a powerful tool that helps you clarify your goals, prioritize your spending, and make informed decisions about your financial future. By taking the time to craft a detailed strategy, you'll gain a deeper understanding of your current financial situation and develop a clear vision of where you want to be in the years to come.

But creating a financial plan isn't just about crunching numbers and setting arbitrary targets. It's a deeply personal process that requires you to reflect on your values, aspirations, and life priorities. What matters most to you? Is it buying your dream home, starting a business, or securing a comfortable retirement? Your financial plan should align with your unique goals and provide a realistic framework for achieving them.

In this section, we'll guide you through the process of developing a comprehensive financial plan that is tailored to your specific needs and circumstances. We'll explore the key components of a successful plan, including setting realistic milestones, aligning your budget with your goals, and preparing for potential obstacles along the way. By the end of this section, you'll have the tools and knowledge you need to create a robust financial plan that will serve as your guide on the path to financial success.

So, let's dive in and start building the foundation for a brighter financial future. With a clear plan in place, you'll be empowered to make smart money decisions, stay focused on your goals, and enjoy the peace of mind that comes with knowing you're in control of your financial destiny.

Subsection 3.1: Setting Realistic Milestones and Timelines

When it comes to achieving your financial goals, breaking them down into smaller, manageable milestones is crucial. Just like any long journey, reaching your financial destination requires taking one step at a time. By setting realistic milestones and timelines, you can make steady progress towards your objectives without feeling overwhelmed or discouraged.

The first step in setting milestones is to clearly define your financial goals. Whether you're saving for a down payment on a house, planning for retirement, or aiming to pay off debt, having a specific target in mind will help you create a roadmap to success. Once you have identified your goals, it's time to break them down into smaller, achievable milestones.

Let's say your goal is to save $50,000 for a down payment on a house within the next five years. This may seem like a daunting task, but by breaking it down into milestones, it becomes more manageable. You could set a milestone to save $10,000 each year, which translates to approximately $833 per month. By focusing on this smaller monthly target, you can make consistent progress towards your larger goal.

When setting milestones, it's important to be realistic about your timeline. Consider your current financial situation, income, and expenses to determine what is feasible for you. Setting overly ambitious milestones can lead to frustration and burnout, while setting the bar too low may not provide enough motivation to keep you on track.

One effective strategy for setting realistic timelines is to use the SMART goal framework. SMART stands for Specific, Measurable, Achievable, Relevant, and Time-bound. By ensuring that your milestones meet these criteria, you can create a clear and actionable plan for achieving your financial goals.

For example, instead of setting a vague milestone like "save more money," a SMART milestone would be "save $500 per month for the next 12 months to accumulate an emergency fund of $6,000." This milestone is specific (saving $500 per month), measurable (tracking monthly savings), achievable (based on your current financial situation), relevant (building an emergency fund), and time-bound (12 months).

Another important aspect of setting milestones is to regularly review and adjust your plan as needed. Life is unpredictable, and your financial situation may change over time. By regularly assessing your progress and making necessary adjustments, you can stay on track and adapt to any challenges that arise.

In addition to setting milestones for your savings and investment goals, it's also important to establish timelines for other aspects of your financial plan. This may include paying off debt, reviewing your insurance coverage, or updating your estate plan. By breaking these tasks down into manageable steps and setting realistic timelines, you can ensure that all aspects of your financial life are being addressed.

Remember, setting milestones and timelines is not about perfection, but rather about making steady progress towards your financial goals. Celebrate your successes along the way and don't be too hard on yourself if you encounter setbacks. With persistence, dedication, and a well-crafted plan, you can achieve the financial future you envision.

Subsection 3.2: Aligning Your Budget with Your Financial Goals

Creating a budget is a crucial step in developing a comprehensive financial plan. A well-crafted budget acts as a roadmap, guiding you towards your financial goals and helping you make informed decisions about your money. However, simply having a budget is not enough. To truly harness the power of budgeting, you need to ensure that your budget is aligned with your financial objectives.

Aligning your budget with your financial goals means that your spending and saving habits are designed to support your short-term and long-term aspirations. It involves prioritizing your expenses and allocating your resources in a way that moves you closer to your targets. By creating a budget that is in harmony with your goals, you can make steady progress towards financial success and avoid the pitfalls of aimless spending.

The first step in aligning your budget with your financial goals is to have a clear understanding of your objectives. Take the time to reflect on what you want to achieve financially, both in the near future and in the long run. Do you want to save for a down payment on a house, pay off your student loans, or build a substantial retirement fund? Once you have identified your goals, you can start shaping your budget around them.

Next, review your current spending habits and identify areas where you can make adjustments to better support your goals. Look for opportunities to reduce discretionary expenses, such as dining out or subscription services, and redirect that money towards your financial priorities. Consider setting up automatic transfers to your savings or investment accounts to ensure that you are consistently making progress towards your objectives.

One effective strategy for aligning your budget with your goals is to use the "pay yourself first" approach. This means that before you allocate funds to any other expenses, you prioritize your financial goals by setting aside money for savings and investments. By treating your goals as a non-negotiable expense, you ensure that you are consistently working towards them, even as other financial obligations arise.

Another key aspect of aligning your budget with your goals is to regularly review and adjust your plan. As your financial situation changes, your goals may shift as well. By periodically assessing your budget and making necessary modifications, you can ensure that your spending and saving habits remain in sync with your evolving objectives. This may involve increasing your savings contributions, reallocating funds to different goals, or adjusting your timeline based on your progress.

It's also important to be realistic when aligning your budget with your goals. While it's admirable to have ambitious objectives, setting unrealistic targets can lead to frustration and disappointment. Be honest with yourself about what you can reasonably achieve given your current financial situation, and create a budget that reflects those realities. Remember, progress is more important than perfection, and even small steps towards your goals can add up over time.

In addition to supporting your long-term objectives, aligning your budget with your goals can also help you stay motivated and focused. When you see your money being directed towards the things that matter most to you, it can provide a sense of purpose and satisfaction. Celebrating milestones along the way, such as reaching a savings target or paying off a debt, can further reinforce your commitment to your financial plan.

Aligning your budget with your financial goals is a powerful tool for creating a roadmap to financial success. By prioritizing your objectives, adjusting your spending habits, and regularly reviewing your progress, you can ensure that your money is working hard to support your aspirations. With a goal-oriented budget in place, you'll be well on your way to achieving the financial future you envision.

Subsection 3.3: Identifying Potential Obstacles and Contingency Planning

No matter how well-crafted your financial plan may be, life has a way of throwing curveballs when you least expect them. From unexpected job loss to medical emergencies, there are countless obstacles that can derail even the most meticulously designed plans. That's why identifying potential challenges and developing contingency plans is a crucial component of any comprehensive financial strategy.

Anticipating obstacles requires a combination of realistic thinking and creative foresight. Start by examining your current financial situation and considering the various factors that could impact your ability to achieve your goals. These may include external influences, such as economic downturns or market fluctuations, as well as personal circumstances, like changes in health, family dynamics, or career paths.

One common obstacle that many people face is job instability. In today's rapidly evolving job market, layoffs, company restructuring, and industry shifts can happen unexpectedly, leaving individuals without a steady income. To mitigate this risk, consider building an emergency fund that covers three to six months' worth of living expenses. This financial cushion can provide a safety net during periods of unemployment, allowing you to stay afloat while searching for new opportunities.

Another potential challenge is the impact of major life events on your financial plan. Marriage, divorce, the birth of a child, or the death of a family member can all have significant financial implications. When crafting your plan, consider how these events might affect your goals and budget accordingly. For example, if you're planning to start a family, factor in the costs of childcare, education, and potential changes in household income.

Health-related expenses can also pose a significant threat to your financial well-being. A serious illness or injury can result in substantial medical bills, even with insurance coverage. To protect yourself and your loved ones, make sure you have adequate health insurance and consider establishing a dedicated savings account for medical emergencies. Additionally, explore options like disability insurance, which can provide a portion of your income if you're unable to work due to a covered illness or injury.

Developing contingency plans involves more than just identifying potential obstacles; it also requires creating actionable strategies to overcome them. One effective approach is to create multiple scenarios based on different levels of financial setbacks. For example, consider how you would adjust your budget and financial priorities in the event of a 25%, 50%, or 75% reduction in income. By having these plans in place, you'll be better prepared to navigate challenges and make informed decisions under pressure.

Another key aspect of contingency planning is maintaining flexibility in your financial plan. While it's important to have clear goals and milestones, be open to adjusting your strategy as circumstances change. Regularly review your plan and assess whether your assumptions and projections still hold true. If necessary, make modifications to your budget, savings targets, or investment allocations to ensure that your plan remains relevant and effective.

In addition to financial contingencies, it's also important to plan for the unexpected in other areas of your life. This may include creating a will, establishing a power of attorney, or designating beneficiaries for your accounts. By taking these proactive steps, you can ensure that your wishes are carried out and your loved ones are protected, even in the face of unforeseen events.

Remember, the goal of contingency planning is not to live in fear of potential obstacles, but rather to empower yourself with the knowledge and tools to overcome them. By anticipating challenges and developing flexible strategies, you can navigate life's uncertainties with greater confidence and resilience. Embrace the fact that setbacks are a natural part of the financial journey, and use them as opportunities to learn, grow, and strengthen your plan for the future.

Subsection 3.4: Regularly Reviewing and Adjusting Your Financial Plan

Creating a comprehensive financial plan is a significant milestone in your journey towards financial success. However, it's important to recognize that your plan is not a static document set in stone. Just as life is full of changes and surprises, your financial circumstances and goals may evolve over time. To ensure that your plan remains relevant and effective, it's crucial to regularly review and adjust it to adapt to your changing needs and circumstances.

Think of your financial plan as a living, breathing entity that grows and changes with you. By periodically assessing your progress, reevaluating your objectives, and making necessary modifications, you can keep your plan aligned with your current reality and future aspirations. This proactive approach allows you to stay on track towards your goals, even as the world around you shifts.

One key reason to review your financial plan regularly is to account for changes in your personal life. Major life events, such as getting married, having children, changing careers, or relocating to a new area, can have a significant impact on your financial situation. These milestones may require you to reassess your priorities, adjust your budget, or revise your savings and investment strategies. By reviewing your plan in light of these changes, you can ensure that your financial roadmap accurately reflects your current circumstances and long-term objectives.

Another important factor to consider when reviewing your financial plan is the overall economic and market conditions. Fluctuations in interest rates, inflation, and investment returns can all have an impact on your financial progress. For example, if interest rates rise, you may need to adjust your debt repayment strategy or reconsider your investment allocations. Similarly, if the stock market experiences a downturn, you may need to reassess your risk tolerance and make adjustments to your portfolio. By staying informed about the broader economic landscape and regularly reviewing your plan, you can make proactive decisions to protect and grow your wealth.

In addition to accounting for external factors, regularly reviewing your financial plan also provides an opportunity to assess your own progress and behavior. Are you staying on track with your savings goals? Are you adhering to your budget? Have you made any impulsive financial decisions that may have derailed your progress? By honestly evaluating your own actions and progress, you can identify areas for improvement and make necessary adjustments to get back on course.

When reviewing your financial plan, it's important to be open to making changes as needed. This may involve adjusting your budget to reflect changes in income or expenses, reallocating your investments to better align with your risk tolerance, or revising your timeline for achieving certain goals. While it can be tempting to stick to your original plan, remember that flexibility is key to long-term financial success. By being willing to adapt and make changes as needed, you can ensure that your plan remains relevant and effective, even in the face of unexpected challenges.

To make the review process more manageable, consider setting a regular schedule for assessing your financial plan. This could be quarterly, semi-annually, or annually, depending on your preferences and the complexity of your plan. By establishing a consistent review cycle, you can ensure that you're staying on top of your finances and making informed decisions about your money.

When conducting your review, it can be helpful to involve other stakeholders in the process, such as your spouse, financial advisor, or accountant. By collaborating with others, you can gain valuable insights, perspectives, and support as you navigate the complexities of financial planning. Remember, you don't have to go it alone – seeking guidance and expertise from trusted professionals can help you make sound decisions and stay on track towards your goals.

Ultimately, regularly reviewing and adjusting your financial plan is an essential habit for anyone seeking long-term financial success. By staying proactive, flexible, and informed, you can navigate the ever-changing landscape of personal finance with confidence and clarity. Embrace the opportunity to assess your progress, make necessary adjustments, and keep your financial plan aligned with your evolving needs and aspirations. With a commitment to regular review and adaptation, you'll be well on your way to achieving the financial future you envision.

Summary: Charting Your Course to Financial Success

Developing a comprehensive financial plan is a critical step in taking control of your financial future. By setting realistic milestones, aligning your budget with your goals, and preparing for potential obstacles, you create a roadmap that guides you towards your desired financial destination.

Throughout this section, we've explored the key components of a well-crafted financial plan. We've discussed the importance of breaking down your long-term goals into manageable milestones and establishing realistic timelines for achieving them. By using the SMART goal framework and regularly reviewing your progress, you can ensure that you stay on track and make steady progress towards your objectives.

We've also emphasized the significance of aligning your budget with your financial goals. By prioritizing your spending and allocating your resources in a way that supports your aspirations, you can harness the power of your money to create the life you desire. The "pay yourself first" approach and regular budget reviews are essential tools in keeping your finances in harmony with your goals.

Additionally, we've addressed the need for contingency planning and preparing for potential obstacles. Life is unpredictable, and unexpected events can derail even the most well-laid plans. By anticipating challenges, building emergency funds, and maintaining flexibility in your financial strategy, you can navigate setbacks with greater resilience and adaptability.

Finally, we've stressed the importance of regularly reviewing and adjusting your financial plan. As your life circumstances change and the world around you evolves, your financial plan must adapt to remain relevant and effective. By establishing a consistent review process and being open to making necessary modifications, you can ensure that your plan continues to serve your needs and aspirations.

Developing a comprehensive financial plan is not a one-time event, but rather an ongoing journey of growth, learning, and adaptation. By embracing the principles and strategies outlined in this section, you empower yourself to make informed decisions, overcome obstacles, and achieve the financial success you envision.

As you move forward, remember that your financial plan is a powerful tool for creating the life you desire. With clarity, commitment, and a well-crafted roadmap, you can confidently navigate the path to financial freedom and build a future filled with prosperity, security, and fulfillment. So, take the insights gained from this section, apply them to your unique circumstances, and embark on your journey towards financial success with renewed purpose and determination.

Section 4: Implementing and Staying Committed to Your Financial Plan

Picture this: you've spent hours, perhaps even days, carefully crafting a comprehensive financial plan that outlines your goals, budgets, and investment strategies. You feel a sense of accomplishment and excitement as you envision the financial freedom and security that lies ahead. But then, as time passes, you find yourself straying from the path you've laid out. Old habits creep back in, unexpected expenses arise, and your motivation begins to wane.

This is a common challenge faced by many individuals on their financial journey. Creating a solid financial plan is undoubtedly important, but it's only half the battle. The true test lies in your ability to implement that plan consistently and stay committed to your goals, even in the face of obstacles and temptations.

In this section, we'll explore practical strategies and techniques to help you bridge the gap between planning and execution. You'll discover how to turn your financial plan into a series of actionable steps, creating a clear roadmap to guide you towards your objectives. We'll delve into the power of automation, showing you how to leverage technology to simplify your financial management and stay on track with minimal effort.

But implementation alone isn't enough. Staying motivated and committed to your financial plan is equally crucial. We'll discuss the importance of surrounding yourself with a supportive network of family, friends, and even financial professionals who can offer guidance, accountability, and encouragement along the way. You'll learn how to celebrate your milestones and reward yourself for progress, reinforcing positive habits and keeping yourself inspired.

Throughout this section, we'll emphasize the idea that implementing and staying committed to your financial plan is an ongoing process, not a one-time event. By developing a growth mindset and embracing adaptability, you'll be better equipped to navigate the inevitable challenges and changes that arise on your financial journey.

So, whether you're just starting to put your financial plan into action or you've been struggling to maintain momentum, this section is designed to empower you with the tools, strategies, and mindset needed to stay the course and ultimately achieve the financial success you deserve. Let's dive in and explore how you can transform your financial plan from a static document into a living, breathing guide for your financial future.

Subsection 4.1: Automating Your Finances

In today's fast-paced world, managing your finances can feel like a daunting task. Between juggling multiple accounts, tracking expenses, and remembering to pay bills on time, it's easy to become overwhelmed and let things slip through the cracks. However, with the advent of technology and the rise of automation tools, simplifying your financial management has never been easier.

Automating your finances involves setting up systems and processes that handle various aspects of your money management without requiring constant manual input. By leveraging these tools, you can streamline your financial life, reduce stress, and most importantly, stay consistent with your financial plan.

One of the most powerful ways to automate your finances is through the use of direct deposit and automatic transfers. By setting up your paychecks to be deposited directly into your bank account, you eliminate the need to physically deposit checks and ensure that your money is available to you as soon as possible. From there, you can set up automatic transfers to allocate funds to various accounts, such as your savings, investment, or retirement accounts. This way, you're consistently putting money aside for your goals without having to remember to do it manually each month.

Another key area where automation can be incredibly helpful is in tracking your expenses and budgeting. Many banks and financial institutions offer online tools and mobile apps that allow you to categorize your transactions, set budgets, and receive alerts when you're close to overspending. Some popular budgeting apps even connect to your accounts and automatically update your budget based on your spending habits. By having a clear, real-time picture of where your money is going, you can make informed decisions and stay on track with your financial plan.

Paying bills is another task that can be greatly simplified through automation. Most service providers, such as utility companies, credit card issuers, and subscription services, offer the option to set up automatic payments. By enrolling in these programs, you can ensure that your bills are paid on time each month, avoiding late fees and potential damage to your credit score. Just be sure to regularly review your statements to ensure that the charges are accurate and that you have sufficient funds in your account to cover the payments.

Investing is another area where automation can be a game-changer. Many investment platforms and robo-advisors offer the option to set up automatic contributions to your investment accounts. By consistently investing a fixed amount each month, you can take advantage of dollar-cost averaging, which helps to mitigate the impact of market volatility on your portfolio. Additionally, some platforms offer features like automatic portfolio rebalancing, which ensures that your investments remain aligned with your target asset allocation over time.

While automating your finances can be incredibly beneficial, it's important to remember that it's not a set-it-and-forget-it solution. It's still crucial to regularly review your accounts, update your budget as needed, and make adjustments to your automated systems as your financial situation evolves. By combining the power of automation with a proactive approach to financial management, you'll be well on your way to achieving your goals and staying committed to your financial plan.

Subsection 4.2: Surrounding Yourself with a Support System

Embarking on a financial journey can be a daunting and lonely experience, especially if you're trying to navigate the complexities of money management on your own. However, surrounding yourself with a strong support system can make all the difference in staying motivated, accountable, and on track with your financial goals.

One of the most valuable sources of support is your family and friends. These are the people who know you best, understand your values and aspirations, and want to see you succeed. By sharing your financial goals and plans with your loved ones, you create a sense of accountability and gain a cheering squad that will celebrate your victories and provide encouragement during challenging times. Your family and friends can also serve as sounding boards for ideas, offering fresh perspectives and insights that you may not have considered.

In addition to personal relationships, building a network of like-minded individuals who are also working towards financial success can be incredibly beneficial. Joining local or online communities focused on personal finance, investing, or entrepreneurship can connect you with people who share your interests and goals. These communities often provide a wealth of knowledge, resources, and inspiration, as well as opportunities to learn from others' experiences and collaborate on projects.

Another key component of a strong financial support system is working with professional advisors, such as financial planners, accountants, or attorneys. These experts bring specialized knowledge and objectivity to the table, helping you make informed decisions and navigate complex financial situations. They can provide guidance on creating a comprehensive financial plan, optimizing your tax strategy, protecting your assets, and more. By building a trusted relationship with these professionals, you gain access to valuable insights and support that can help you stay on track and achieve your goals.

Mentors and role models are also powerful additions to your financial support network. Seeking out individuals who have achieved the kind of financial success you aspire to can provide inspiration, guidance, and practical advice. These mentors can share their own experiences, challenges, and lessons learned, helping you avoid common pitfalls and accelerate your progress. They can also introduce you to new opportunities, expand your network, and provide ongoing support and encouragement.

When building your financial support system, it's important to be selective and surround yourself with positive, knowledgeable, and trustworthy individuals. Seek out people who share your values, respect your goals, and have a track record of success in their own financial lives. Be open to feedback, advice, and constructive criticism, but also trust your own instincts and make decisions that align with your unique circumstances and aspirations.

Remember, building a strong financial support system is an ongoing process. As you grow and evolve, so too will your network. Be proactive in seeking out new connections, nurturing existing relationships, and expressing gratitude for the support you receive. By surrounding yourself with a diverse and empowering support system, you'll be better equipped to stay motivated, navigate challenges, and ultimately achieve the financial success you deserve.

Subsection 4.3: Celebrating Milestones and Rewarding Yourself

As you embark on your financial journey, it's essential to recognize that progress is not always linear. There will be ups and downs, challenges and triumphs along the way. Amidst the hard work and dedication required to stick to your financial plan, it's crucial to take a step back and celebrate your milestones, no matter how small they may seem.

Acknowledging your progress serves as a powerful motivator, reinforcing positive habits and keeping you engaged in the pursuit of your financial goals. When you reach a milestone, whether it's paying off a debt, reaching a savings target, or achieving a specific investment goal, take a moment to reflect on your accomplishment. Recognize the effort and discipline it took to get there, and allow yourself to feel a sense of pride and satisfaction.

Celebrating your financial milestones doesn't have to be extravagant or expensive. It can be as simple as treating yourself to a favorite meal, sharing the news with a supportive friend or family member, or taking a well-deserved break to engage in a hobby you enjoy. The key is to mark the occasion in a way that feels meaningful and rewarding to you.

In addition to celebrating milestones, it's important to build in rewards for yourself along your financial journey. These rewards serve as positive reinforcement, helping to maintain your motivation and commitment to your financial plan. When setting your financial goals, consider incorporating small rewards at various checkpoints. For example, if you're working towards saving for a down payment on a house, you might treat yourself to a weekend getaway or a spa day when you reach the halfway point.

When choosing rewards, it's important to strike a balance between enjoyment and financial responsibility. Avoid rewards that derail your progress or undermine your hard work. Instead, opt for experiences or purchases that align with your values and bring you genuine happiness without breaking the bank.

Remember, celebrating milestones and rewarding yourself is not about perfection or reaching the finish line. It's about recognizing the progress you've made, no matter how incremental, and acknowledging the effort and dedication you've put into improving your financial life. By taking the time to celebrate your victories and reward your commitment, you'll find yourself more motivated, inspired, and resilient on your path to financial success.

Summary: Turning Your Financial Plan into a Lifelong Journey of Success

As we conclude this section on implementing and staying committed to your financial plan, it's important to recognize that the strategies and techniques we've discussed are not one-time solutions, but rather essential tools to be used throughout your lifelong financial journey. By automating your finances, surrounding yourself with a supportive network, and celebrating your milestones along the way, you'll be well-equipped to turn your financial plan into a reality.

Remember, the path to financial success is not always smooth or straightforward. There will be challenges, setbacks, and moments of doubt. However, by staying focused on your goals, adaptable in your approach, and committed to your plan, you'll be able to navigate these obstacles and emerge stronger and more financially secure.

As you move forward, continue to educate yourself, seek out new opportunities for growth, and embrace the power of incremental progress. Every small step you take towards your financial goals is a victory worth celebrating, and each lesson learned is a valuable asset in your journey.

Ultimately, implementing and staying committed to your financial plan is about taking control of your financial destiny. It's about creating a life of abundance, security, and freedom on your own terms. By putting the strategies and mindset shifts we've discussed into practice, you'll be empowered to make informed decisions, build lasting wealth, and create a financial legacy that extends far beyond your own lifetime.

So, as you embark on this exciting new chapter of your financial journey, remember that you have the knowledge, tools, and support you need to succeed. Stay committed to your vision, trust in the process, and never lose sight of the incredible potential that lies ahead. With dedication, perseverance, and a steadfast commitment to your financial plan, there's no limit to what you can achieve.

Chapter Summary: Charting Your Financial Future

Setting financial goals and creating a comprehensive plan to achieve them is a crucial step in taking control of your financial future. By understanding the importance of goal setting, assessing your current financial situation, and developing a detailed roadmap, you can transform your financial aspirations into reality.

Throughout this chapter, we explored the benefits of setting clear financial priorities and learned how to differentiate between short-term and long-term goals. The SMART goal setting framework provided a structured approach to defining specific, measurable, achievable, relevant, and time-bound objectives that align with your values and aspirations.

We also emphasized the significance of evaluating your current financial standing, including calculating your net worth, tracking your income and expenses, and conducting a financial health checkup. This assessment serves as a foundation for creating a tailored financial plan that addresses your unique circumstances and challenges.

Developing a comprehensive financial plan involves breaking down your goals into manageable milestones, establishing realistic timelines, and aligning your budget with your objectives. We discussed the importance of anticipating potential obstacles and creating contingency plans to overcome them, as well as regularly reviewing and adjusting your plan to adapt to changing circumstances.

Implementing and staying committed to your financial plan is key to long-term success. By automating your finances, surrounding yourself with a supportive network, and celebrating your progress along the way, you can maintain motivation and stay on track towards achieving your financial goals.

Remember, setting financial goals and creating a plan is not a one-time event, but an ongoing process that requires dedication, discipline, and flexibility. By embracing the strategies and concepts discussed in this chapter, you can take meaningful steps towards building a solid financial foundation and securing a brighter financial future for yourself and your loved ones.

Chapter 3: Budgeting and Expense Management

Picture this: you're steering a ship across a vast ocean, navigating through calm waters and rough seas alike. Your destination? Financial freedom. But to reach that distant shore, you need a reliable compass and a well-charted course. That's where budgeting and expense management come in.

Budgeting is the foundation upon which your financial journey is built. It's the process of creating a plan for your money, ensuring that every dollar has a purpose and that your spending aligns with your goals and values. By taking control of your finances through effective budgeting, you'll gain a clearer understanding of where your money is going and how you can optimize your spending to achieve your dreams.

But creating a budget is only half the battle. Sticking to it requires discipline, commitment, and a keen eye for expense management. It's about making conscious choices about your spending, distinguishing between needs and wants, and finding ways to stretch your dollars further. Whether you're saving for a rainy day, paying off debt, or investing in your future, effective expense management is key to staying on track and avoiding financial pitfalls.

In this chapter, we'll dive deep into the world of budgeting and expense management. We'll explore proven strategies for creating a budget that works for you, no matter your income level or financial situation. You'll learn how to track your spending, identify areas where you can cut back, and find creative ways to save money without sacrificing your quality of life.

We'll also tackle common budgeting challenges and provide practical tips for overcoming them. From dealing with unexpected expenses to staying motivated when times get tough, we'll equip you with the tools and mindset you need to stay the course and reach your financial goals.

So, whether you're just starting out on your financial journey or looking to take your budgeting skills to the next level, this chapter is your guide. Get ready to set sail towards a brighter financial future, one dollar at a time.

Section 1: Understanding the Importance of Budgeting

Imagine a world where you have complete control over your financial life, where every dollar you earn works towards your goals and dreams. A world where you don't have to worry about unexpected expenses or living paycheck to paycheck. This is the power of budgeting.

Many people view budgeting as a restrictive and tedious task, but in reality, it is a liberating tool that empowers you to take charge of your money. By creating and maintaining a budget, you gain a clear understanding of your income and expenses, allowing you to make informed decisions about how to allocate your resources.

Think of your budget as a roadmap to financial success. It helps you navigate the complex landscape of personal finance, guiding you towards your desired destination. Whether you're saving for a down payment on a house, planning for retirement, or simply trying to make ends meet, a well-crafted budget is essential.

In this section, we'll explore the numerous benefits of budgeting and how it can transform your financial life. We'll dispel common myths and misconceptions that may have held you back from embracing this powerful tool. By the end of this section, you'll have a solid foundation for creating and maintaining a budget that works for you.

So, let's dive in and discover how budgeting can help you take control of your money, achieve your financial goals, and live the life you've always wanted. Your journey to financial success starts here.

Subsection 1.1: Defining a Budget and Its Purpose

At its core, a budget is a financial plan that helps you manage your money effectively. It is a tool that allows you to take control of your income and expenses, ensuring that you are making the most of your financial resources. A budget is essentially a roadmap that guides you towards your financial goals, whether they are short-term, like saving for a vacation, or long-term, like planning for retirement.

Creating a budget involves tracking your income from all sources, such as your salary, investments, or side hustles, and then allocating that income towards your expenses. These expenses can be divided into two main categories: fixed expenses, which remain relatively constant each month, such as rent or mortgage payments, and variable expenses, which can fluctuate, like groceries or entertainment.

The purpose of a budget is to help you gain a clear understanding of your financial situation. By seeing how much money you have coming in and how much you are spending, you can make informed decisions about where to allocate your funds. This awareness is crucial for managing your finances effectively, as it allows you to identify areas where you may be overspending and make adjustments accordingly.

Moreover, a budget helps you prioritize your spending based on your values and goals. By setting clear financial objectives and incorporating them into your budget, you can ensure that your money is being used in a way that aligns with what matters most to you. This could mean setting aside funds for a down payment on a house, contributing to your children's education, or saving for a comfortable retirement.

In addition to helping you manage your day-to-day finances, a budget also serves as a tool for financial planning and preparedness. By regularly reviewing and adjusting your budget, you can anticipate potential challenges and opportunities, such as changes in income or unexpected expenses. This proactive approach to money management can help you build financial resilience and weather any storms that may come your way.

Ultimately, the purpose of a budget is to empower you to take control of your financial life. By understanding your income and expenses, setting clear goals, and making informed decisions about your money, you can build a strong foundation for long-term financial success and security. In the following subsections, we will explore the benefits of budgeting in more detail and provide practical strategies for creating and maintaining a budget that works for you.

Subsection 1.2: The Relationship Between Budgeting and Financial Goals

Budgeting is not just about tracking your income and expenses; it is a powerful tool that can help you achieve your financial goals, both short-term and long-term. By creating a budget that aligns with your objectives, you can ensure that your money is working for you, rather than against you.

Think of your financial goals as destinations on a map, and your budget as the route that will get you there. Without a clear path, it's easy to get lost or sidetracked, spending money on things that don't contribute to your overall financial well-being. By establishing a budget that prioritizes your goals, you can make conscious decisions about how to allocate your resources and make steady progress towards your objectives.

For example, let's say you have a short-term goal of saving for a down payment on a house. By incorporating this goal into your budget, you can determine how much you need to save each month and adjust your spending accordingly. This might mean cutting back on discretionary expenses, such as dining out or entertainment, and redirecting that money towards your savings account. By consistently following your budget and making these trade-offs, you'll be able to watch your down payment fund grow over time, bringing you closer to your goal of homeownership.

Similarly, budgeting can help you achieve long-term financial goals, such as saving for retirement or building an emergency fund. By setting aside a portion of your income each month and treating these contributions as non-negotiable expenses, you can ensure that you're making steady progress towards these important objectives. Over time, the power of compound interest and consistent savings can help you build a substantial nest egg, providing you with financial security and peace of mind.

Budgeting also helps you prioritize your goals and make tough decisions when resources are limited. By having a clear understanding of your income and expenses, you can determine which goals are most important to you and allocate your money accordingly. This might mean temporarily putting some goals on hold while you focus on others, or finding creative ways to balance multiple objectives simultaneously.

Ultimately, the relationship between budgeting and financial goals is one of empowerment and control. By creating a budget that aligns with your objectives, you're taking an active role in shaping your financial future. Rather than letting your money control you, you're making intentional decisions about how to use your resources to achieve the things that matter most to you. With a clear plan in place and the discipline to stick to it, you can turn your financial dreams into reality, one budget at a time.

Subsection 1.3: Overcoming Common Budgeting Misconceptions

Despite the numerous benefits of budgeting, many people are hesitant to embrace this powerful financial tool. This reluctance often stems from common myths and misconceptions about what budgeting entails and how it can impact one's life. In this subsection, we'll address and dispel these misconceptions, empowering you to overcome any mental obstacles that may be hindering your progress.

One of the most pervasive budgeting myths is that it's restrictive and constraining, leaving no room for spontaneity or enjoyment. However, this couldn't be further from the truth. A well-designed budget is not about deprivation; it's about making conscious choices that align with your values and goals. By allocating your money intentionally, you can ensure that you're spending on the things that matter most to you, whether that's experiences, hobbies, or indulgences. Budgeting is not about saying "no" to everything; it's about saying "yes" to the things that truly bring you joy and fulfillment.

Another common misconception is that budgeting is only for people with low incomes or those struggling financially. In reality, budgeting is a valuable tool for everyone, regardless of their income level or financial situation. Even high earners can benefit from the clarity and control that budgeting provides, ensuring that they're making the most of their resources and avoiding lifestyle creep. Whether you're just starting out or well-established in your career, budgeting can help you make informed decisions about your money and achieve your financial goals.

Some people also believe that budgeting is too time-consuming or complicated to be worth the effort. While creating a budget does require some initial time investment, it's a small price to pay for the long-term benefits it provides. With the abundance of budgeting apps, tools, and resources available today, the process has never been more streamlined or user-friendly. Once you've established your budget, maintaining it becomes a simple matter of tracking your spending and making adjustments as needed. The time you invest in budgeting will pay dividends in the form of increased financial awareness, reduced stress, and a clearer path to your goals.

Finally, there's the misconception that budgeting is a one-size-fits-all solution, with rigid rules that must be followed to the letter. In truth, budgeting is a highly personal process that should be tailored to your unique circumstances, preferences, and goals. What works for one person may not work for another, and that's okay. The key is to find a budgeting approach that resonates with you and that you can stick with over time. Whether you prefer a detailed, line-item budget or a more flexible, envelope-based system, the best budget is the one that helps you take control of your money and achieve your financial objectives.

By recognizing and overcoming these common budgeting misconceptions, you can break free from the mental barriers that may be holding you back from embracing this powerful financial tool. Remember, budgeting is not about restriction or deprivation; it's about empowerment, clarity, and control. With an open mind and a willingness to experiment, you can create a budget that works for you and that supports your unique financial journey. So, let go of any preconceived notions and embrace the transformative power of budgeting – your future self will thank you.

Summary: Embracing the Power of Budgeting for Financial Success

In this section, we've explored the fundamental importance of budgeting in achieving financial success. By understanding what a budget is and its purpose, you've gained a solid foundation for taking control of your money and making informed decisions about your financial future.

We've seen how budgeting is not just about tracking numbers, but about aligning your spending with your values and goals. By creating a budget that reflects your priorities, you can ensure that your money is working for you, helping you achieve your short-term and long-term objectives. Whether you're saving for a down payment on a house, planning for retirement, or simply trying to make ends meet, a well-crafted budget is an essential tool in your financial toolkit.

We've also addressed common misconceptions about budgeting, such as the belief that it's restrictive, complicated, or only for those with low incomes. By dispelling these myths, we've empowered you to overcome any mental barriers that may have been holding you back from embracing this transformative financial practice.

Remember, budgeting is not about deprivation or rigidity; it's about empowerment, flexibility, and control. By finding a budgeting approach that works for you and staying committed to the process, you can experience the numerous benefits of financial clarity, reduced stress, and a clearer path to your goals.

As we move forward in this book, we'll dive deeper into the practical strategies and tools for creating and maintaining a budget that supports your unique financial journey. With the knowledge and mindset gained from this section, you're well-equipped to take the next steps towards financial success.

So, embrace the power of budgeting and get ready to transform your relationship with money. Your future self will thank you for the commitment and discipline you show today. Let's continue this journey together, one budget at a time.

Section 2: Creating a Comprehensive Budget

Imagine having a roadmap that guides you towards your financial goals, helping you navigate through the twists and turns of everyday expenses. That's exactly what a well-crafted budget can do for you. A budget is not just a list of numbers; it's a powerful tool that puts you in control of your money and empowers you to make informed decisions about your financial future.

In this section, we'll walk you through the process of creating a comprehensive budget that is tailored to your unique needs and circumstances. Whether you're a seasoned budgeter or new to the concept, you'll discover practical strategies and insights that will help you build a solid foundation for your financial journey.

Creating a budget may seem daunting at first, but it's a crucial step towards achieving financial stability and reaching your long-term goals. By taking the time to understand your income and expenses, you'll gain a clear picture of where your money is going and identify opportunities to optimize your spending and saving habits.

Throughout this section, we'll explore the key components of a comprehensive budget, from gathering your financial information to categorizing your expenses and allocating funds for savings and investments. You'll learn how to differentiate between fixed and variable expenses, and how to prioritize your spending based on your values and goals.

But a budget is more than just a set of numbers on a spreadsheet. It's a reflection of your priorities and a tool for aligning your financial decisions with your values. By creating a budget that works for you, you'll be able to make more intentional choices about how you earn, spend, and save your money.

So, let's dive in and discover the power of a comprehensive budget. With the right tools and mindset, you'll be well on your way to taking control of your finances and building a brighter financial future.

Subsection 2.1: Gathering Financial Information and Documents

Before you can create a comprehensive budget, you need to gather all the necessary financial information and documents. This crucial first step lays the foundation for an accurate and effective budget that reflects your true financial situation. Without a clear picture of your income, expenses, and financial obligations, it's impossible to create a realistic plan for managing your money.

Start by collecting all the documents that detail your income sources. This may include pay stubs from your employer, invoices from freelance work, or statements from rental properties or investments. Don't forget to account for any additional sources of income, such as side hustles, bonuses, or tax refunds. Having a complete understanding of your income is essential for determining how much money you have available to allocate towards expenses and savings.

Next, gather all the documents related to your expenses. This includes bills for utilities, rent or mortgage payments, insurance premiums, and subscriptions. Collect receipts for groceries, dining out, entertainment, and other discretionary spending. If you have any debts, such as student loans, credit card balances, or car payments, make sure to include statements that show your current balances and minimum payment amounts.

It's also important to gather documents related to your savings and investments. This may include bank statements for your savings accounts, retirement account statements, and investment portfolio reports. Understanding how much money you have saved and invested will help you determine your net worth and assess your progress towards your financial goals.

Once you have collected all the necessary documents, take some time to review them carefully. Look for any discrepancies or errors, such as incorrect charges or missing payments. If you notice any issues, contact the relevant financial institution or service provider to resolve them before proceeding with your budget.

Organizing your financial documents can be a time-consuming process, but it's a critical step in creating a comprehensive budget. Consider using a filing system or digital storage solution to keep your documents organized and easily accessible. You may also want to set up a schedule for regularly updating your financial information, such as reviewing your credit card statements monthly or tracking your investment portfolio quarterly.

By gathering all your financial information and documents upfront, you'll have a solid foundation for creating a budget that accurately reflects your income, expenses, and financial goals. This clarity and transparency will empower you to make informed decisions about how to allocate your money and take control of your financial future.

Subsection 2.2: Categorizing Income and Expenses

With your financial documents in hand, it's time to start categorizing your income and expenses. This essential step in creating a comprehensive budget involves grouping your financial transactions into distinct categories, making it easier to track, analyze, and manage your money.

Categorizing your income is relatively straightforward. Start by identifying your main sources of income, such as your salary from your primary job, freelance work, investments, or rental properties. Assign each income source to a specific category, such as "Primary Income," "Side Hustle," or "Passive Income." This categorization will help you understand where your money is coming from and how diversified your income streams are.

Next, turn your attention to categorizing your expenses. This process may seem more complex, as you likely have numerous transactions to sort through. Begin by identifying your major expense categories, such as housing, transportation, food, utilities, and entertainment. These broad categories will serve as the foundation for your expense tracking.

Within each main category, you can create subcategories to provide a more detailed breakdown of your spending. For example, under the "Food" category, you might have subcategories like "Groceries," "Dining Out," and "Snacks." This level of detail will help you pinpoint areas where you may be overspending and identify opportunities to cut back.

As you categorize your expenses, consider creating separate categories for fixed and variable expenses. Fixed expenses, such as rent or mortgage payments, remain relatively constant from month to month, while variable expenses, like dining out or entertainment, can fluctuate. Understanding the difference between these two types of expenses will be crucial when it comes to budgeting and financial planning.

Don't forget to include categories for savings and debt repayment. Treating these financial priorities as separate categories will help you ensure that you're consistently allocating money towards your long-term goals and financial obligations.

When categorizing your income and expenses, it's essential to be consistent and thorough. Develop a system that works for you, whether it's using a spreadsheet, budgeting app, or old-fashioned pen and paper. Make sure to assign every transaction to a category, even if it means creating a "Miscellaneous" category for those hard-to-classify expenses.

As you work through this process, you may discover expenses that you didn't realize were adding up or income sources that you hadn't fully considered. This newfound awareness is one of the key benefits of categorizing your financial transactions. By bringing clarity to your income and expenses, you'll be better equipped to make informed decisions about how to allocate your money and reach your financial goals.

Remember, categorizing your income and expenses is an ongoing process. As your financial situation evolves, you may need to adjust your categories or create new ones to reflect your changing circumstances. Regularly reviewing and updating your categories will help you stay on top of your finances and ensure that your budget remains relevant and effective.

By taking the time to categorize your income and expenses, you're laying the groundwork for a comprehensive budget that will serve as a roadmap for your financial journey. With a clear understanding of where your money is coming from and where it's going, you'll be well on your way to making informed decisions and achieving your financial goals.

Subsection 2.3: Determining Fixed and Variable Expenses

When creating a comprehensive budget, it's crucial to understand the difference between fixed and variable expenses. This knowledge will help you prioritize your spending, identify areas where you can cut back, and create a more accurate and realistic budget that aligns with your financial goals.

Fixed expenses are costs that remain relatively constant from month to month. These expenses are often essential and non-negotiable, such as rent or mortgage payments, car payments, insurance premiums, and subscriptions. While the exact amounts may vary slightly, you can generally count on these expenses remaining stable over time. When budgeting for fixed expenses, it's important to account for them first, as they typically make up a significant portion of your monthly expenditure.

To determine your fixed expenses, review your financial documents and identify the costs that occur regularly and remain fairly consistent. Make a list of these expenses, along with their corresponding amounts, and total them up. This sum represents the minimum amount you need to allocate each month to cover your fixed expenses.

On the other hand, variable expenses are costs that fluctuate from month to month based on your consumption, habits, and lifestyle choices. These expenses are often more discretionary and can be adjusted based on your financial situation and goals. Examples of variable expenses include groceries, dining out, entertainment, clothing, and travel. While some variable expenses, such as food and gas, are necessary, others, like entertainment and shopping, are more flexible and can be reduced if needed.

Determining your variable expenses can be more challenging, as they tend to vary from month to month. To get a clear picture of your variable expenses, track your spending for several months, categorizing each expense as fixed or variable. Look for patterns in your spending habits and identify areas where you may be able to cut back or make adjustments.

When accounting for variable expenses in your budget, consider using a range rather than a fixed amount. For example, if your monthly grocery expenses typically fall between $300 and $400, budget for the higher end of that range to ensure you have enough funds allocated. This approach provides flexibility while still encouraging you to be mindful of your spending.

It's important to note that some expenses may have both fixed and variable components. For example, your phone bill may have a fixed monthly service charge, but your data usage may vary based on your consumption. In these cases, separate the fixed and variable components and account for them accordingly in your budget.

Understanding the difference between fixed and variable expenses is a key step in creating a comprehensive budget. By categorizing your expenses and accounting for them appropriately, you'll be better equipped to make informed decisions about your spending, adjust your habits as needed, and ultimately reach your financial goals. Remember, a budget is a living document that should be regularly reviewed and updated to reflect changes in your income, expenses, and priorities. By staying on top of your fixed and variable expenses, you'll be well on your way to creating a budget that works for you.

Subsection 2.4: Allocating Funds for Savings and

Investments

Creating a comprehensive budget is not just about managing your day-to-day expenses; it's also about planning for your future. One of the most critical aspects of a well-rounded budget is allocating funds for savings and investments. By setting aside a portion of your income for these purposes, you're taking a proactive step towards achieving your short-term and long-term financial goals.

When it comes to saving money, it's essential to have a clear understanding of what you're saving for. Are you building an emergency fund to cover unexpected expenses? Are you saving for a down payment on a house or planning for a dream vacation? By identifying your specific savings goals, you can determine how much you need to allocate each month to reach those targets.

A good rule of thumb is to save at least 10-20% of your income, but the exact percentage will depend on your individual circumstances and goals. If you're just starting out, aim to save a smaller percentage and gradually increase it over time as you adjust your spending habits and find more room in your budget.

One effective strategy for saving money is to treat your savings allocation as a fixed expense in your budget. Just as you would with rent or a car payment, determine a set amount to transfer to your savings account each month and consider it non-negotiable. By automating your savings through direct deposit or scheduled transfers, you can ensure that you consistently prioritize your savings goals without the temptation to spend that money elsewhere.

In addition to saving for specific goals, it's crucial to allocate funds for long-term investments. Investing your money allows you to take advantage of compound interest and potentially grow your wealth over time. Whether you're contributing to a retirement account, such as a 401(k) or IRA, or investing in stocks, bonds, or mutual funds, setting aside money for investments can help you build a more secure financial future.

When allocating funds for investments, consider your risk tolerance and time horizon. If you're younger and have a longer investment timeline, you may be able to afford to take on more risk in exchange for potentially higher returns. As you near retirement age, however, you may want to shift your investments to more conservative options to protect your principal.

It's also important to educate yourself on the different types of investment vehicles available and understand the fees and costs associated with each one. Consider seeking the advice of a financial professional who can help you develop a personalized investment strategy that aligns with your goals and risk profile.

As you allocate funds for savings and investments in your budget, remember to be realistic and flexible. It may take time to adjust your spending habits and find the right balance between your current needs and your future goals. Don't be discouraged if you can't save as much as you'd like right away; the key is to start somewhere and remain consistent.

Regularly review your budget and assess your progress towards your savings and investment goals. Celebrate your successes along the way and make adjustments as needed to stay on track. By prioritizing savings and investments in your comprehensive budget, you're taking a significant step towards building a solid financial foundation and creating a brighter future for yourself and your loved ones.

Summary: Laying the Foundation for Financial Success

Creating a comprehensive budget is a critical step in taking control of your finances and achieving your short-term and long-term goals. By gathering your financial information, categorizing your income and expenses, distinguishing between fixed and variable costs, and allocating funds for savings and investments, you're laying the foundation for a solid financial future.

Remember, a budget is not a one-time task, but an ongoing process that requires regular review and adjustment. As your life circumstances change, so too will your financial priorities and needs. By staying engaged with your budget and making updates as necessary, you'll be better equipped to navigate the ups and downs of your financial journey.

The process of creating a budget may seem daunting at first, but the rewards are well worth the effort. With a clear understanding of your income and expenses, you'll be able to make informed decisions about how to allocate your resources and prioritize your spending. You'll also be better positioned to identify areas where you can cut back or make changes to improve your financial health.

But perhaps most importantly, a comprehensive budget gives you the power to take control of your financial destiny. By setting clear goals and creating a roadmap to achieve them, you'll be able to make meaningful progress towards the things that matter most to you, whether that's saving for a down payment on a house, funding your children's education, or building a comfortable retirement.

So embrace the process of creating a budget, and approach it with a spirit of curiosity and empowerment. With the right tools, mindset, and commitment, you'll be well on your way to achieving the financial freedom and security you deserve.

Section 3: Implementing and Sticking to Your Budget

Picture this: you've put in the time and effort to create a comprehensive budget that aligns with your financial goals and priorities. You've categorized your income and expenses, determined your fixed and variable costs, and even allocated funds for savings and investments. But now comes the real challenge—actually implementing and sticking to your budget consistently.

It's a common struggle faced by many people, as the excitement of creating a budget can quickly fade when faced with the day-to-day realities of managing money. Temptations to overspend, unexpected expenses, and a lack of motivation can all contribute to budget derailment. However, the key to successful budgeting lies not just in the planning stage but in the execution and adherence to the plan over time.

In this section, we'll explore a range of techniques and tools that can help you bridge the gap between budgeting in theory and budgeting in practice. From tracking your spending habits and using budgeting apps to involving family members and handling financial emergencies, we'll cover strategies that can make the process of sticking to your budget more manageable and sustainable.

By implementing these techniques and tools, you'll be better equipped to navigate the challenges that come with budgeting and stay committed to your financial plan. Remember, budgeting is not a one-time event but an ongoing process that requires consistent effort and adaptation. With the right mindset, support, and tools, you can transform your budget from a mere document into a powerful catalyst for achieving your financial goals and building long-term financial stability.

So, let's dive in and discover how you can make your budget work for you, not against you, as you embark on this journey towards better financial management and a more secure future.

Subsection 3.1: Tracking Your Spending Habits

One of the most crucial aspects of successfully implementing and sticking to your budget is developing a keen awareness of your spending habits. It's easy to create a budget on paper, but it's an entirely different challenge to monitor and control your actual spending in real life. This is where tracking your spending habits comes into play.

Tracking your spending involves systematically recording and categorizing every dollar you spend, whether it's on essential expenses like rent and groceries or discretionary purchases like entertainment and dining out. By doing so, you gain a clear and accurate picture of where your money is going and can identify areas where you may be overspending or have room for improvement.

There are various methods for tracking your spending, ranging from traditional pen and paper to modern digital tools. One popular approach is to use a spending journal, where you manually record every transaction you make throughout the day. This method can be particularly effective in helping you become more mindful of your spending decisions and identifying any impulsive or unnecessary purchases.

Another option is to use spreadsheet software, such as Microsoft Excel or Google Sheets, to create a digital record of your expenses. This allows you to categorize your spending, create formulas to automatically calculate totals, and generate visual charts and graphs to better understand your spending patterns over time.

In addition to manual tracking, there are numerous budgeting apps and online tools available that can automate the process of recording and categorizing your expenses. These apps often sync with your bank accounts and credit cards, automatically importing transactions and providing real-time insights into your spending habits. Some popular examples include Mint, YNAB (You Need A Budget), and PocketGuard.

Regardless of the method you choose, the key is to be consistent and diligent in tracking your spending. Make it a daily habit to record your expenses, whether it's immediately after making a purchase or setting aside dedicated time each evening to update your records. The more consistently you track your spending, the more accurate and informative your data will be.

As you track your spending over time, patterns and trends will emerge. You may discover that you're spending more than you realized on certain categories, such as dining out or subscription services. Or you may find that you have a tendency to make impulsive purchases when you're stressed or emotional. By identifying these patterns, you can take steps to address them and make adjustments to your spending habits.

For example, if you notice that you're spending a significant amount on takeout coffee each month, you could consider investing in a quality coffee maker and brewing your own coffee at home instead. Or if you find that you're prone to overspending on online shopping when you're bored, you could explore alternative activities or hobbies that don't involve spending money.

Tracking your spending habits is not about judging or punishing yourself for your financial decisions. Rather, it's about gaining self-awareness, identifying areas for improvement, and making informed choices that align with your budget and financial goals. By regularly monitoring your spending, you'll be better equipped to make adjustments as needed and stay on track with your budget over the long term.

Remember, change doesn't happen overnight, and it's normal to have setbacks and challenges along the way. The important thing is to remain committed to the process and use the insights gained from tracking your spending to continuously refine and optimize your budget. With patience, persistence, and a willingness to learn and adapt, you can transform your spending habits and take control of your financial life.

Subsection 3.2: Using Budgeting Apps and Tools

In today's digital age, technology has revolutionized the way we manage our finances, and budgeting is no exception. Gone are the days of manually tracking expenses with pen and paper or relying on cumbersome spreadsheets. Now, a plethora of budgeting apps and tools are available at our fingertips, making the process of creating, implementing, and sticking to a budget more convenient and efficient than ever before.

Budgeting apps and tools offer a range of features and benefits that can simplify the budgeting process and help you stay on track with your financial goals. These digital solutions often provide a centralized platform for managing your income, expenses, and savings, allowing you to see a comprehensive picture of your financial situation in real-time.

One of the key advantages of using budgeting apps is the automation they provide. Many apps can sync with your bank accounts, credit cards, and investment accounts, automatically importing transactions and categorizing them based on your predefined budget categories. This eliminates the need for manual data entry and reduces the risk of errors or omissions in your budget tracking.

Popular budgeting apps like Mint, YNAB (You Need A Budget), and PocketGuard offer user-friendly interfaces and intuitive features that make budgeting accessible and engaging. These apps often provide visual dashboards and charts that display your spending patterns, budget progress, and financial goals in a clear and concise manner. They may also offer personalized insights and recommendations based on your spending habits, helping you identify areas where you can cut back or save more.

In addition to tracking expenses, many budgeting apps also offer tools for setting financial goals and monitoring your progress towards them. Whether you're saving for a down payment on a house, planning a dream vacation, or working towards paying off debt, these apps can help you break down your goals into manageable milestones and track your progress along the way. Some apps even offer features like bill reminders, savings challenges, and investment tracking to help you stay on top of all aspects of your financial life.

Another benefit of using budgeting apps and tools is the accessibility and portability they provide. With mobile apps, you can access your budget anytime, anywhere, whether you're at home, at work, or on the go. This makes it easier to make informed spending decisions in the moment, such as checking your budget before making a purchase or quickly logging an expense after a transaction.

When choosing a budgeting app or tool, it's important to consider your specific needs and preferences. Some apps may be more suitable for beginners, offering a simplified interface and basic features, while others may cater to more advanced users with complex budgeting requirements. It's also important to consider factors such as cost (some apps offer free versions with limited features, while others require a subscription), security (look for apps with strong data encryption and privacy measures), and compatibility with your devices and financial institutions.

While budgeting apps and tools can be incredibly helpful in simplifying the budgeting process, it's important to remember that they are not a magic solution. Ultimately, the success of your budget will depend on your commitment to regularly updating and monitoring your finances, making adjustments as needed, and staying disciplined in your spending habits. However, by leveraging the power of technology and choosing the right budgeting app or tool for your needs, you can streamline the process and make it easier to stay on track with your financial goals.

In conclusion, budgeting apps and tools offer a convenient and efficient way to manage your finances and stick to your budget. By automating expense tracking, providing visual insights, and offering goal-setting and progress monitoring features, these digital solutions can help you take control of your financial life and work towards a more secure and prosperous future. So why not explore the various options available and find the budgeting app or tool that works best for you?

Subsection 3.3: Involving Family Members in the Budgeting Process

Budgeting is not just a solitary endeavor; it's a collaborative process that involves all members of a household. Whether you're managing finances as a couple, a single parent, or a multigenerational family, involving your loved ones in the budgeting process is crucial for fostering financial harmony, accountability, and success.

When you involve family members in budgeting discussions and decision-making, you create a shared sense of ownership and responsibility for the household's financial well-being. By openly communicating about money matters, you can align your financial goals, priorities, and expectations, reducing the potential for conflicts and misunderstandings down the line.

One of the key benefits of involving family members in the budgeting process is increased transparency and trust. When everyone is aware of the household's income, expenses, and financial objectives, there is less room for secrecy or resentment. Family members can hold each other accountable for sticking to the budget and making responsible spending choices, providing a built-in support system for financial discipline.

Involving children in age-appropriate budgeting discussions can also be incredibly valuable. By teaching kids about money management from a young age, you can help them develop essential financial skills and habits that will serve them well throughout their lives. Children can learn the importance of saving, distinguishing between needs and wants, and making informed spending decisions by observing and participating in family budgeting practices.

To effectively involve family members in the budgeting process, start by scheduling regular financial meetings or "money dates." These dedicated times allow everyone to come together, review the household's financial situation, and discuss any concerns or challenges. Encourage open and honest communication, creating a safe space for family members to express their thoughts and ideas without judgment.

During these meetings, review your budget categories, track your progress towards financial goals, and make any necessary adjustments based on changing circumstances or priorities. Celebrate successes together, such as reaching a savings milestone or paying off a debt, to maintain motivation and a positive outlook.

Consider assigning specific budgeting tasks or responsibilities to each family member based on their skills and interests. For example, one person might be in charge of tracking expenses, while another focuses on finding ways to save money on groceries or utilities. By actively contributing to the budgeting process, family members can feel more invested in the outcome and take pride in their role in the household's financial success.

It's important to recognize that involving family members in the budgeting process may not always be easy. There may be differing opinions, priorities, or spending habits that need to be addressed and reconciled. However, by approaching these discussions with patience, empathy, and a willingness to compromise, you can work together to find solutions that benefit the entire household.

Remember, budgeting as a family is not about perfection but about progress. There will be ups and downs, successes and setbacks, but by involving your loved ones in the process, you can navigate the financial journey together, strengthening your relationships and building a more secure financial future for all.

Subsection 3.4: Handling Unexpected Expenses and Emergencies

Even with the most meticulous budgeting and expense tracking, life has a way of throwing curveballs that can disrupt your financial plans. Unexpected expenses and emergencies, such as car repairs, medical bills, or job loss, can quickly derail your budget and leave you feeling overwhelmed and stressed. However, by developing strategies to manage these unforeseen circumstances, you can minimize their impact on your financial well-being and stay on track with your long-term goals.

One of the most crucial steps in handling unexpected expenses and emergencies is to build an emergency fund. An emergency fund is a separate savings account that is specifically designated for unexpected financial needs. Ideally, your emergency fund should cover three to six months' worth of living expenses, providing a safety net in case of job loss, illness, or other major disruptions to your income. By having this financial cushion in place, you can avoid relying on high-interest credit cards or loans to cover unexpected costs, which can quickly spiral into debt.

To build your emergency fund, start by setting a realistic savings goal based on your monthly expenses and income. Consider automating your savings by setting up a recurring transfer from your checking account to your emergency fund each month. Even small contributions can add up over time, so don't be discouraged if you can only save a little bit at first. As you adjust your budget and find ways to cut expenses or increase your income, you can gradually increase your emergency fund contributions.

In addition to building an emergency fund, it's important to have a plan in place for how you will handle unexpected expenses when they arise. One strategy is to prioritize your expenses based on their urgency and importance. For example, a necessary car repair that impacts your ability to get to work would take precedence over a less urgent expense, such as a home improvement project. By focusing on the most pressing needs first, you can allocate your limited resources effectively and minimize the overall impact on your budget.

Another strategy for managing unexpected expenses is to look for ways to reduce their cost or spread them out over time. For example, if you're faced with a large medical bill, contact the healthcare provider to see if they offer payment plans or discounts for patients who pay in cash. Similarly, if your car needs a costly repair, shop around for the best prices and consider whether the repair can be delayed or if there are alternative transportation options available.

In some cases, unexpected expenses may be too large to cover with your emergency fund or other savings. In these situations, it's important to explore your options carefully and avoid making rash decisions that could worsen your financial situation. If you need to borrow money, consider low-interest options such as personal loans from a credit union or borrowing from family or friends. Be sure to have a clear plan for how you will repay the borrowed funds and communicate openly with your lender to avoid straining relationships or damaging your credit.

Finally, it's important to remember that unexpected expenses and emergencies are a normal part of life, and experiencing them does not mean that you have failed at budgeting or managing your money. Instead, view these challenges as opportunities to reassess your financial priorities, adjust your budget as needed, and build resilience for the future. By staying flexible, proactive, and committed to your long-term financial goals, you can weather any financial storm and emerge stronger on the other side.

Summary: Embracing the Journey of Budgeting Success

Implementing and sticking to a budget is a transformative journey that requires dedication, discipline, and a willingness to embrace change. By tracking your spending habits, utilizing budgeting apps and tools, involving family members in the process, and developing strategies to handle unexpected expenses and emergencies, you can create a solid foundation for long-term financial success.

Remember, budgeting is not about deprivation or restriction, but rather about aligning your spending with your values, goals, and priorities. It's a tool that empowers you to take control of your financial life, make informed decisions, and build the future you desire.

As you embark on this journey, be patient with yourself and celebrate the small victories along the way. Recognize that setbacks and challenges are a normal part of the process, and use them as opportunities to learn, grow, and refine your approach.

By consistently applying the techniques and tools discussed in this section, you can transform your relationship with money and create a life of financial abundance and security. Embrace the power of budgeting, and watch as your dreams and aspirations become a reality, one purposeful spending decision at a time.

Section 4: Expense Management Techniques

Picture this: you've created a budget, you're tracking your spending, and you're feeling pretty good about your financial progress. But then, life happens. An unexpected car repair, a medical bill, or a sudden urge to splurge on that designer handbag you've been eyeing. Before you know it, your carefully crafted budget is in shambles, and you're left wondering where all your money went.

Sound familiar? Don't worry; you're not alone. Managing expenses is a challenge that many of us face, regardless of our income level or financial savvy. It's easy to get caught up in the daily grind of life and lose sight of our spending habits, leading to financial stress and anxiety.

But what if I told you that there are effective strategies you can use to take control of your expenses and keep more money in your pocket? In this section, we'll explore a range of expense management techniques that can help you reduce your spending, make smart purchasing decisions, and ultimately achieve your financial goals.

From distinguishing between needs and wants to finding creative ways to cut costs and save money, we'll cover all the bases. We'll also delve into the art of negotiation, showing you how to secure better rates on bills, subscriptions, and services. And, perhaps most importantly, we'll discuss the concept of mindful spending and how adopting this mindset can transform your relationship with money.

By the end of this section, you'll be armed with a toolkit of expense management strategies that you can implement immediately. Whether you're looking to pay off debt, save for a big purchase, or simply improve your overall financial health, these techniques will put you on the path to success.

So, are you ready to take control of your expenses and start making every dollar count? Let's dive in and discover how you can become a master of expense management!

Subsection 4.1: Differentiating Between Needs and Wants

In the pursuit of effective expense management, one of the most crucial skills to develop is the ability to distinguish between needs and wants. This fundamental distinction lies at the heart of making sound financial decisions and prioritizing your spending in a way that aligns with your goals and values.

At first glance, it may seem like a simple task to differentiate between the two categories. Needs are often thought of as the essentials required for survival, such as food, shelter, and clothing. Wants, on the other hand, are typically associated with desires, luxuries, and non-essential items that enhance our lives but are not strictly necessary.

However, in reality, the line between needs and wants can often blur, leading to confusion and overspending. For instance, while food is undeniably a need, dining out at expensive restaurants or indulging in gourmet ingredients falls into the category of wants. Similarly, while clothing is a necessity, splurging on designer labels or following every fashion trend is a discretionary choice.

To effectively distinguish between needs and wants, it's important to take a step back and ask yourself some key questions. First, consider whether the item or experience is essential for your basic well-being and functioning. Will your life be significantly impacted if you don't have it? Next, evaluate whether there are more affordable alternatives that can fulfill the same purpose. Finally, reflect on your motivation for making the purchase. Is it driven by a genuine need or influenced by emotions, peer pressure, or temporary desires?

By honestly assessing your spending through this lens, you can begin to identify areas where you may be allocating too much money towards discretionary expenses. This awareness is the first step towards making more intentional and mindful choices about your spending.

Once you have a clearer understanding of your needs and wants, you can prioritize your budget allocations accordingly. Start by ensuring that your essential needs are met, such as housing, utilities, groceries, and healthcare. These non-negotiable expenses should be the foundation of your budget.

Next, allocate funds towards important financial goals, such as saving for emergencies, paying off debt, or investing for the future. These priorities may not feel as pressing as immediate wants, but they are crucial for long-term financial stability and success.

Only after your needs and financial goals are accounted for should you consider allocating money towards discretionary spending. By giving yourself a limited budget for wants, you can still enjoy life's pleasures without compromising your overall financial health.

Mastering the art of differentiating between needs and wants is an ongoing process that requires self-awareness, discipline, and a commitment to your financial priorities. By continually evaluating your spending through this framework, you can make more purposeful decisions, reduce unnecessary expenses, and ultimately achieve a more balanced and fulfilling financial life.

Subsection 4.2: Finding Ways to Cut Costs and Save Money

In the quest for effective expense management, one of the most powerful strategies is to actively seek out ways to reduce your spending and save money. By adopting a proactive approach to cutting costs, you can free up more of your hard-earned income to allocate towards your financial goals, such as paying off debt, building an emergency fund, or investing for the future.

The good news is that opportunities to save money can be found in virtually every aspect of your life, from your daily habits to your major purchases. The key is to develop a keen eye for identifying these cost-saving opportunities and to be willing to make small changes that can add up to significant savings over time.

One of the first places to start when looking to cut costs is your everyday expenses. Take a close look at your spending patterns and identify areas where you may be able to trim the fat. For example, you might consider bringing your lunch to work instead of eating out, brewing your own coffee at home rather than stopping at a café, or opting for generic brands over name-brand products at the grocery store. These small changes may not seem like much in isolation, but over the course of a month or a year, they can make a noticeable impact on your budget.

Another area ripe for cost-cutting is your recurring bills and subscriptions. Take inventory of all the services you pay for on a regular basis, such as cable TV, streaming platforms, gym memberships, or magazine subscriptions. Ask yourself which of these are truly essential and which ones you could live without. Consider canceling or downgrading services that you don't use frequently or that don't bring you significant value. You might also explore more affordable alternatives, such as switching to a lower-cost cell phone plan or opting for free workout videos on YouTube instead of a pricey gym membership.

When it comes to major purchases, such as appliances, electronics, or furniture, a little research and patience can go a long way in helping you save money. Before making a significant purchase, take the time to compare prices across multiple retailers, both online and in-store. Look for sales, discounts, or promotions that can help you snag a better deal. Consider timing your purchases strategically, such as waiting for end-of-season sales or holiday promotions when prices are likely to be lower.

Another cost-saving strategy is to embrace the concept of "buying used." While new items can be tempting, opting for second-hand goods can often result in substantial savings without sacrificing quality. Explore options like thrift stores, consignment shops, or online marketplaces like Craigslist or Facebook Marketplace to find gently used items at a fraction of the cost of buying new.

In addition to these specific tactics, cultivating a mindset of frugality and resourcefulness can help you identify even more opportunities to save money in your daily life. Challenge yourself to find creative ways to repurpose or repair items instead of automatically buying new ones. Learn to negotiate prices or ask for discounts when appropriate. Embrace the art of DIY and take on projects yourself instead of paying for professional services when possible.

Remember, the goal of cutting costs is not to deprive yourself or live a life of austerity, but rather to be intentional and strategic about your spending. By finding ways to save money on the things that matter less to you, you can free up more resources to allocate towards the things that bring you true joy and fulfillment.

As you embark on your cost-cutting journey, be patient with yourself and celebrate the small victories along the way. Every dollar saved is a step closer to your financial goals and a testament to your commitment to taking control of your expenses. With persistence and creativity, you'll be amazed at how much you can save and how empowered you'll feel in the process.

Subsection 4.3: Negotiating Bills and Subscriptions

In the quest to reduce monthly expenses and take control of your finances, one often overlooked strategy is negotiating better rates on your existing bills and subscriptions. Many people assume that the prices they pay for services like cable TV, internet, cell phone plans, and streaming platforms are set in stone, but the truth is that there is often room for negotiation.

The first step in successfully negotiating your bills is to do your research. Take the time to explore the current market rates for the services you use, including any promotions or discounts being offered by your provider or their competitors. This information will serve as valuable leverage when it comes time to negotiate.

Next, prepare a compelling case for why you deserve a better rate. This could include factors such as your loyalty as a long-time customer, your consistent on-time payments, or your willingness to bundle multiple services together. If you have received offers from competing providers, mention these as well, as they can demonstrate that you have other options available.

When you're ready to negotiate, contact your service provider's customer retention department. These representatives are often empowered to offer discounts and incentives to keep customers from canceling their services. Be polite but firm in your request, and don't be afraid to ask for a supervisor if the initial representative is unable to meet your needs.

During the negotiation process, be prepared to compromise and consider alternative solutions. For example, your provider may offer a temporary promotional rate rather than a permanent discount, or they may suggest bundling additional services to provide more value for your money.

Evaluate these offers carefully to determine whether they align with your financial goals and priorities.

It's important to remember that negotiation is a skill that improves with practice. If your first attempt at negotiating a bill is unsuccessful, don't be discouraged. Instead, take note of what worked and what didn't, and use this knowledge to inform your approach in future negotiations.

In addition to negotiating with your current providers, it's also worth regularly reassessing your subscriptions and memberships to ensure that you're still getting value from them. Take inventory of all the services you pay for on a monthly or annual basis, and ask yourself whether they continue to align with your needs and priorities. If you find that you're no longer using a particular service or that a less expensive alternative is available, don't hesitate to cancel or make a change.

By being proactive and strategic in your approach to bills and subscriptions, you can potentially save hundreds of dollars each year without sacrificing the services that matter most to you. Remember, every dollar saved is a dollar that can be redirected towards your other financial goals, such as paying off debt, building an emergency fund, or investing for the future.

Subsection 4.4: Adopting a Mindful Spending Mindset

In the journey towards effective expense management, one of the most transformative strategies is to embrace the concept of mindful spending. Mindful spending is a philosophy that encourages individuals to approach their purchasing decisions with intention, awareness, and alignment with their values and long-term financial goals. By adopting a mindful spending mindset, you can cultivate a more conscious and purposeful relationship with money, ultimately leading to greater financial well-being and satisfaction.

At its core, mindful spending is about being present and deliberate in your financial choices. It involves taking a moment to pause before making a purchase and asking yourself a series of reflective questions. These questions might include: "Do I truly need this item, or is it merely a want?", "Does this purchase align with my values and priorities?", "Will this expense contribute to my long-term financial goals, or will it derail my progress?" By engaging in this introspective process, you can gain clarity on the underlying motivations behind your spending habits and make more intentional decisions.

One of the key benefits of mindful spending is that it helps you differentiate between purchases that bring genuine value and fulfillment to your life and those that provide only fleeting satisfaction. In our consumer-driven society, it's easy to fall into the trap of emotional or impulsive spending, where we seek to fill a void or cope with stress through retail therapy. However, this type of spending often leads to feelings of regret, guilt, and financial strain in the long run. By practicing mindfulness, you can learn to recognize and resist these temptations, instead focusing on purchases that genuinely enhance your quality of life and align with your values.

Another important aspect of mindful spending is being aware of the broader impact of your financial choices. In today's globalized world, our purchasing decisions have far-reaching consequences that extend beyond our personal lives. By being mindful of the environmental, social, and ethical implications of our spending, we can make more responsible and sustainable choices. This might involve supporting local businesses, choosing eco-friendly products, or investing in companies that prioritize social responsibility. By aligning our spending with our values, we can use our financial power to create positive change and contribute to a more equitable and sustainable world.

Adopting a mindful spending mindset also requires a shift in our relationship with money itself. Rather than viewing money as a source of stress, scarcity, or competition, mindful spending encourages us to see money as a tool for creating the life we desire. By focusing on abundance, gratitude, and purposeful use of our financial resources, we can cultivate a more positive and empowered mindset around money. This shift in perspective can help alleviate financial anxiety, improve our decision-making, and ultimately lead to greater financial resilience and security.

To put mindful spending into practice, consider implementing some of the following strategies:

1. Before making a purchase, take a moment to pause and reflect on whether the item aligns with your values, needs, and long-term goals.
2. Keep a journal or log of your spending, noting how each purchase made you feel and whether it contributed to your overall well-being and satisfaction.
3. Set clear financial boundaries and priorities, and communicate these with your loved ones to ensure that your spending habits are aligned and supportive of your shared goals.
4. Practice gratitude for the resources and possessions you already have, focusing on contentment rather than constant acquisition.
5. Regularly review your spending patterns and adjust your habits as needed to ensure ongoing alignment with your values and goals.

By embracing a mindful spending mindset, you can transform your relationship with money and make more intentional, fulfilling financial choices. While it may require some initial effort and self-reflection, the benefits of mindful spending are well worth the investment. By aligning your spending with your values, priorities, and long-term goals, you can create a more abundant, purposeful, and satisfying financial life.

Summary: Mastering Your Expenses for Financial Freedom

Throughout this section, we've explored a range of powerful strategies and techniques for managing your expenses effectively. From distinguishing between needs and wants to finding creative ways to cut costs, negotiating better rates on bills, and cultivating a mindful spending mindset, you now have a comprehensive toolkit for taking control of your financial life.

By implementing these strategies consistently and with dedication, you can experience a profound shift in your relationship with money. No longer will you feel controlled by your expenses or trapped in a cycle of overspending. Instead, you'll gain a sense of empowerment and freedom, knowing that every dollar you spend is aligned with your values, priorities, and long-term goals.

As you embark on this journey of expense management, remember that change doesn't happen overnight. It takes time, patience, and perseverance to rewire your financial habits and build a strong foundation for success. Celebrate your progress along the way, no matter how small, and use any setbacks as opportunities for learning and growth.

The path to financial freedom is paved with intentional choices, mindful actions, and a commitment to your own well-being. By mastering your expenses and aligning your spending with your deepest values, you'll not only improve your financial health but also create a life of abundance, purpose, and joy.

So, take a deep breath, trust in your ability to transform your financial life, and embrace the power of effective expense management. Your future self will thank you for the choices you make today, as you build a brighter, more secure, and more fulfilling tomorrow.

Section 5: Regularly Reviewing and Adjusting Your Budget

Picture this: you've put in the hard work of creating a comprehensive budget, diligently tracking your expenses, and implementing smart money management strategies. You're feeling confident and in control of your finances. But as time goes by, you start to notice that your budget isn't quite aligning with your reality. Perhaps your income has changed, or your expenses have shifted in unexpected ways. This is where the power of regularly reviewing and adjusting your budget comes into play.

Just like a ship navigating the open seas, your financial journey requires constant course corrections to stay on track. Life is full of changes, both big and small, and your budget must adapt to these changes to remain effective. By periodically assessing your budget and making necessary modifications, you can ensure that your financial plan remains relevant, realistic, and aligned with your goals.

In this section, we'll dive into the importance of conducting regular budget reviews and explore practical strategies for analyzing variances and making adjustments. You'll learn how to fine-tune your budget to accommodate changes in your income, expenses, or financial objectives. We'll also discuss the value of maintaining a flexible mindset and being proactive in adapting your budget to changing circumstances.

Whether you're facing a major life transition, such as starting a new job or welcoming a child, or simply dealing with the everyday fluctuations of life, this section will equip you with the tools and knowledge you need to stay on top of your finances. By embracing the habit of regularly reviewing and adjusting your budget, you'll develop a deeper understanding of your financial situation and be better prepared to navigate any challenges that come your way.

So, let's embark on this crucial aspect of your financial journey together. Get ready to discover the power of adaptability and learn how to make your budget a dynamic, living document that evolves with you over time. By mastering the art of regular budget reviews and adjustments, you'll be well on your way to achieving your financial goals and securing a brighter financial future.

Subsection 5.1: Conducting Regular Budget Reviews

In the grand scheme of your financial journey, creating a budget is just the beginning. To truly harness the power of budgeting and ensure that you stay on track, it's crucial to conduct regular budget reviews. These periodic check-ins provide an opportunity to assess your progress, identify areas for improvement, and make necessary adjustments to keep your financial plan aligned with your goals.

But how often should you review your budget, and what should you look for during these evaluations? The answer may vary depending on your individual circumstances and financial situation. However, a good rule of thumb is to conduct a thorough budget review at least once a month. This frequency allows you to stay on top of your spending, catch any discrepancies early on, and make timely corrections before small issues snowball into larger problems.

When scheduling your budget reviews, choose a time that works best for you and treat it as a non-negotiable commitment. Whether it's the first Sunday of every month or the last Friday evening, dedicate a specific time slot to sit down and focus solely on your budget. Create a calm and distraction-free environment, gather all the necessary financial documents, and approach the review process with a clear and objective mindset.

During your budget review, start by comparing your actual income and expenses against your planned budget. Look for any variances or deviations from your original allocations. Did you overspend in certain categories or underspend in others? Were there any unexpected expenses that threw your budget off balance? Take note of these discrepancies and investigate the reasons behind them. This analysis will help you identify patterns, habits, or circumstances that may be hindering your financial progress.

As you assess your spending, don't just focus on the numbers; consider the broader context of your financial goals. Are your current spending habits aligned with your short-term and long-term objectives? Are you allocating enough money towards savings, investments, and debt repayment? Use your budget review as an opportunity to evaluate your priorities and ensure that your financial decisions are supporting your overall vision.

In addition to reviewing your past performance, use your budget review to plan for the future. Look ahead to the coming month and anticipate any upcoming expenses or changes in income. Consider any seasonal or one-time costs that may impact your budget, such as holidays, birthdays, or annual subscriptions. By proactively planning for these events, you can adjust your budget accordingly and avoid any surprises down the line.

Throughout the review process, maintain an open and honest dialogue with yourself and any family members involved in your financial decision-making. Celebrate your successes and acknowledge areas where you may have fallen short. Use these insights to set new goals, adjust your strategies, and recommit to your financial plan with renewed motivation.

Remember, conducting regular budget reviews is not about perfection; it's about progress. By consistently monitoring your financial health and making informed adjustments, you'll develop a deeper understanding of your money management habits and gain the confidence to navigate any challenges that come your way. Embrace the power of regular budget reviews and watch as your financial journey becomes more intentional, empowered, and aligned with your dreams.

Subsection 5.2: Analyzing Variances and Making Adjustments

Conducting regular budget reviews is an essential step in maintaining financial control, but simply glancing at the numbers isn't enough. To truly maximize the benefits of these periodic check-ins, it's crucial to dive deeper into the data and analyze any variances between your planned budget and actual spending. By scrutinizing these discrepancies and understanding the factors that contribute to them, you can make informed adjustments to your budget and ensure that you stay on track towards your financial goals.

When reviewing your budget, pay close attention to any categories where your actual expenses deviate significantly from your allocated amounts. These variances can be either positive (underspending) or negative (overspending), and both warrant careful examination. Start by identifying the categories with the most substantial variances and prioritize your analysis accordingly.

Once you've pinpointed the areas of concern, ask yourself a series of probing questions to uncover the root causes of the discrepancies. Were there any unexpected events or expenses that threw off your budget? Did you underestimate the cost of certain items or activities? Were there any changes in your income or lifestyle that impacted your spending patterns? By honestly assessing the factors that contributed to the variances, you can gain valuable insights into your financial habits and identify opportunities for improvement.

As you analyze your variances, it's important to approach the process with a growth mindset. Rather than viewing deviations from your budget as failures, treat them as learning experiences and opportunities for growth. Recognize that budgeting is an ongoing process of refinement and adaptation, and that setbacks are a natural part of the journey. By maintaining a positive and proactive attitude, you'll be better equipped to make the necessary adjustments and stay motivated in the face of challenges.

Armed with a clear understanding of your variances, the next step is to make strategic adjustments to your budget. These modifications should be based on your analysis and aligned with your financial priorities. If you consistently overspend in a particular category, consider reallocating funds from other areas to better reflect your actual needs. Alternatively, if you find that you're consistently underspending in certain categories, you may want to reassess your allocations and redirect those funds towards your savings or debt repayment goals.

When making adjustments to your budget, it's essential to strike a balance between flexibility and discipline. While it's important to adapt your budget to changing circumstances, be cautious not to abandon your financial plan entirely. Make sure that any modifications you make are sustainable and aligned with your long-term objectives. Consider setting realistic boundaries for discretionary spending and establishing clear guidelines for when and how to adjust your budget.

As you implement these adjustments, keep in mind that budgeting is not a one-time event, but rather an ongoing process of monitoring, analyzing, and adapting. Regularly review the impact of your modifications and assess whether they are yielding the desired results. If necessary, continue to fine-tune your approach until you find a budgeting strategy that works best for your unique financial situation.

In addition to making adjustments based on your variance analysis, consider incorporating contingencies into your budget to prepare for unexpected expenses or changes in income. Building an emergency fund, for example, can provide a financial cushion to absorb unforeseen costs without derailing your budget. Similarly, setting aside a portion of your income for discretionary spending can help you manage occasional splurges or spontaneous purchases without compromising your overall financial plan.

By mastering the art of variance analysis and strategic budget adjustments, you'll develop a deeper understanding of your financial patterns and gain the confidence to navigate any challenges that come your way. Remember, the goal of budgeting is not to achieve perfection, but rather to create a flexible and sustainable framework for managing your money and achieving your financial aspirations. Embrace the process of continuous improvement and watch as your financial skills and resilience grow with each passing month.

Subsection 5.3: Adapting Your Budget to Changing Circumstances

Life is full of surprises, and your financial circumstances are no exception. Whether it's a change in your income, unexpected expenses, or a shift in your personal goals, it's essential to have a budget that can adapt to these evolving situations. By learning how to modify your budget in response to changing circumstances, you can maintain financial stability and continue making progress towards your long-term objectives.

One of the most common reasons to adjust your budget is a change in income. If you receive a raise or bonus at work, it's an excellent opportunity to reassess your financial priorities and allocate the additional funds strategically. Consider increasing your savings contributions, paying down debt, or investing in your future goals, such as buying a home or starting a business. On the other hand, if you experience a reduction in income, whether due to job loss, reduced work hours, or other factors, you'll need to adapt your budget accordingly. Look for areas where you can cut back on expenses, such as discretionary spending or subscription services, and prioritize essential needs like housing, food, and healthcare.

Unexpected expenses can also throw your budget off balance. Whether it's a car repair, medical emergency, or home renovation, these unplanned costs can quickly drain your financial resources. To prepare for these situations, it's crucial to build an emergency fund that can cover three to six months' worth of living expenses. By having a financial safety net in place, you can weather unexpected expenses without resorting to high-interest credit card debt or loans. When faced with an unforeseen cost, adjust your budget by temporarily reducing non-essential expenses and redirecting those funds towards the emergency.

As your life evolves, so too may your financial goals. Perhaps you're saving for a down payment on a house, planning for a child's education, or working towards an early retirement. When your priorities shift, it's important to align your budget with these new objectives. Take the time to reassess your current spending and saving patterns, and make adjustments that support your updated goals. This may involve increasing your savings rate, reallocating funds from one category to another, or finding new ways to boost your income.

To effectively adapt your budget to changing circumstances, it's essential to maintain a flexible and proactive mindset. Regularly review your financial situation and be prepared to make adjustments as needed. Use budgeting tools and apps to track your spending, monitor your progress, and identify areas for improvement. Engage in open and honest communication with your partner or family members about your financial priorities and work together to make decisions that support your shared goals.

Remember, adapting your budget is not a sign of failure, but rather a demonstration of your financial resilience and adaptability. By embracing change and being willing to adjust your financial strategies, you'll be better equipped to navigate life's ups and downs and ultimately achieve your long-term aspirations. Trust in your ability to adapt, stay focused on your goals, and maintain a positive outlook as you navigate the ever-changing landscape of your financial journey.

Summary: Embracing the Power of Adaptability in Your Financial Journey

Regularly reviewing and adjusting your budget is a crucial habit that empowers you to take control of your financial life. By conducting periodic check-ins, analyzing variances, and adapting to changing circumstances, you develop a deep understanding of your money management patterns and gain the confidence to navigate any challenges that come your way.

Throughout this section, we've explored the importance of treating your budget as a living, breathing document that evolves alongside your life. We've discussed the value of setting aside dedicated time for monthly budget reviews, diving deep into your spending habits, and honestly assessing your progress towards your financial goals. By embracing a growth mindset and viewing variances as opportunities for learning and improvement, you can make strategic adjustments that keep you on track and aligned with your priorities.

As you continue on your financial journey, remember that adaptability is key. Life is full of surprises, and your ability to modify your budget in response to changes in income, expenses, or personal goals will be a crucial factor in your long-term success. By maintaining a flexible and proactive approach, you can weather any financial storms and emerge stronger and more resilient.

The power to shape your financial future lies in your hands. By regularly reviewing and adjusting your budget, you are taking an active role in creating the life you desire. Embrace the process of continuous improvement, trust in your abilities, and know that every step you take brings you closer to your ultimate financial aspirations.

As you move forward, carry with you the lessons and insights gained from this section. Let the habit of regular budget reviews become a non-negotiable part of your financial routine. Embrace the power of adaptability, and watch as your financial skills and confidence grow with each passing month. Remember, the journey to financial success is not about perfection, but rather about progress. Stay committed, stay curious, and keep moving forward, one budget review at a time.

Chapter Summary: Mastering Your Money Through Effective Budgeting and Expense Management

Throughout this chapter, we have explored the crucial role that budgeting and expense management play in achieving financial success. By understanding the importance of creating and sticking to a budget, you have taken the first step towards gaining control over your finances. We have covered the essential steps in crafting a comprehensive budget, from gathering financial information and categorizing expenses to allocating funds for savings and investments.

Implementing and adhering to your budget is key to making it work for you. By tracking your spending habits, utilizing budgeting tools and apps, involving family members in the process, and developing strategies for handling unexpected expenses, you can ensure that your budget becomes a powerful tool for financial management.

Additionally, we have delved into effective expense management techniques that can help you reduce costs and prioritize your spending. By differentiating between needs and wants, finding ways to cut expenses, negotiating bills and subscriptions, and adopting a mindful spending mindset, you can optimize your budget and make the most of your financial resources.

Remember, budgeting is not a one-time event but an ongoing process. Regularly reviewing and adjusting your budget is essential to account for changes in your income, expenses, and financial goals. By staying proactive and adaptable, you can ensure that your budget remains a relevant and effective tool for managing your finances.

Armed with the knowledge and strategies presented in this chapter, you are now equipped to take control of your expenses, make informed financial decisions, and pave the way for a more secure and prosperous financial future. Embrace the power of budgeting and expense management, and watch as your financial goals become more attainable with each passing day.

Chapter 4: Earning Income and Building Your Career

In the grand scheme of personal finance, earning income is the foundation upon which all other financial strategies are built. Your ability to generate a steady and growing income stream is crucial to achieving your short-term and long-term financial goals. Whether you're just starting your career or looking to take your professional life to the next level, understanding the various ways to increase your income and build a successful career is essential.

In this chapter, we'll explore the diverse landscape of earning income and building a rewarding career. We'll start by examining the current job market and identifying potential career paths that align with your skills, interests, and values. You'll learn how to research different industries and sectors to uncover job opportunities that match your unique talents and aspirations.

Next, we'll dive into the importance of developing your human capital. Investing in your personal and professional growth is one of the most effective ways to increase your earning potential over time. We'll discuss the benefits of pursuing education and training, acquiring certifications and licenses, gaining practical experience through internships and volunteering, and embracing a mindset of continuous learning.

Armed with the knowledge and skills to succeed, we'll then explore strategies for maximizing your earning potential. From negotiating salary and benefits to pursuing promotions and career advancement, you'll discover proven techniques for increasing your income within your current job or by exploring new opportunities. We'll also delve into the world of side hustles and freelance work, showing you how to supplement your primary income and diversify your revenue streams.

For those with an entrepreneurial spirit, we'll explore the path of starting your own business. We'll assess the skills and mindset required for successful entrepreneurship, identify promising business opportunities, and guide you through the process of developing a comprehensive business plan and securing funding. You'll learn how to manage and grow your venture, turning your passion into a profitable enterprise.

Finally, we'll examine the changing nature of work in the modern era. With rapid technological advancements and the growing influence of globalization, it's crucial to adapt and thrive in an evolving job market. We'll discuss the importance of embracing digital skills, navigating remote work and flexible arrangements, and cultivating resilience and adaptability in the face of change.

By the end of this chapter, you'll have a deep understanding of the various strategies and approaches to earning income and building a successful career. Whether you're an employee, freelancer, or entrepreneur, you'll be equipped with the knowledge and tools to take control of your professional life and unlock your full earning potential. Let's embark on this exciting journey together and discover the many paths to financial success.

Section 1: Understanding the Job Market and Employment Opportunities

In the ever-changing landscape of the modern workforce, navigating the job market and identifying potential career paths can be a daunting task. With new industries emerging, traditional roles evolving, and the impact of technology on employment, it's crucial to have a clear understanding of the current job market to make informed decisions about your career. This section will provide you with the tools and knowledge needed to explore the vast array of employment opportunities available and identify the career paths that align with your skills, interests, and goals.

As you embark on your journey to build a successful career, it's essential to recognize that the job market is not a static entity. It is constantly shifting and adapting to economic, social, and technological changes. By staying attuned to these changes and understanding the forces that shape the job market, you can position yourself to seize opportunities and thrive in your chosen field.

In the following subsections, we will delve into the strategies and techniques for researching industries and sectors, identifying your unique skills and strengths, and building a strong professional network. Whether you're just starting your career, looking to make a change, or seeking advancement in your current field, the insights and guidance provided in this section will empower you to navigate the job market with confidence and purpose.

So, let's begin our exploration of the job market and uncover the wealth of employment opportunities that await you. By the end of this section, you'll be equipped with the knowledge and tools to make informed decisions about your career path and take the first steps towards building a fulfilling and prosperous future.

Subsection 1.1: Researching Industries and Sectors

Embarking on a successful career journey begins with a deep understanding of the various industries and sectors that make up the modern economy. By researching and exploring these different areas, you can uncover a wealth of job opportunities and identify the fields that align with your interests, skills, and values.

To start your research, it's essential to grasp the distinction between industries and sectors. An industry refers to a specific group of companies that produce similar goods or services, such as the automotive industry or the healthcare industry. On the other hand, a sector is a broader category that encompasses multiple industries with shared characteristics, such as the technology sector or the financial sector.

One of the most effective ways to research industries and sectors is to utilize online resources. Government websites, such as the Bureau of Labor Statistics (BLS) in the United States, provide comprehensive data on employment trends, job growth projections, and wage information for various industries. These resources can help you identify industries with promising job prospects and understand the skills and qualifications required for success in those fields.

In addition to government resources, industry associations and trade organizations offer valuable insights into specific industries. These groups often publish reports, newsletters, and articles that highlight trends, challenges, and opportunities within their respective fields. By engaging with these resources, you can gain a deeper understanding of the dynamics and requirements of different industries.

Another powerful tool for researching industries and sectors is networking. Attending industry events, conferences, and workshops can provide you with opportunities to connect with professionals working in your fields of interest. These interactions can yield valuable insights into the day-to-day realities of working in specific industries, as well as potential job openings and career paths.

As you explore different industries and sectors, it's important to consider factors beyond job growth and salary potential. Take the time to assess the alignment between your personal values and the values and mission of companies within each industry. Consider the work culture, work-life balance, and opportunities for professional development and advancement.

Remember that your research into industries and sectors is an ongoing process. As you gain more experience and exposure to different fields, your interests and priorities may evolve. By staying curious and open to new opportunities, you can continuously refine your career path and find industries that truly resonate with your goals and passions.

Investing time and effort into researching industries and sectors is a crucial step in building a fulfilling and successful career. By understanding the landscape of opportunities available to you, you can make informed decisions about your professional journey and position yourself for long-term growth and satisfaction in your chosen field.

Subsection 1.2: Identifying Your Skills and Strengths

Discovering your unique skills and strengths is a crucial step in aligning your career path with your natural abilities and passions. By taking the time to assess your strengths, you can identify industries and roles that allow you to leverage your talents and excel in your chosen field. This process of self-discovery not only enhances your job satisfaction but also increases your chances of success and fulfillment in your professional life.

One effective way to identify your skills and strengths is to reflect on your past experiences and achievements. Consider the tasks and projects that you have undertaken, both in your personal and professional life, and analyze the skills that contributed to your success. Perhaps you have a knack for problem-solving, a talent for communication, or a keen eye for detail. By examining your accomplishments, you can begin to recognize patterns and themes that highlight your unique strengths.

Another powerful tool for assessing your skills is to seek feedback from others. Reach out to colleagues, mentors, friends, and family members who have witnessed your abilities in action. Ask them to provide honest and constructive feedback on your strengths and areas where you excel. Often, others can offer valuable insights and perspectives that you may have overlooked or taken for granted.

In addition to reflecting on your experiences and seeking feedback, there are various assessments and personality tests that can help you identify your skills and strengths. These tools, such as the Myers-Briggs Type Indicator (MBTI), the StrengthsFinder assessment, or the Holland Code (RIASEC) test, provide structured frameworks for understanding your personality traits, work preferences, and natural abilities. By completing these assessments and analyzing the results, you can gain a clearer picture of your unique strengths and how they can be applied in different career contexts.

As you identify your skills and strengths, it's important to consider how they align with your interests and values. Reflect on the activities and subjects that naturally capture your attention and ignite your passion. Consider the causes and issues that you care deeply about and the type of work environment that energizes you. By combining your skills and strengths with your interests and values, you can narrow down potential career paths that offer the greatest opportunity for fulfillment and success.

Once you have a clearer understanding of your skills and strengths, it's time to research industries and roles that align with your abilities. Explore job descriptions and career profiles that highlight the skills and strengths you possess. Investigate companies and organizations that value and cultivate the talents you bring to the table. By proactively seeking out opportunities that match your unique skill set, you can position yourself for a rewarding and satisfying career journey.

Remember that identifying your skills and strengths is an ongoing process. As you gain new experiences, take on new challenges, and learn new things, your abilities and interests may evolve. Embrace the journey of self-discovery and be open to exploring new possibilities as your skills and strengths continue to grow and develop over time.

By dedicating time and effort to identifying your skills and strengths, you lay the foundation for a career that not only showcases your talents but also brings you joy and fulfillment. Embrace the process of self-reflection, seek feedback and guidance, and align your abilities with your passions. With a clear understanding of your unique strengths, you can confidently navigate the job market and build a career that truly resonates with who you are and what you have to offer.

Subsection 1.3: Networking and Building Professional Relationships

In the modern job market, networking and building professional relationships are essential components of career success. Gone are the days when a strong resume and a solid set of skills were enough to secure your dream job. Today, who you know is often just as important as what you know. By cultivating a robust network of professional contacts, you open doors to new opportunities, gain valuable insights and advice, and position yourself for long-term career growth.

At its core, networking is about building genuine connections with others in your industry or field of interest. It involves engaging in meaningful conversations, sharing knowledge and resources, and establishing mutually beneficial relationships. Effective networking is not about collecting business cards or adding connections on LinkedIn; rather, it's about fostering authentic interactions and creating a supportive community of professionals who can help you navigate the challenges and opportunities of your career journey.

One of the most powerful benefits of networking is access to hidden job opportunities. Many positions are never advertised publicly, and instead, are filled through referrals and personal recommendations. By building strong relationships with professionals in your field, you increase your chances of being considered for these "hidden" jobs. Your network can also provide valuable insights into company cultures, industry trends, and the skills and experiences that employers are looking for, allowing you to tailor your job search and professional development accordingly.

Networking also serves as a valuable source of mentorship and guidance. Connecting with experienced professionals who have already navigated the challenges you face can provide invaluable wisdom and support. These mentors can offer advice on career decisions, help you develop new skills, and provide constructive feedback on your work. By building relationships with mentors and sponsors, you gain access to a wealth of knowledge and experience that can accelerate your professional growth and help you avoid common pitfalls.

To build a strong professional network, it's important to be proactive and strategic in your approach. Attend industry events, conferences, and workshops where you can connect with like-minded professionals. Join relevant professional associations and participate in their activities and discussions. Engage with your alumni network and reconnect with former colleagues and classmates. Leverage social media platforms, such as LinkedIn, to expand your online presence and connect with professionals in your field.

When networking, focus on building genuine, reciprocal relationships. Show interest in others' work and experiences, and be generous with your own knowledge and resources. Follow up with the people you meet, and find ways to stay in touch and provide value to your connections. Remember that networking is a long-term investment in your career, and the relationships you build today can pay dividends for years to come.

In addition to external networking, it's equally important to build strong relationships within your current organization. Collaborate with colleagues across different departments, and seek out opportunities to work on cross-functional projects. Participate in company events and initiatives, and take the time to get to know your coworkers on a personal level. By building a strong internal network, you not only enhance your job satisfaction and performance but also position yourself for future growth and advancement within the company.

Ultimately, networking and building professional relationships are essential skills for navigating the modern job market and achieving long-term career success. By cultivating a robust network of contacts, mentors, and sponsors, you gain access to valuable opportunities, insights, and support that can help you thrive in your chosen field. Embrace the power of human connection, and invest in building meaningful, mutually beneficial relationships with those around you. Your network is one of your most valuable career assets, and the effort you put into nurturing it today will pay off in countless ways throughout your professional journey.

Summary: Navigating the Job Market with Confidence and Purpose

Navigating the job market and identifying potential career paths can be a daunting task, but by understanding the dynamics of industries, sectors, and your own unique strengths, you can approach your career journey with confidence and purpose. Researching industries and sectors provides valuable insights into employment trends, job growth projections, and the skills and qualifications required for success in various fields. By exploring government resources, industry associations, and networking opportunities, you can gain a comprehensive understanding of the landscape of opportunities available to you.

Equally important is the process of identifying your own skills and strengths. Through self-reflection, seeking feedback from others, and utilizing assessment tools, you can uncover your natural abilities and align them with your interests and values. This self-discovery process lays the foundation for a fulfilling career that showcases your talents and brings you joy.

However, success in the modern job market goes beyond individual skills and knowledge. Building a strong professional network is crucial for accessing hidden job opportunities, gaining valuable insights and advice, and positioning yourself for long-term career growth. By cultivating genuine relationships with professionals in your field, participating in industry events, and leveraging online platforms, you can create a supportive community that helps you navigate the challenges and opportunities of your career journey.

As you embark on your career path, remember that the job market is constantly evolving. By staying attuned to industry trends, continuously developing your skills, and adapting to change, you can position yourself for success in the face of uncertainty. Embrace the journey of self-discovery, be proactive in your approach, and trust in your unique strengths and abilities.

Understanding the job market and employment opportunities is the first step towards building a rewarding and fulfilling career. By combining industry research, self-reflection, and strategic networking, you can navigate the job market with confidence and purpose, and unlock a world of possibilities for your professional growth and success. As you move forward, keep an open mind, stay curious, and be ready to seize the opportunities that align with your goals and passions. Your dream career awaits, and with the right knowledge and approach, you have the power to make it a reality.

Section 2: Developing Your Human Capital

Imagine for a moment that you are a highly sought-after professional, commanding a top salary in your field. What sets you apart from the competition? Is it your innate talents, your years of experience, or something more? The answer lies in your human capital—the knowledge, skills, and abilities that you bring to the table. Just like any other form of capital, your human capital is an asset that can be developed, refined, and leveraged to increase your earning potential and achieve your career goals.

In today's rapidly evolving job market, simply having a degree or a few years of experience is no longer enough to guarantee success. Employers are looking for candidates who possess a diverse range of skills, are adaptable to change, and are committed to continuous learning and growth. By investing in your personal and professional development, you can position yourself as a valuable asset to any organization and command a higher price for your services.

But where do you start? How can you identify the skills and knowledge that will be most valuable in your chosen field? And what are the most effective ways to acquire and develop those skills? In this section, we will explore the various strategies and techniques you can use to build your human capital and increase your earning potential. From pursuing advanced education and training to gaining practical experience through internships and volunteering, we will cover all the key areas you need to focus on to take your career to the next level.

So whether you are just starting out in your career or looking to make a mid-career pivot, developing your human capital is an investment that will pay dividends for years to come. By taking a proactive approach to your personal and professional growth, you can position yourself for success in any economic environment and build a career that is both fulfilling and financially rewarding. Let's dive in and discover how you can unlock your full potential and achieve your career dreams.

Subsection 2.1: Pursuing Education and Training

In the pursuit of developing your human capital, education and training play a crucial role. Whether you are just starting your career or looking to advance in your current field, investing in your knowledge and skills can open up new opportunities and increase your earning potential.

One of the most obvious ways to pursue education is through formal schooling, such as earning a degree or certificate from a college or university. Higher education can provide you with a strong foundation in your chosen field, as well as expose you to new ideas and perspectives. It can also signal to potential employers that you have the dedication and discipline to complete a rigorous program of study.

However, education doesn't always have to take place in a traditional classroom setting. With the rise of online learning platforms and massive open online courses (MOOCs), it's easier than ever to access high-quality educational content from anywhere in the world. These online courses can be a cost-effective way to gain new skills and knowledge, and many of them offer certificates of completion that can be added to your resume.

Another way to pursue education is through professional development workshops and seminars. These short-term programs can provide targeted training in specific areas, such as project management, leadership, or technical skills. Many employers offer professional development opportunities to their employees, but you can also seek out workshops and seminars on your own.

In addition to formal education and training programs, there are many informal ways to continue learning and developing your skills. Reading books and articles in your field, attending conferences and networking events, and seeking out mentors and advisors can all contribute to your ongoing education and professional growth.

Investing in education and training can pay off in many ways. It can help you stay current with the latest trends and technologies in your field, making you a more valuable asset to your employer. It can also open up new career paths and opportunities for advancement, as well as increase your confidence and job satisfaction.

Of course, pursuing education and training requires an investment of time and money. It's important to carefully consider your goals and budget when deciding which educational opportunities to pursue. But with careful planning and a commitment to lifelong learning, investing in your education can be one of the best decisions you make for your career and your future earning potential.

Subsection 2.2: Acquiring Certifications and Licenses

In today's competitive job market, having the right certifications and licenses can set you apart from other candidates and demonstrate your expertise in your field. These credentials serve as proof of your knowledge, skills, and commitment to your profession, and can often lead to higher salaries, better job opportunities, and increased credibility among colleagues and clients.

Certifications are typically awarded by professional organizations or industry associations after completing a specific course of study or passing an examination. They indicate that you have met a set of standards or qualifications in your field, and have the necessary knowledge and skills to perform your job effectively. For example, a project manager might pursue a Project Management Professional (PMP) certification from the Project Management Institute (PMI), while a financial analyst might obtain a Chartered Financial Analyst (CFA) certification from the CFA Institute.

Licenses, on the other hand, are usually granted by government agencies or regulatory bodies, and are required to legally practice certain professions. They ensure that professionals meet minimum standards of competency and adhere to ethical guidelines in their work. Examples of licensed professions include doctors, lawyers, nurses, teachers, and architects.

Obtaining certifications and licenses often requires a significant investment of time and money, but the benefits can be substantial. In many industries, having these credentials is not just a bonus, but a necessity for career advancement. They can open doors to higher-level positions, increase your earning potential, and provide access to exclusive job opportunities.

Moreover, the process of acquiring certifications and licenses can be a valuable learning experience in itself. It can expose you to the latest trends, best practices, and technologies in your field, and provide opportunities to network with other professionals and expand your knowledge base. Many certification programs also require ongoing education and recertification, ensuring that you stay current and continue to develop your skills over time.

When considering which certifications or licenses to pursue, it's important to research the requirements and benefits carefully. Look for credentials that are widely recognized and respected in your industry, and that align with your career goals and interests. Consider the time and financial commitments required, and weigh them against the potential returns on investment.

In some cases, your employer may be willing to support your pursuit of certifications or licenses, either by providing financial assistance or allowing time off for study and exams. If not, there are often scholarships, grants, or loans available to help offset the costs.

Ultimately, acquiring certifications and licenses is a powerful way to invest in your human capital and demonstrate your value to potential employers. By taking the initiative to develop your skills and knowledge, you can set yourself apart in a crowded job market and position yourself for long-term career success.

Subsection 2.3: Gaining Practical Experience Through Internships and Volunteering

While education and certifications provide a solid foundation for your career, nothing quite compares to the value of hands-on experience in your field. Internships and volunteer work offer invaluable opportunities to gain practical skills, build your professional network, and explore different career paths.

Internships are typically short-term, structured programs designed to provide students or recent graduates with real-world experience in a particular industry or company. They can be paid or unpaid, and may range from a few weeks to several months in duration. Internships allow you to apply the knowledge and skills you've acquired in school to actual projects and tasks, giving you a taste of what it's like to work in your chosen field.

Not only do internships provide practical experience, but they also offer a chance to make valuable connections within your industry. You'll have the opportunity to work alongside experienced professionals, learn from their expertise, and build relationships that can lead to future job opportunities or mentorship. Many companies use internships as a way to identify and recruit promising talent, so excelling in your internship can often lead to a full-time job offer.

Volunteering is another excellent way to gain practical experience and make a positive impact in your community. While volunteer work may not always be directly related to your chosen career path, it can still provide valuable skills and experiences that transfer to the workplace. For example, volunteering for a local nonprofit organization can help you develop leadership, communication, and project management skills, all of which are highly valued by employers.

Volunteering can also help you explore different career options and gain exposure to new industries or sectors. By working with a variety of organizations and causes, you can discover new passions and interests that may influence your career choices. Additionally, volunteering demonstrates your commitment to social responsibility and community engagement, which can set you apart from other candidates in a competitive job market.

When seeking internships or volunteer opportunities, it's important to be strategic and proactive. Research companies or organizations that align with your career goals and values, and don't be afraid to reach out and express your interest. Attend job fairs, networking events, and industry conferences to make connections and learn about potential opportunities.

Once you've secured an internship or volunteer position, make the most of the experience by taking on new challenges, asking questions, and seeking feedback from your supervisors and colleagues. Keep a record of your accomplishments and the skills you've developed, as these can be valuable additions to your resume and portfolio.

Remember, gaining practical experience through internships and volunteering is not just about building your resume; it's about discovering your strengths, exploring your passions, and making a meaningful contribution to the world around you. By embracing these opportunities with enthusiasm and dedication, you'll not only develop your human capital but also set yourself on the path to a fulfilling and successful career.

Subsection 2.4: Continuous Learning and Staying Up-to-Date

In today's rapidly evolving world, the skills and knowledge that were once sufficient to succeed in your career may no longer be enough. Industries are constantly changing, new technologies are emerging, and best practices are continuously being refined. To stay competitive and relevant in your field, it's essential to embrace a mindset of continuous learning and commit to staying up-to-date with the latest trends and developments.

Continuous learning involves proactively seeking out opportunities to expand your knowledge and skills, even after you've completed your formal education or training. It means taking responsibility for your own professional growth and recognizing that learning is a lifelong process. By continuously learning and adapting to change, you can position yourself as a valuable asset to your organization and increase your earning potential over time.

One of the most effective ways to stay current in your field is to regularly read industry publications, blogs, and news sources. These resources can help you stay informed about the latest trends, challenges, and opportunities in your industry, as well as provide insights into how other professionals are adapting to change. Consider subscribing to relevant newsletters, following thought leaders on social media, and attending industry conferences and events to stay connected and engaged.

Another important aspect of continuous learning is seeking out opportunities to develop new skills and knowledge. This might involve taking online courses, attending workshops or seminars, or pursuing additional certifications in your field. Many employers offer professional development programs or tuition reimbursement for employees who want to continue their education, so be sure to explore these options and take advantage of them when possible.

In addition to formal learning opportunities, there are many informal ways to continue growing and developing as a professional. Seeking out mentors or coaches who can provide guidance and support, participating in professional networks or associations, and volunteering for projects or initiatives that stretch your skills are all excellent ways to learn and grow.

It's also important to stay curious and open-minded, and to approach learning with a growth mindset. This means embracing challenges and seeing failures as opportunities to learn and improve, rather than as setbacks or limitations. By cultivating a love of learning and a willingness to step outside your comfort zone, you can continue to grow and develop throughout your career.

Of course, staying up-to-date and continuously learning requires an investment of time and effort. It can be challenging to find the motivation and discipline to prioritize learning when you're already juggling the demands of work and life. However, by setting clear goals, creating a plan, and building learning into your daily routine, you can make continuous learning a habit and a priority.

Ultimately, the key to staying relevant and valuable in your career is to never stop learning and growing. By embracing a mindset of continuous learning, staying up-to-date with industry trends and developments, and proactively seeking out opportunities to develop new skills and knowledge, you can position yourself for long-term success and fulfillment in your chosen field.

Summary: Investing in Yourself for a Brighter Financial Future

Throughout this section, we've explored the various ways in which you can invest in your human capital to increase your earning potential and achieve your career goals. From pursuing education and training to acquiring certifications and licenses, gaining practical experience through internships and volunteering, and embracing continuous learning, the path to professional growth is multifaceted and ongoing.

By taking a proactive approach to your personal and professional development, you can position yourself as a valuable asset in the job market and command higher salaries and better opportunities. Investing in your education, skills, and knowledge is not just a short-term strategy, but a lifelong commitment to excellence and adaptability in the face of change.

As you embark on this journey of self-improvement, remember that the process is not always easy or straightforward. It requires dedication, discipline, and a willingness to step outside your comfort zone. You may face challenges and setbacks along the way, but by staying focused on your goals and persisting through adversity, you can overcome any obstacle and emerge stronger and more resilient.

Ultimately, developing your human capital is about more than just increasing your earning potential. It's about unlocking your full potential, discovering your passions, and building a career that aligns with your values and aspirations. By investing in yourself, you are not only securing your financial future but also paving the way for a more fulfilling and meaningful life.

So take the first step today. Identify the skills and knowledge you need to succeed in your chosen field, and start exploring the many opportunities available to you. Whether it's enrolling in a course, seeking out a mentor, or volunteering for a cause you believe in, every action you take brings you one step closer to your goals.

Remember, your human capital is your most valuable asset. By nurturing and developing it over time, you can achieve the financial security, professional success, and personal fulfillment you deserve. The power to transform your life lies within you – all you have to do is invest in yourself and watch your potential unfold.

Section 3: Maximizing Your Earning Potential

Picture this: you're sitting across the table from your boss, ready to discuss your annual performance review. Your palms are sweaty, and your heart is racing. You know you've worked hard and deserve a raise, but the thought of negotiating your salary fills you with dread. Sound familiar? You're not alone. Many people struggle with advocating for their worth in the workplace, leaving money on the table and limiting their earning potential.

But what if I told you that maximizing your earning potential is within your reach? That by implementing a few key strategies, you can increase your income, negotiate better compensation, and take control of your financial future? In this section, we'll explore the art of salary negotiation, the importance of pursuing promotions and career advancement, and the potential of supplementing your income through side hustles and freelance work.

We'll dive into the psychology behind successful negotiation techniques, arming you with the tools and confidence needed to articulate your value and secure the compensation you deserve. You'll learn how to research market rates for your position, build a compelling case for your achievements, and navigate common objections and pushback from employers.

But maximizing your earning potential goes beyond just negotiating your salary. We'll also examine the importance of proactively pursuing promotions and career advancement within your organization. You'll discover strategies for showcasing your skills, taking on additional responsibilities, and positioning yourself as a valuable asset to your company.

And in today's gig economy, there's never been a better time to explore the world of side hustles and freelance work. Whether you're looking to turn a passion project into a profitable venture or simply supplement your primary income, we'll provide guidance on identifying opportunities, marketing your services, and managing your time effectively.

By the end of this section, you'll have a comprehensive toolkit for maximizing your earning potential and taking control of your financial future. So, let's roll up our sleeves and get started on the path to a more prosperous and fulfilling career.

Subsection 3.1: Negotiating Salary and Benefits

Picture this: you've just received a job offer, and you're thrilled about the opportunity. But there's one thing standing between you and your dream job – the salary. You know you're worth more than what they're offering, but the thought of negotiating makes your palms sweat and your heart race. Sound familiar?

Negotiating salary and benefits is a crucial skill that can have a significant impact on your long-term earning potential. However, many people feel uncomfortable or even afraid to negotiate, worrying that they might appear greedy or ungrateful. But the truth is, negotiating your compensation package is a normal and expected part of the hiring process.

The key to successful negotiation is preparation. Before you even step into the negotiation room, you need to do your homework. Research the market rates for your position, taking into account factors such as your experience, education, and location. Websites like Glassdoor, PayScale, and Salary.com can provide valuable insights into the compensation ranges for your role.

Armed with this information, you can begin to build a compelling case for why you deserve a higher salary or better benefits. Start by making a list of your accomplishments, skills, and experiences that make you a valuable asset to the company. Quantify your achievements wherever possible, using metrics such as revenue generated, costs saved, or projects completed.

When it comes time to negotiate, it's essential to approach the conversation with confidence and professionalism. Begin by expressing your excitement about the job offer and your appreciation for the opportunity. Then, calmly and assertively state your case for a higher salary or better benefits package, using the evidence you've gathered to support your request.

It's also important to be prepared for pushback or objections from the employer. They may argue that the salary is non-negotiable or that they don't have room in the budget for additional benefits. In these cases, it's crucial to remain calm and respectful while continuing to advocate for your worth. Consider negotiating for alternative forms of compensation, such as a signing bonus, additional vacation time, or professional development opportunities.

Remember, negotiation is a two-way street. Be willing to listen to the employer's perspective and find a mutually beneficial solution. And if the company is unable or unwilling to meet your requests, be prepared to walk away. While it can be disappointing to turn down a job offer, it's important to know your worth and not settle for less than you deserve.

In the end, negotiating your salary and benefits is about more than just the numbers on your paycheck. It's about advocating for your worth, setting yourself up for long-term financial success, and ensuring that you're fairly compensated for the value you bring to the company. By approaching the negotiation process with preparation, confidence, and professionalism, you can maximize your earning potential and take control of your financial future.

Subsection 3.2: Pursuing Promotions and Career Advancement

You've landed your dream job, and you're excelling in your role. But as time passes, you start to feel a sense of stagnation. You're eager to take on new challenges, expand your skills, and climb the corporate ladder. However, promotions and career advancement don't always come easily. It takes a proactive approach, strategic planning, and a willingness to go above and beyond to catch the attention of your superiors and demonstrate your value to the organization.

First and foremost, it's essential to understand that promotions are earned, not given. Simply showing up to work and completing your assigned tasks is not enough to warrant a promotion. You need to consistently demonstrate exceptional performance, take initiative, and contribute to the success of your team and the organization as a whole.

One effective strategy for pursuing promotions is to actively seek out opportunities to expand your responsibilities and take on new challenges. Volunteer for projects outside your normal scope of work, particularly those that are high-profile or strategically important to the company. By stepping up and taking on additional tasks, you showcase your willingness to grow and your ability to handle increased responsibility.

Another key aspect of career advancement is continuous learning and skill development. Stay up-to-date with the latest industry trends, technologies, and best practices. Attend workshops, conferences, and training sessions to expand your knowledge and expertise. By investing in your own professional development, you demonstrate your commitment to your career and your value as an employee.

Networking is also crucial for career advancement. Build strong relationships with colleagues, managers, and leaders within your organization. Attend company events, participate in employee resource groups, and engage in informal conversations with coworkers. By establishing a positive reputation and cultivating a network of allies, you increase your visibility and create opportunities for growth and advancement.

When it comes to seeking promotions, timing is everything. Pay attention to the company's business cycles and strategic priorities. Look for opportunities to showcase your achievements and make a case for your promotion when the company is in a position to recognize and reward top performers. Schedule regular check-ins with your manager to discuss your career goals, seek feedback on your performance, and express your interest in taking on additional responsibilities.

It's also important to be proactive in communicating your achievements and the value you bring to the organization. Keep a record of your accomplishments, quantifying your results whenever possible. Share your successes with your manager and other key stakeholders, highlighting how your contributions have positively impacted the company's bottom line.

However, it's important to approach the pursuit of promotions with a balanced perspective. While it's essential to advocate for yourself and your career growth, it's equally important to be a team player and support the success of your colleagues. Avoid engaging in office politics or undermining others in your quest for advancement. Instead, focus on collaborating, mentoring, and contributing to a positive work environment.

Remember that career advancement is a marathon, not a sprint. It may take time, patience, and persistence to secure the promotion you desire. Stay focused on your goals, continue to deliver exceptional work, and seize opportunities as they arise. By consistently demonstrating your value, expanding your skills, and building strong relationships, you'll position yourself for long-term career success and financial growth within your organization.

Subsection 3.3: Exploring Side Hustles and Freelance Opportunities

In today's fast-paced, digital world, the traditional 9-to-5 job is no longer the only way to earn a living. With the rise of the gig economy and the increasing popularity of remote work, more and more people are turning to side hustles and freelance opportunities to supplement their income and achieve greater financial freedom.

Side hustles are part-time jobs or projects that you take on in addition to your primary source of income. These can range from driving for a ride-sharing service, selling handmade crafts online, or offering tutoring services in your area of expertise. The beauty of side hustles is that they allow you to leverage your skills and passions to earn extra money on your own terms, often with flexible hours and the ability to work from home.

Freelancing, on the other hand, involves offering your professional services to clients on a project-by-project basis. This can include writing, graphic design, web development, consulting, or any other skill that businesses or individuals are willing to pay for. As a freelancer, you have the freedom to choose your clients, set your own rates, and work on projects that align with your interests and values.

One of the biggest advantages of side hustles and freelance work is the potential to significantly boost your income without the need to commit to a full-time job or long-term contract. By diversifying your income streams and taking on additional work outside of your primary job, you can increase your financial stability and create a safety net for yourself in case of job loss or other unexpected events.

However, it's important to approach side hustles and freelance opportunities with a strategic mindset. Before diving in, take the time to assess your skills, interests, and the demand for your services in the market. Research potential clients or platforms where you can offer your services, and develop a clear plan for how you will manage your time and resources to balance your side hustle with your other commitments.

It's also crucial to set realistic expectations and goals for your side hustle or freelance work. While the potential for earning extra income is significant, it's important to remember that building a successful side hustle or freelance career takes time, effort, and persistence. Be prepared to invest in your skills, market yourself effectively, and deliver high-quality work to attract and retain clients.

Another key consideration when exploring side hustles and freelance opportunities is the legal and financial implications of your work. Depending on your location and the nature of your side hustle, you may need to obtain licenses, permits, or insurance to operate legally. You'll also need to keep accurate records of your income and expenses, and set aside money for taxes and other business-related costs.

Despite these challenges, the rewards of side hustles and freelance work can be significant. Not only can you increase your income and achieve greater financial stability, but you can also gain valuable skills, build your professional network, and explore new career paths that align with your passions and goals.

In the end, whether you choose to pursue a side hustle or freelance work depends on your individual circumstances, skills, and goals. But by carefully considering your options, developing a strategic plan, and staying committed to your vision, you can unlock the potential of these alternative income streams and take control of your financial future.

Summary: Unlocking Your Full Financial Potential

Congratulations! You've taken a significant step towards maximizing your earning potential and securing a brighter financial future. By mastering the art of salary negotiation, pursuing strategic career advancement, and exploring the world of side hustles and freelance opportunities, you're well on your way to unlocking your full financial potential.

Remember, negotiating your salary and benefits is not about being greedy or ungrateful; it's about advocating for your worth and ensuring that you're fairly compensated for the value you bring to your employer. With the right preparation, confidence, and approach, you can successfully navigate the negotiation process and secure the compensation package you deserve.

But your earning potential doesn't stop there. By proactively seeking out promotions and career advancement opportunities, you can continue to grow your skills, take on new challenges, and climb the corporate ladder. Stay focused on delivering exceptional work, building strong relationships, and consistently demonstrating your value to your organization.

And in today's dynamic and ever-evolving job market, side hustles and freelance work offer a compelling way to diversify your income streams and achieve greater financial freedom. By leveraging your skills and passions, you can create additional sources of revenue that align with your interests and goals.

As you embark on this journey of maximizing your earning potential, remember that success rarely happens overnight. It takes time, effort, and persistence to build the career and financial life you desire. But by staying committed to your goals, continuously investing in your personal and professional growth, and seizing opportunities as they arise, you'll be well on your way to achieving the financial success you deserve.

So, take a moment to celebrate how far you've come and the valuable insights you've gained throughout this section. But don't stop here. Keep pushing forward, stay curious, and never stop learning. The world of personal finance is vast and ever-changing, and there's always more to discover.

In the next section, we'll dive into the fascinating world of entrepreneurship and explore what it takes to start and grow your own business. Get ready to unleash your inner entrepreneur and discover the rewards and challenges of being your own boss. The journey towards financial freedom continues, and the best is yet to come!

Section 4: Entrepreneurship and Starting Your Own Business

Have you ever dreamed of being your own boss, turning your passion into a thriving business, and taking control of your financial future?

Entrepreneurship is a path that many have taken to achieve their goals and create a life of freedom and fulfillment. In this section, we will explore the exciting world of entrepreneurship and guide you through the process of starting your own business.

Starting a business can be a daunting task, but with the right mindset, skills, and knowledge, anyone can embark on this rewarding journey. We will begin by helping you assess your entrepreneurial skills and mindset, ensuring that you have what it takes to succeed as a business owner. From there, we will dive into the process of identifying viable business opportunities and assessing market needs, so you can create a product or service that truly resonates with your target audience.

Once you have a solid business idea, we will walk you through the crucial steps of developing a comprehensive business plan and exploring various funding options. Whether you choose to bootstrap your venture, seek investors, or explore alternative financing methods, we will provide you with the insights and resources you need to secure the necessary capital to bring your vision to life.

But starting a business is just the beginning. To truly succeed as an entrepreneur, you must learn how to effectively manage and grow your business over time. From building a strong team and establishing efficient operations to marketing your products and services and scaling your venture, we will cover all the essential aspects of running a successful business.

Throughout this section, we will share inspiring stories of successful entrepreneurs who have paved the way and offer practical advice and actionable strategies that you can implement in your own entrepreneurial journey. Whether you are a first-time entrepreneur or an experienced business owner looking to take your venture to the next level, this section will provide you with the tools, knowledge, and motivation you need to turn your dreams into reality.

So, if you are ready to take the leap into entrepreneurship and start building the business of your dreams, let's dive in and explore the exciting possibilities that await you on this transformative journey.

Subsection 4.1: Assessing Your Entrepreneurial Skills and Mindset

Before embarking on the exciting journey of starting your own business, it's crucial to take a step back and honestly assess your entrepreneurial skills and mindset. Entrepreneurship is not for everyone, and it requires a unique set of qualities, abilities, and attitudes to succeed. By taking the time to evaluate yourself, you can determine whether starting a business is the right path for you and identify areas where you may need to develop further.

One of the key traits of successful entrepreneurs is a strong sense of self-awareness. They understand their strengths, weaknesses, passions, and motivations, and they use this knowledge to guide their decision-making and actions. To assess your own self-awareness, consider questions such as: What are my core values and beliefs? What are my natural talents and skills? What motivates me to take action? What are my biggest fears and limitations?

In addition to self-awareness, successful entrepreneurs possess a range of other essential skills and qualities. These include:

1. Creativity and innovation: The ability to generate new ideas, spot opportunities, and think outside the box.
2. Resilience and perseverance: The capacity to bounce back from setbacks, learn from failures, and keep pushing forward in the face of challenges.
3. Adaptability and flexibility: The willingness to embrace change, pivot when necessary, and adjust to new circumstances and market conditions.
4. Leadership and communication: The ability to inspire and motivate others, build strong teams, and effectively communicate your vision and goals.

5. Risk-taking and decision-making: The courage to take calculated risks, make tough decisions, and navigate uncertainty and ambiguity.

To evaluate your own entrepreneurial skills, consider taking self-assessment tests, seeking feedback from colleagues and mentors, and reflecting on your past experiences and achievements. Look for patterns in your behavior and performance that demonstrate your strengths and areas for improvement.

In addition to skills, having the right mindset is essential for entrepreneurial success. This means cultivating a growth mindset, where you view challenges as opportunities for learning and development, rather than as threats or limitations. It also means embracing failure as a natural part of the entrepreneurial process and using it as a stepping stone to success.

Other key aspects of an entrepreneurial mindset include:

1. Passion and purpose: Having a deep sense of commitment and enthusiasm for your business idea and a clear understanding of the value and impact you want to create.
2. Confidence and self-belief: Believing in yourself, your abilities, and your vision, even in the face of doubt, rejection, or setbacks.
3. Proactivity and initiative: Taking ownership of your goals and actions, and actively seeking out opportunities and solutions, rather than waiting for things to happen.
4. Curiosity and continuous learning: Having an open and inquisitive mind, and a willingness to constantly learn, grow, and adapt to new knowledge and insights.

By honestly assessing your entrepreneurial skills and mindset, you can gain a clearer understanding of your strengths, weaknesses, and areas for development. This self-awareness can help you make informed decisions about whether starting a business is the right path for you, and what steps you need to take to set yourself up for success. Remember, entrepreneurship is a journey of continuous learning and growth, and by cultivating the right skills and mindset, you can unlock your full potential as a business owner and leader.

Subsection 4.2: Identifying Business Opportunities and Market Needs

One of the most crucial aspects of starting a successful business is identifying viable opportunities and understanding the needs of your target market. Many aspiring entrepreneurs make the mistake of rushing into a business idea without thoroughly assessing its potential or considering whether there is a genuine demand for their product or service. To avoid this pitfall, it's essential to take a systematic approach to opportunity identification and market research.

The first step in identifying business opportunities is to stay alert and observant of the world around you. Keep an eye out for problems or challenges that people face in their daily lives, as these can often be translated into business ideas. For example, if you notice that many people in your community struggle to find reliable and affordable pet care services, this could be an opportunity to start a pet-sitting or dog-walking business.

Another way to identify potential business opportunities is to stay up-to-date with the latest trends and developments in your industry or area of interest. Attend trade shows, conferences, and networking events to learn about emerging technologies, changing consumer preferences, and new market segments. By staying informed and connected, you'll be better positioned to spot opportunities as they arise.

Once you've identified a potential business opportunity, the next step is to assess its viability by conducting thorough market research. This involves gathering and analyzing data about your target market, competitors, and industry trends to determine whether there is a sufficient demand for your product or service, and whether you can realistically compete in the market.

One key aspect of market research is identifying your target customer. Who are the people most likely to buy your product or service? What are their demographics, preferences, and purchasing behaviors? By developing a clear understanding of your ideal customer, you can tailor your offerings and marketing strategies to better meet their needs and preferences.

Another important consideration is the size and growth potential of your target market. Is there a large enough customer base to support your business in the long term? Is the market growing or shrinking? By researching market trends and projections, you can assess the overall viability and scalability of your business idea.

It's also crucial to research your competition. Who are the other businesses operating in your market, and what are their strengths and weaknesses? How do their products or services compare to yours in terms of quality, price, and features? By conducting a thorough competitive analysis, you can identify gaps in the market and opportunities to differentiate your business from the competition.

In addition to traditional market research methods such as surveys and focus groups, there are many online tools and resources available to help you gather valuable insights about your target market and industry. These include social media platforms, online forums, and industry-specific databases and reports. By leveraging these resources, you can gain a deeper understanding of your customers' needs, preferences, and pain points, and use this knowledge to refine your business idea and strategy.

Ultimately, the key to identifying viable business opportunities and assessing market needs is to approach the process with curiosity, openness, and a willingness to learn. By staying alert to potential opportunities, conducting thorough research, and continuously refining your understanding of your target market, you can increase your chances of success as an entrepreneur and build a business that truly resonates with your customers.

Subsection 4.3: Developing a Business Plan and Securing Funding

Once you have identified a viable business opportunity and conducted thorough market research, the next crucial step in your entrepreneurial journey is to develop a comprehensive business plan. A well-crafted business plan serves as a roadmap for your venture, outlining your goals, strategies, and financial projections. It is also an essential tool for securing funding from investors, lenders, or other sources.

A typical business plan includes several key components, such as an executive summary, company description, market analysis, competitive analysis, product or service description, marketing and sales strategy, operations plan, management team, and financial projections. Each of these sections should be carefully researched and thoughtfully written to provide a clear and compelling case for your business.

The executive summary is perhaps the most critical part of your business plan, as it is the first thing that potential investors or lenders will read. This section should succinctly summarize the key points of your plan, including your business concept, target market, unique value proposition, financial highlights, and funding requirements. It should be engaging, persuasive, and no more than a few pages long.

In the company description section, you will provide a detailed overview of your business, including its history, mission statement, legal structure, and key milestones. This section should also highlight your team's expertise and experience, as well as any competitive advantages or unique selling points that set your business apart from others in the market.

The market analysis section will present the findings of your market research, including information on your target customers, market size and trends, and potential opportunities and threats. This section should demonstrate a deep understanding of your industry and the needs and preferences of your target audience.

In the competitive analysis section, you will assess the strengths and weaknesses of your key competitors and explain how your business will differentiate itself in the market. This may involve highlighting unique features or benefits of your product or service, or identifying underserved market segments that you can target.

The product or service description section will provide a detailed overview of your offerings, including their features, benefits, and pricing. This section should also address any intellectual property or regulatory issues related to your products or services.

In the marketing and sales strategy section, you will outline your plans for promoting and selling your products or services to your target customers. This may include a mix of online and offline marketing tactics, such as social media advertising, content marketing, email campaigns, trade shows, or direct sales. You should also discuss your pricing strategy and any partnerships or distribution channels you plan to leverage.

The operations plan section will describe how your business will function on a day-to-day basis, including details on your production processes, supply chain, inventory management, and quality control measures. This section should also address any staffing or technology requirements needed to support your operations.

In the management team section, you will highlight the skills and experience of your key team members and explain how their expertise will contribute to the success of your business. This section should also discuss any gaps in your team and how you plan to fill them, such as through hiring or partnerships.

Finally, the financial projections section will provide detailed financial statements and forecasts for your business, typically for the next three to five years. This may include income statements, balance sheets, cash flow statements, and break-even analyses. These projections should be based on realistic assumptions and supported by your market research and competitive analysis.

Once you have developed a comprehensive business plan, the next step is to explore funding options to bring your vision to life. There are several common sources of funding for startups, each with its own advantages and disadvantages.

One option is to bootstrap your business, which means funding it through your own savings, revenue, or credit. This approach allows you to maintain full control over your business and avoid giving up equity to outside investors. However, it may also limit your growth potential and put your personal finances at risk.

Another option is to seek funding from friends and family, who may be willing to invest in your business based on their personal relationship with you. While this can be a quick and easy way to secure funding, it can also strain personal relationships if the business does not perform as expected.

Angel investors and venture capitalists are another common source of funding for startups. These are typically high-net-worth individuals or firms that invest in early-stage companies in exchange for equity ownership. While this can provide a significant infusion of capital and valuable expertise and connections, it also means giving up some control over your business and potentially diluting your ownership stake.

Crowdfunding platforms, such as Kickstarter or Indiegogo, have also become popular in recent years as a way for entrepreneurs to raise money from a large number of small investors. This approach can be effective for businesses with a compelling story or innovative product, but it also requires significant marketing and outreach efforts to attract backers.

Finally, traditional bank loans or government grants may be available to some startups, particularly those in certain industries or with a strong track record of success. However, these options often require collateral, a personal guarantee, or a detailed business plan and financial projections.

Ultimately, the key to securing funding for your business is to develop a strong and compelling business plan that demonstrates the viability and growth potential of your venture. By thoroughly researching your market, developing a clear and differentiated value proposition, and presenting a realistic and achievable financial plan, you can increase your chances of attracting the capital you need to turn your entrepreneurial dreams into reality.

Subsection 4.4: Managing and Growing Your Business

Congratulations! You've taken the leap into entrepreneurship, identified a viable business opportunity, developed a comprehensive plan, and secured the necessary funding to bring your vision to life. Now, the real work begins – managing and growing your business over time. As a business owner, your ability to effectively manage operations, make strategic decisions, and adapt to changing circumstances will be crucial to your long-term success and sustainability.

One of the first key considerations in managing your business is to establish clear goals and objectives. What do you want to achieve in the short term and long term? What are your targets for revenue, profitability, market share, and customer satisfaction? By setting specific, measurable, achievable, relevant, and time-bound (SMART) goals, you can create a roadmap for your business and ensure that everyone on your team is working towards the same objectives.

To effectively manage your business, it's also essential to develop strong financial management skills. This includes creating and sticking to a budget, monitoring cash flow, managing expenses, and making informed financial decisions. Regularly reviewing your financial statements, such as your income statement, balance sheet, and cash flow statement, can help you identify areas for improvement and make data-driven decisions about investments, pricing, and resource allocation.

Another critical aspect of managing your business is building and leading a strong team. As your business grows, you'll likely need to hire employees or contractors to help you manage the workload and bring new skills and expertise to the table. When building your team, look for individuals who share your values, work ethic, and vision for the business. Provide clear expectations, regular feedback, and opportunities for growth and development to keep your team motivated and engaged.

As you manage your day-to-day operations, it's also important to keep an eye on the bigger picture and look for opportunities to scale and grow your business over time. This may involve expanding into new markets, developing new products or services, or forming strategic partnerships with other businesses. When considering growth opportunities, always refer back to your business plan and ensure that any new initiatives align with your overall goals and objectives.

One effective strategy for scaling your business is to focus on building strong relationships with your customers. By providing exceptional products, services, and customer experiences, you can foster loyalty, encourage repeat business, and generate positive word-of-mouth referrals. Regularly seeking feedback from your customers and using their insights to improve your offerings can help you stay ahead of the competition and adapt to changing market needs.

Another key to growing your business is to stay agile and adaptable in the face of change. Markets, technologies, and consumer preferences are constantly evolving, and successful entrepreneurs are those who can quickly pivot and adjust their strategies in response. By staying informed about industry trends, seeking out new learning opportunities, and being open to feedback and constructive criticism, you can position your business for long-term success and resilience.

Finally, as you manage and grow your business, don't forget to take care of yourself and maintain a healthy work-life balance. Running a business can be all-consuming, but it's essential to prioritize self-care, set boundaries, and make time for the people and activities that matter most to you. By taking care of yourself and your team, you'll be better equipped to handle the challenges and opportunities that come with entrepreneurship and build a thriving, sustainable business over time.

Summary: Embarking on Your Entrepreneurial Journey

Throughout this section, we have explored the exciting world of entrepreneurship and the process of starting your own business. We began by emphasizing the importance of assessing your entrepreneurial skills and mindset, ensuring that you have the necessary qualities and attitudes to succeed as a business owner. By understanding your strengths, weaknesses, and areas for improvement, you can make informed decisions about whether entrepreneurship is the right path for you.

Next, we delved into the crucial step of identifying viable business opportunities and assessing market needs. By staying alert to potential problems or challenges in your daily life and staying informed about industry trends and developments, you can spot opportunities for new products or services. Conducting thorough market research, including analyzing your target customers, market size, and competition, is essential to determining the viability of your business idea.

Once you have identified a promising opportunity, we discussed the importance of developing a comprehensive business plan. This roadmap for your venture should include key components such as an executive summary, company description, market analysis, competitive analysis, product or service description, marketing and sales strategy, operations plan, management team, and financial projections. A well-crafted business plan is not only essential for guiding your business decisions but also for securing funding from investors or lenders.

We then explored various funding options for your startup, including bootstrapping, seeking investments from friends and family, angel investors, venture capitalists, crowdfunding platforms, bank loans, and government grants. Each option has its advantages and disadvantages, and the key to securing funding is to present a compelling and well-researched business plan that demonstrates the growth potential of your venture.

Finally, we emphasized the importance of effectively managing and growing your business over time. Setting clear goals and objectives, developing strong financial management skills, building a talented team, focusing on customer relationships, staying adaptable in the face of change, and maintaining a healthy work-life balance are all critical factors in the long-term success and sustainability of your business.

As you embark on your entrepreneurial journey, remember that starting and running a business is not a sprint, but a marathon. It requires dedication, perseverance, and a willingness to learn and grow. By leveraging the knowledge and strategies presented in this section, you can increase your chances of success and build a thriving, impactful business that not only supports your personal goals but also makes a positive difference in the world.

So, take the insights you've gained, trust in your abilities, and dare to pursue your entrepreneurial dreams. The path ahead may be challenging, but with the right mindset, skills, and support, you have the power to turn your vision into reality. Embrace the journey, learn from your experiences, and never stop believing in yourself and the value you bring to the market. Your entrepreneurial success story starts now.

Section 5: Adapting to the Changing Nature of Work

In today's rapidly evolving world, the nature of work is undergoing a profound transformation. The advent of new technologies and the increasing globalization of the economy are reshaping the job market, creating both opportunities and challenges for workers across all industries. To thrive in this dynamic landscape, it is essential to understand the impact of these changes and develop the skills and mindset needed to adapt and succeed.

As automation and artificial intelligence continue to advance, many traditional jobs are being disrupted or even eliminated, while new roles are emerging that require a different set of skills and competencies. At the same time, the rise of remote work and flexible work arrangements is blurring the lines between work and life, offering new possibilities for work-life balance but also presenting new challenges for communication, collaboration, and productivity.

In this section, we will explore the key trends and forces driving the future of work, and provide practical guidance on how to navigate this changing landscape. We will examine the importance of embracing technology and developing digital skills, as well as the strategies for effectively managing remote work and flexible work arrangements. We will also discuss the crucial role of resilience and adaptability in the face of change and uncertainty, and provide tips for cultivating these essential qualities.

By understanding the changing nature of work and taking proactive steps to adapt and grow, you can position yourself for success in the years ahead. Whether you are just starting your career or looking to make a change, this section will provide you with the insights and tools you need to thrive in the new world of work.

Subsection 5.1: Embracing Technology and Digital Skills

In the rapidly evolving modern workplace, technology has become an integral part of almost every job and industry. As automation, artificial intelligence, and digital tools continue to transform the way we work, it is crucial for professionals to recognize the importance of developing digital skills and embracing technology to remain competitive and adaptable.

One of the most significant benefits of embracing technology in the workplace is increased efficiency and productivity. By leveraging digital tools and platforms, workers can streamline tasks, collaborate more effectively with colleagues, and access information and resources quickly and easily. For example, cloud-based project management software allows teams to work together seamlessly, even when working remotely, while automation tools can handle repetitive tasks, freeing up time for more strategic and creative work.

Moreover, as technology continues to advance, new job opportunities are emerging that require specialized digital skills. From data analysis and digital marketing to software development and cybersecurity, these roles are in high demand and offer competitive salaries and growth potential. By investing in developing these skills, professionals can position themselves for success in the digital economy and open up new career paths that may not have existed before.

However, embracing technology and digital skills is not just about learning how to use specific tools or platforms. It also requires a mindset shift towards continuous learning, experimentation, and adaptability. As technology evolves at a rapid pace, professionals must be willing to learn and unlearn skills throughout their careers, staying up-to-date with the latest trends and best practices in their field.

To cultivate this mindset, professionals can seek out learning opportunities both within and outside of their organizations. Many companies offer training and development programs to help employees build digital skills, while online learning platforms like Coursera, Udemy, and LinkedIn Learning provide a wealth of courses and certifications in various digital disciplines. By proactively investing in their own skill development, professionals can take control of their careers and remain valuable assets to their organizations.

In addition to technical skills, embracing technology also requires strong soft skills, such as communication, collaboration, and problem-solving. As teams become more distributed and digital-first, the ability to communicate effectively across different channels, work collaboratively with colleagues from diverse backgrounds, and think critically to solve complex problems is becoming increasingly important.

Ultimately, embracing technology and digital skills is not just a nice-to-have in the modern workplace – it is a necessity for professionals who want to thrive and succeed in the years ahead. By recognizing the importance of these skills, investing in their own development, and cultivating a mindset of continuous learning and adaptability, professionals can position themselves for long-term success and fulfillment in their careers.

Subsection 5.2: Navigating Remote Work and Flexible Work Arrangements

The rise of remote work and flexible work arrangements has been one of the most significant changes in the modern workplace, accelerated by advances in technology and the global shift towards digital collaboration. While these new ways of working offer numerous benefits, such as greater autonomy, improved work-life balance, and reduced commuting time, they also present unique challenges that require careful navigation.

One of the key challenges of remote work is maintaining effective communication and collaboration with colleagues and team members. When working remotely, it is essential to establish clear channels of communication, such as regular video conferences, instant messaging, and project management platforms, to ensure that everyone is on the same page and working towards common goals. It is also important to set expectations around response times, availability, and deliverables to avoid misunderstandings and maintain productivity.

Another challenge of remote work is managing time and staying focused in the face of distractions and competing priorities. Without the structure and routine of a traditional office environment, it can be easy to fall into unproductive habits or struggle with motivation. To overcome this, remote workers must develop strong time management and self-discipline skills, such as setting clear boundaries between work and personal life, creating a dedicated workspace, and using techniques like the Pomodoro method to stay focused and avoid burnout.

Flexible work arrangements, such as part-time or variable schedules, can also present challenges in terms of coordination and fairness. When team members are working on different schedules, it is important to establish clear protocols for communication and collaboration, such as regular check-ins and status updates, to ensure that everyone is aligned and accountable. It is also important to ensure that flexible arrangements are applied fairly and consistently across the team, to avoid resentment or perceptions of favoritism.

Despite these challenges, remote work and flexible work arrangements also offer significant opportunities for personal and professional growth. By developing the skills and mindset needed to thrive in these new ways of working, professionals can increase their autonomy, creativity, and job satisfaction, while also opening up new possibilities for work-life balance and career advancement.

To effectively navigate remote work and flexible work arrangements, professionals can take several proactive steps, such as:

1. Investing in the right tools and technology, such as a reliable internet connection, ergonomic workspace, and digital collaboration platforms.
2. Establishing clear boundaries and routines, such as setting regular work hours, taking breaks, and communicating availability to colleagues and family members.
3. Developing strong communication and collaboration skills, such as active listening, clear writing, and effective meeting facilitation.
4. Cultivating a growth mindset and embracing continuous learning, such as seeking out new skills and knowledge related to remote work and digital collaboration.
5. Building a supportive network of colleagues, mentors, and peers who can provide guidance, feedback, and accountability in navigating the challenges of remote work.

By taking these steps and approaching remote work and flexible work arrangements with a proactive and adaptable mindset, professionals can not only survive but thrive in the new world of work, achieving greater success, fulfillment, and balance in their careers and personal lives.

Subsection 5.3: Developing Resilience and Adaptability

In the face of rapid change and uncertainty in the job market, cultivating resilience and adaptability has become more important than ever for professionals seeking to thrive in their careers. Resilience refers to the ability to bounce back from setbacks, challenges, and failures, while adaptability involves being able to adjust and respond effectively to new situations, demands, and opportunities.

One key aspect of developing resilience is maintaining a positive and growth-oriented mindset. This means viewing challenges and setbacks as opportunities for learning and improvement, rather than as threats or failures. By embracing a growth mindset, professionals can reframe negative experiences as chances to develop new skills, gain valuable insights, and become stronger and more capable in the face of adversity.

Another important component of resilience is building a strong support network of colleagues, mentors, friends, and family members who can provide encouragement, advice, and perspective during difficult times. By cultivating meaningful relationships and seeking out guidance and support when needed, professionals can tap into a valuable source of resilience and motivation, helping them to persevere and stay focused on their goals even in the face of obstacles and setbacks.

Adaptability, on the other hand, involves being proactive and flexible in the face of change, and being willing to take on new roles, responsibilities, and challenges as needed. This may involve learning new skills, taking on new projects or assignments, or even changing careers or industries altogether in response to shifting market demands or personal interests.

To develop adaptability, professionals can focus on continuously learning and growing, both within and outside of their current roles. This may involve taking on new assignments or projects that stretch their skills and knowledge, attending workshops or conferences to stay up-to-date with the latest trends and best practices, or pursuing additional education or certifications to expand their expertise and marketability.

Another key aspect of adaptability is being open to feedback and willing to adjust one's approach or strategy as needed. This means actively seeking out input and guidance from colleagues, supervisors, and mentors, and being receptive to constructive criticism and suggestions for improvement.

By maintaining a flexible and open-minded approach, professionals can more easily navigate changing circumstances and find new opportunities for growth and success.

Ultimately, developing resilience and adaptability requires a combination of mindset, skills, and support. By cultivating a positive and growth-oriented outlook, building strong relationships and networks, continuously learning and growing, and being open to feedback and change, professionals can position themselves to thrive in the face of uncertainty and succeed in the rapidly evolving world of work.

Summary: Embracing Change and Thriving in the Future of Work

In this section, we have explored the profound impact of technology and globalization on the modern workplace, and the importance of adapting to these changes in order to thrive in the future of work. From embracing digital skills and navigating remote work to developing resilience and adaptability, we have covered a range of strategies and mindsets that can help professionals succeed in the face of uncertainty and change.

The key takeaway from this section is that the nature of work is evolving rapidly, and those who are willing to learn, grow, and adapt will be best positioned to seize the opportunities that arise. By continuously investing in our own development, staying open to new possibilities, and cultivating a strong support network, we can navigate the challenges of the changing job market with confidence and resilience.

As we move forward into an increasingly digital and interconnected world, it is clear that the skills and mindsets we have discussed in this section will only become more valuable and essential. Whether you are just starting your career or looking to make a change, embracing these strategies and taking proactive steps to prepare for the future of work can help you achieve greater success, fulfillment, and impact in your professional life.

So let this section be a call to action – to embrace change, to invest in yourself, and to approach the future with curiosity, courage, and optimism.

By doing so, you will not only survive but thrive in the new world of work, and make a meaningful contribution to the organizations and communities you serve.

Chapter Summary: Unlocking Your Earning Potential and Achieving Career Success

Throughout this chapter, we have explored various strategies and approaches to help you maximize your earning potential and build a successful career. By understanding the job market, developing your human capital, and exploring entrepreneurial opportunities, you can take control of your financial future and achieve your professional goals.

Investing in your education, skills, and experience is crucial for increasing your value in the job market and opening up new opportunities for career advancement. Whether through formal education, certifications, or practical experience, continuously learning and staying up-to-date with industry trends will help you remain competitive and adaptable in the ever-changing world of work.

Negotiating your salary, pursuing promotions, and exploring side hustles are all effective ways to boost your income and achieve financial success. By advocating for your worth and seeking out new opportunities, you can take charge of your career trajectory and reach new heights in your professional life.

For those with an entrepreneurial spirit, starting your own business can be a rewarding and lucrative path to financial independence. By identifying market needs, developing a solid business plan, and securing the necessary funding, you can turn your passion and skills into a successful venture.

As technology continues to shape the future of work, embracing digital skills and adapting to new ways of working will be essential for thriving in the modern job market. By cultivating resilience, adaptability, and a growth mindset, you can navigate the challenges and opportunities that come with a rapidly evolving professional landscape.

Remember, building a successful career and maximizing your earning potential is a lifelong journey. By staying focused on your goals, continuously investing in yourself, and seizing opportunities as they arise, you can create a fulfilling and financially rewarding professional life. With the strategies and insights gained from this chapter, you are well-equipped to take control of your career and unlock your full earning potential.

Chapter 5: Saving Money and Building an Emergency Fund

Saving money is a fundamental pillar of financial stability and security. It is the foundation upon which you can build a strong financial future, weather unexpected storms, and achieve your long-term goals. In a world filled with uncertainties and unforeseen expenses, having a solid savings plan and an emergency fund is not just a luxury but a necessity.

Many people understand the importance of saving money, yet they struggle to make it a consistent habit. The reasons are varied, from the allure of instant gratification to the pressure of keeping up with societal expectations. However, the benefits of saving money far outweigh the short-term sacrifices it may require.

When you save money, you are essentially paying yourself first. You are prioritizing your future self over the temptations of the present. By setting aside a portion of your income regularly, you create a safety net that can protect you from financial shocks, such as job loss, medical emergencies, or unexpected repairs. This peace of mind is invaluable and can significantly reduce stress in your life.

Moreover, saving money opens up a world of opportunities. It allows you to invest in yourself, whether through education, starting a business, or pursuing your passions. It gives you the freedom to make choices based on your values and goals, rather than being constrained by financial limitations.

Building an emergency fund is a crucial aspect of saving money. An emergency fund is a separate savings account that is specifically designated for unexpected expenses. It acts as a buffer between you and life's curveballs, ensuring that you don't have to rely on credit cards or loans when faced with a financial emergency.

The size of your emergency fund will depend on your individual circumstances, such as your income, expenses, and family size. However, a general rule of thumb is to aim for saving three to six months' worth of living expenses. This may seem daunting at first, but by starting small and consistently contributing to your emergency fund, you can gradually build a robust financial safety net.

Throughout this chapter, we will explore the various strategies and techniques for saving money effectively and building a solid emergency fund. We will delve into the psychological barriers that often hinder saving habits and provide practical solutions to overcome them. By the end of this chapter, you will have the knowledge and tools necessary to take control of your financial future and create a life of greater security and freedom.

Section 1: The Importance of Saving Money

Imagine a life where you have the freedom to pursue your dreams, the security to handle unexpected expenses, and the peace of mind that comes with a stable financial future. This is the power of saving money. In a world where financial uncertainties lurk around every corner, cultivating a habit of saving can be your key to unlocking a life of prosperity and abundance.

Saving money is not just about putting aside a few dollars each month; it's a fundamental pillar of personal finance that lays the foundation for your long-term financial well-being. By consistently setting aside a portion of your income, you are taking control of your financial destiny and creating a safety net that can cushion you against life's inevitable ups and downs.

But the benefits of saving money extend far beyond just having a rainy day fund. When you prioritize saving, you are making a conscious choice to value your future self over instant gratification. You are developing the discipline and mindset necessary to achieve your financial goals, whether it's buying your first home, starting a business, or retiring comfortably.

Moreover, the act of saving money can have a profound impact on your overall quality of life. When you have a robust savings account, you have the freedom to make choices based on your values and aspirations, rather than being held hostage by financial constraints. You can pursue your passions, invest in your personal growth, and create a life that aligns with your deepest desires.

In the following subsections, we will delve deeper into the myriad benefits of saving money and explore practical strategies for making saving a non-negotiable part of your financial plan. Whether you're just starting your savings journey or looking to take your financial game to the next level, the insights and tools you'll gain in this section will empower you to build a solid foundation for a lifetime of financial stability and prosperity. So, let's dive in and discover the transformative power of saving money!

Subsection 1.1: The Power of Compound Interest

Have you ever wondered how a small seed can grow into a mighty tree? The answer lies in the power of compounding. Just as a tree grows exponentially over time, your money can grow exponentially through the magic of compound interest.

Compound interest is the interest calculated on the initial principal and the accumulated interest from previous periods. In other words, it's the interest you earn on your interest. This may sound simple, but the effects of compound interest over time can be truly astonishing.

Let's consider an example to illustrate the power of compound interest. Imagine you invest $1,000 in an account that earns 5% interest per year. After the first year, you will have $1,050 ($1,000 + $50 in interest). In the second year, you will earn interest not only on your initial $1,000 but also on the $50 in interest from the first year. This means you will earn $52.50 in interest ($1,050 x 5%), bringing your total to $1,102.50.

As time goes on, the compounding effect becomes even more powerful. After 10 years, your initial $1,000 investment will have grown to $1,628.89. After 20 years, it will be $2,653.30, and after 30 years, it will have more than quadrupled to $4,321.94. This growth is due to the power of compound interest, which allows your money to grow at an increasing rate over time.

The formula for compound interest is:

$$A = P(1 + r)^n$$

Where:

- A is the final amount

- P is the initial principal balance

- r is the annual interest rate (expressed as a decimal)

- n is the number of years the amount is invested

The key to harnessing the power of compound interest is time. The earlier you start saving and investing, the more time your money has to grow. Even small amounts, when consistently invested over a long period, can yield substantial results.

Another factor that amplifies the power of compound interest is the frequency of compounding. In our example, we assumed annual compounding. However, if the interest is compounded more frequently, such as monthly or daily, the growth rate accelerates even further.

It's important to note that compound interest works both ways. While it can be a powerful tool for growing your savings, it can also work against you if you have debt. Credit card balances, for example, can quickly spiral out of control due to high-interest rates and daily compounding.

The power of compound interest is a fundamental concept in personal finance. By understanding and harnessing its potential, you can make your money work harder for you and achieve your long-term financial goals. Whether you're saving for retirement, a down payment on a house, or your child's education, compound interest can be a valuable ally in building wealth over time.

In the next subsection, we'll explore how to set specific financial goals and create a plan to achieve them, leveraging the power of compound interest along the way.

Subsection 1.2: Saving for Short-Term and Long-Term Goals

Saving money is not just about setting aside funds for a rainy day; it's also about strategically allocating your savings to achieve your short-term and long-term financial goals. By clearly defining your objectives and creating a savings plan that aligns with your priorities, you can turn your dreams into reality and build a secure financial future.

Short-term goals are typically defined as objectives you want to achieve within the next one to three years. These goals may include saving for a down payment on a car, planning a dream vacation, or building an emergency fund to cover unexpected expenses. When saving for short-term goals, it's essential to choose savings vehicles that offer liquidity and stability, such as high-yield savings accounts or short-term certificates of deposit (CDs). These options allow you to access your funds quickly when needed while still earning a competitive interest rate.

On the other hand, long-term goals are those that require a longer time horizon, usually five years or more. These goals may include saving for retirement, purchasing a home, or funding your children's education. When saving for long-term goals, you have the advantage of time on your side, which allows you to take on more risk in exchange for potentially higher returns. Investment vehicles such as stocks, bonds, and mutual funds can be suitable options for long-term savings, as they have the potential to outpace inflation and grow your wealth over time.

To effectively save for both short-term and long-term goals, it's crucial to prioritize your objectives and create a savings plan that reflects your values and aspirations. Start by listing your goals and assigning a specific dollar amount and target date to each one. Then, evaluate your current financial situation and determine how much you can realistically allocate towards each goal on a monthly or yearly basis.

One effective strategy for saving towards multiple goals is to use the "pay yourself first" approach. This means treating your savings as a non-negotiable expense and automatically transferring a fixed amount from your paycheck to your savings accounts before allocating funds to other expenses. By making saving a priority and automating the process, you can ensure consistent progress towards your goals without relying on willpower or discretionary income.

Another key aspect of saving for short-term and long-term goals is regularly reviewing and adjusting your savings plan as your circumstances and priorities change. Life events such as marriage, the birth of a child, or a career change may require you to reassess your goals and modify your savings strategy accordingly. By staying flexible and adaptable, you can ensure that your savings plan remains aligned with your evolving needs and aspirations.

In addition to setting specific goals and creating a savings plan, it's also essential to educate yourself on the various savings and investment options available to you. Research different account types, such as traditional and Roth IRAs for retirement savings, 529 plans for education savings, and health savings accounts (HSAs) for medical expenses. Understanding the features, benefits, and limitations of each option can help you make informed decisions and optimize your savings strategy.

Saving for short-term and long-term goals is a crucial component of achieving financial stability and success. By prioritizing your objectives, creating a tailored savings plan, and leveraging the right savings and investment vehicles, you can turn your dreams into tangible realities and build a secure financial future for yourself and your loved ones. Remember, the key to successful saving is consistency, discipline, and a clear vision of what you want to achieve. With these elements in place, you can harness the power of saving to transform your financial landscape and create the life you've always imagined.

Subsection 1.3: The Relationship Between Saving and Financial Freedom

Imagine a life where you have the freedom to make choices based on your desires and values, rather than being constrained by financial limitations. A life where you can pursue your passions, take risks, and seize opportunities without the constant worry of making ends meet. This is the essence of financial freedom, and it all begins with a simple yet powerful habit: saving money.

Saving money is not just about accumulating wealth for the sake of it; it's about creating a foundation of financial security that allows you to live life on your own terms. When you consistently set aside a portion of your income, you are not only building a safety net for unexpected expenses but also laying the groundwork for a future of endless possibilities.

The relationship between saving and financial freedom is rooted in the concept of delayed gratification. By choosing to prioritize your future financial well-being over immediate desires, you are developing the discipline and mindset necessary to achieve long-term success. Every dollar you save is a step towards greater autonomy, flexibility, and peace of mind.

One of the most powerful ways that saving contributes to financial freedom is by providing you with options. When you have a substantial savings account, you have the ability to make choices that align with your values and goals, rather than being forced into decisions based on financial necessity. For example, if you're unhappy with your current job, a robust savings cushion can give you the confidence to explore new career opportunities or even start your own business. If you've always dreamed of traveling the world, your savings can turn that fantasy into a reality.

Moreover, the act of saving money can help you break free from the cycle of living paycheck to paycheck. When you have a financial buffer in place, you're less likely to rely on credit cards or loans to cover unexpected expenses or indulgences. This, in turn, can help you avoid the trap of high-interest debt, which can quickly erode your financial stability and hinder your progress towards financial freedom.

But the benefits of saving extend beyond just financial security and flexibility. The process of saving money can also have a profound impact on your mental and emotional well-being. When you know that you have a strong financial foundation, you can approach life with a greater sense of confidence, resilience, and optimism. You're less likely to experience stress and anxiety related to money, and more likely to focus on the things that truly matter to you, such as relationships, personal growth, and making a positive impact in the world.

Of course, achieving financial freedom through saving requires more than just good intentions; it requires a strategic and disciplined approach. This means setting clear financial goals, creating a budget that prioritizes saving, and automating your savings contributions to ensure consistency. It also means being mindful of your spending habits and making informed choices about how you allocate your resources.

One effective strategy for building a strong savings habit is to treat your savings contributions like a non-negotiable expense, just like rent or utilities. By paying yourself first and allocating a fixed percentage of your income to savings before discretionary spending, you can ensure steady progress towards your financial goals. Over time, as your savings grow and compound, you'll begin to see the tangible rewards of your efforts in the form of greater financial freedom and security.

In essence, the relationship between saving and financial freedom is one of empowerment. By taking control of your financial destiny through consistent saving, you are not only creating a safety net for the future but also unlocking a world of possibilities in the present. Every dollar saved is a declaration of your commitment to living life on your own terms, free from the constraints of financial stress and limitations.

As you embark on your own journey towards financial freedom, remember that saving money is not about deprivation or sacrifice; it's about making a conscious choice to prioritize your long-term well-being and happiness. With discipline, strategy, and a clear vision of what you want to achieve, you can harness the power of saving to create a life of abundance, joy, and endless possibility. So start today, and watch as your financial freedom unfolds one dollar at a time.

Summary: Embracing the Power of Saving for a Brighter Financial Future

Throughout this section, we have explored the fundamental importance of saving money and how it serves as the bedrock of financial stability. From understanding the awe-inspiring potential of compound interest to strategically allocating savings towards short-term and long-term goals, we have seen how every dollar saved can contribute to a more secure and prosperous future.

But the true power of saving money lies not just in the numbers on a bank statement or the size of an investment portfolio. It lies in the profound impact that a strong savings habit can have on your overall quality of life. When you prioritize saving, you are not only building a financial safety net, but you are also cultivating a mindset of discipline, resilience, and empowerment.

By consistently setting aside a portion of your income, you are taking control of your financial destiny and creating a world of possibilities. You are giving yourself the freedom to pursue your dreams, weather life's unexpected storms, and create a legacy that extends beyond your own lifetime. You are embracing the power of delayed gratification and investing in your future self, one dollar at a time.

As we move forward in this book, we will delve deeper into the practical strategies and tools that can help you supercharge your savings and achieve your financial goals. But always remember that the foundation of any successful financial journey begins with a simple, yet profound, commitment to saving.

So, whether you are just starting your savings journey or looking to take your financial game to the next level, know that every choice you make to prioritize saving is a powerful step towards a brighter, more abundant future. Embrace the power of saving, and watch as your financial dreams transform into a beautiful reality.

Section 2: Developing a Saving Mindset

Picture this: you're standing at a crossroads, one path leading to a life of financial stress and uncertainty, the other to a future of stability and security. The choice may seem obvious, but for many, taking that first step towards a saving mindset can be daunting. Developing a saving mindset is not about depriving yourself of life's joys or living a frugal existence; rather, it's about making conscious decisions that prioritize your long-term financial well-being.

In a world where instant gratification is just a click away, cultivating a saving mindset requires a shift in perspective. It means looking beyond the present moment and understanding the power of small, consistent actions over time. By adopting a saving mindset, you take control of your financial destiny and create a safety net that can weather life's unexpected storms.

But how do you develop a saving mindset when temptation lurks around every corner? The answer lies in understanding the psychological barriers that hinder saving behavior and developing strategies to overcome them. It's about creating habits that make saving second nature and finding the motivation to stay the course even when the going gets tough.

In this section, we'll explore the tools and techniques you need to cultivate a saving mindset that will serve you for a lifetime. We'll delve into the psychology of saving, learn how to automate your savings, and discover the power of setting clear financial goals. By the end of this section, you'll have the knowledge and inspiration to transform your relationship with money and build a foundation for lasting financial success.

Subsection 2.1: Overcoming Psychological Barriers to Saving

Saving money is often easier said than done. Despite our best intentions, we may find ourselves struggling to set aside funds for the future. This difficulty can often be attributed to psychological barriers that hinder our saving behavior. These mental obstacles are deeply ingrained in our minds, shaped by our experiences, emotions, and societal influences.

Understanding and overcoming these barriers is crucial to developing a strong saving mindset.

One common psychological barrier is the concept of present bias. As humans, we tend to prioritize immediate gratification over long-term rewards. We may find it challenging to resist the temptation of a new gadget or a fancy dinner, even if it means compromising our saving goals. This bias can be particularly strong when we're faced with stress or emotional triggers, leading us to seek comfort in short-term pleasures.

Another significant barrier is the influence of social comparison. In a world where social media highlights the lavish lifestyles of others, it's easy to fall into the trap of "keeping up with the Joneses." We may feel pressure to match the spending habits of our peers, even if it means sacrificing our own financial well-being. This desire to fit in and maintain a certain image can be a powerful obstacle to saving.

Overcoming these psychological barriers requires a combination of self-awareness, mindset shifts, and practical strategies. One effective approach is to reframe our thinking about saving. Instead of viewing it as a sacrifice or deprivation, we can see it as an investment in our future selves. By focusing on the long-term benefits of saving, such as financial security and the ability to pursue our dreams, we can create a more compelling motivation to resist short-term temptations.

Another key strategy is to create a system of accountability and rewards. Setting clear saving goals and tracking our progress can help us stay motivated and focused. Celebrating milestones along the way, such as reaching a specific saving target, can provide a sense of accomplishment and reinforce positive habits. Additionally, surrounding ourselves with supportive individuals who share our financial values can provide encouragement and help us stay on track.

Developing a saving mindset also requires a willingness to challenge societal norms and expectations. By defining our own measures of success and happiness, we can break free from the pressure to keep up with others and focus on what truly matters to us. This may involve learning to find joy in experiences rather than material possessions or cultivating a sense of contentment with what we already have.

Ultimately, overcoming psychological barriers to saving is a continuous process of self-reflection and growth. By becoming aware of our mental obstacles, reframing our mindset, and implementing practical strategies, we can gradually transform our relationship with money and build a strong foundation for long-term financial success. With persistence and practice, we can develop the resilience and discipline needed to prioritize our saving goals and create a brighter financial future.

Subsection 2.2: Creating a Saving Habit and Automating Savings

Developing a saving habit is one of the most powerful tools in your financial arsenal. By consistently setting aside a portion of your income, you build a solid foundation for your financial future. However, forming a new habit can be challenging, especially when it comes to money. That's where the power of automation comes in.

Automating your savings means setting up a system where a predetermined amount of money is transferred from your checking account to your savings account on a regular basis, without requiring any manual intervention. This simple strategy takes the decision-making process out of your hands and ensures that you're consistently saving, even when life gets busy or temptation strikes.

One of the most effective ways to automate your savings is to set up a direct deposit from your paycheck. Many employers offer the option to split your paycheck between multiple accounts, allowing you to allocate a specific percentage or dollar amount to your savings account each pay period. By saving before the money even reaches your checking account, you reduce the temptation to spend it on non-essential items.

Another powerful automation tool is to set up recurring transfers from your checking account to your savings account. Most banks and credit unions offer online banking features that allow you to schedule automatic transfers on a weekly, biweekly, or monthly basis. By aligning these transfers with your pay schedule or budget, you can ensure that you're consistently saving without having to remember to do it manually.

When setting up your automated savings plan, it's essential to choose an amount that is both meaningful and sustainable. Start by reviewing your budget and identifying areas where you can cut back on expenses, freeing up more money to allocate towards savings. Consider starting with a small percentage of your income, such as 5-10%, and gradually increasing it over time as you adjust to your new saving habit.

It's also important to choose the right savings vehicle for your automated transfers. High-yield savings accounts and money market accounts often offer higher interest rates than traditional savings accounts, allowing your money to grow faster over time. Do your research and compare options from different financial institutions to find the account that best aligns with your saving goals and preferences.

In addition to automating your savings, there are other strategies you can use to reinforce your saving habit. One effective approach is to set clear, specific savings goals for yourself. Whether you're saving for an emergency fund, a down payment on a house, or a dream vacation, having a tangible target in mind can help you stay motivated and focused on your saving journey.

Another strategy is to make saving a game or challenge. Consider setting up a friendly competition with friends or family members to see who can save the most over a specific period, or challenge yourself to find creative ways to cut expenses and boost your savings each month. By making saving fun and engaging, you're more likely to stick with it over the long term.

Ultimately, creating a saving habit and automating your savings is about making your financial well-being a priority. By taking a proactive approach and leveraging the power of automation, you can build a strong foundation for your financial future, one dollar at a time. With consistency, discipline, and a commitment to your saving goals, you can transform your relationship with money and achieve the financial freedom you've always dreamed of.

Subsection 2.3: Finding Motivation and Accountability in Saving

Embarking on a saving journey can be an exciting and empowering experience, but it's not without its challenges. As with any long-term goal, staying motivated and accountable is crucial to success. When the initial enthusiasm wears off and the temptation to spend arises, it's essential to have strategies in place to keep yourself on track.

One powerful way to stay motivated is to connect your saving goals to your personal values and aspirations. Take some time to reflect on what truly matters to you, whether it's financial security, travel, entrepreneurship, or providing for your family. By aligning your saving objectives with your deepest desires and passions, you create a compelling reason to stay committed, even in the face of obstacles.

Visualization is another effective technique for maintaining motivation. Create a vivid mental picture of what your life will look like when you achieve your saving goals. Imagine the sense of pride, freedom, and accomplishment you'll feel. Use this mental image as a source of inspiration, regularly reminding yourself of the bigger picture and the rewards that await you.

Accountability is also key to staying on track with your saving journey. While internal motivation is important, external accountability can provide an extra layer of support and encouragement. Consider finding a saving buddy or joining a community of like-minded individuals who share your financial goals. Having someone to check in with, share progress, and celebrate milestones can make the journey feel less daunting and more enjoyable.

Another way to foster accountability is to make your saving goals public. Share your aspirations with friends, family, or even on social media. By putting your intentions out there, you create a sense of commitment and responsibility to follow through. Knowing that others are aware of your goals can provide a powerful incentive to stay on track, as you won't want to let yourself or others down.

Tracking your progress is another essential component of staying motivated and accountable. Regularly review your saving achievements and celebrate your successes, no matter how small. Use visual aids like charts or graphs to illustrate your progress over time, making the abstract concept of saving more tangible and rewarding. By seeing the fruits of your efforts, you'll be more likely to stay committed and motivated to continue.

It's also important to be kind to yourself and maintain a growth mindset. Saving is a skill that develops over time, and setbacks are a normal part of the journey. If you encounter a challenge or fall short of your goals, don't be too hard on yourself. Instead, view it as an opportunity to learn, adjust, and improve. Celebrate your resilience and determination to keep going, even in the face of adversity.

Finally, consider incorporating rewards into your saving plan. While the ultimate reward is achieving your financial goals, smaller incentives along the way can help keep you motivated. Set milestones for yourself and plan enjoyable treats or experiences to look forward to when you reach them. These rewards should be meaningful to you but not derail your overall saving progress.

Remember, finding motivation and accountability in saving is an ongoing process. It requires consistent effort, self-reflection, and a willingness to adapt as needed. By connecting your goals to your values, visualizing success, seeking support, tracking progress, maintaining a growth mindset, and celebrating milestones, you'll be well-equipped to stay the course and achieve the financial future you envision.

Summary: Embracing a Saving Mindset for Lifelong Financial Success

Developing a saving mindset is a transformative journey that requires introspection, discipline, and a willingness to challenge deeply ingrained habits and beliefs. By understanding the psychological barriers that hinder our saving behavior, we can develop effective strategies to overcome them and cultivate a mindset that prioritizes long-term financial well-being.

Through the power of automation and the creation of consistent saving habits, we can make the process of setting aside money feel effortless and rewarding. By aligning our saving goals with our deepest values and aspirations, we can tap into a well of intrinsic motivation that propels us forward, even in the face of temptation or setbacks.

As we navigate this path, it's essential to surround ourselves with a supportive network of individuals who share our financial vision and can provide accountability and encouragement along the way. By celebrating our progress, maintaining a growth mindset, and embracing the lessons that come with challenges, we can develop the resilience and adaptability needed to thrive in our saving journey.

Ultimately, developing a saving mindset is about reclaiming control over our financial destiny and creating a life of abundance, security, and freedom. By making the choice to prioritize our long-term financial well-being, we open the door to a world of possibilities and lay the foundation for a brighter, more prosperous future.

As we move forward, armed with the knowledge and tools to cultivate a saving mindset, we can approach the rest of our financial journey with renewed confidence and purpose. In the next section, we'll explore practical strategies for increasing our savings and optimizing our financial resources, building upon the mindset shifts we've established and taking our saving success to new heights.

Section 3: Strategies for Increasing Your Savings

Picture this: you're standing at the foot of a mountain, gazing up at the summit. Your goal is to reach the top, where financial freedom and security await. Saving money is the path that will lead you there, but the climb can seem daunting at times. Just like any mountain climb, increasing your savings requires strategy, determination, and a clear plan of action.

In this section, we'll explore practical methods to boost your savings rate and make steady progress towards your financial goals. We'll look at ways to reduce expenses without sacrificing your quality of life, and how to make the most of your income by directing extra funds towards savings. You'll discover the benefits of employer-sponsored savings plans and learn about savings vehicles that can help your money grow faster.

By implementing these strategies and making saving a priority, you'll be amazed at how quickly your savings can accumulate. Whether you're saving for a rainy day, a down payment on a house, or a comfortable retirement, the key is to start now and stay consistent. With each step you take, you'll be closer to reaching that financial summit and enjoying the view from the top.

So, let's dive in and explore the practical steps you can take to increase your savings and build a strong financial foundation. Get ready to lace up your hiking boots and embark on a transformative journey towards a more secure and prosperous future.

Subsection 3.1: Reducing Expenses and Cutting Unnecessary Costs

One of the most effective ways to boost your savings is by reducing your expenses and eliminating unnecessary spending. This process involves taking a close look at your current spending habits and identifying areas where you can cut back without significantly impacting your quality of life.

Start by creating a detailed budget that tracks all of your income and expenses. Review your spending over the past few months and categorize each expense as either essential or non-essential. Essential expenses include items like housing, food, transportation, and healthcare, while non-essential expenses might include dining out, entertainment, or subscription services.

Once you've identified your non-essential expenses, consider which ones you can reduce or eliminate entirely. For example, you might choose to cook more meals at home instead of eating out, cancel subscriptions you don't use frequently, or opt for free or low-cost entertainment options like hiking or visiting local parks.

Another area where many people can cut costs is in their monthly bills. Take the time to review your bills for services like cable TV, internet, and cell phone plans. Research competitors' prices and don't be afraid to negotiate with your current providers for better rates or discounts. You may be surprised at how much you can save by simply asking.

When it comes to essential expenses, look for ways to reduce costs without sacrificing quality. For example, you might choose to buy generic or store-brand groceries instead of name-brand items, or shop around for better rates on insurance policies. Small changes like these can add up to significant savings over time.

It's important to remember that reducing expenses doesn't mean depriving yourself of the things you enjoy. Instead, it's about being mindful of your spending and making intentional choices that align with your financial goals. By cutting unnecessary costs and finding ways to save on essential expenses, you'll be able to redirect more money towards your savings and build a stronger financial foundation over time.

Subsection 3.2: Maximizing Your Income and Saving Windfalls

Increasing your savings isn't just about cutting expenses; it's also about making the most of your income. Whether you receive a raise, a bonus, or an unexpected windfall, how you allocate that extra money can have a significant impact on your financial future.

When you find yourself with additional income, it's tempting to indulge in a shopping spree or treat yourself to a luxurious vacation. While there's nothing wrong with enjoying the fruits of your labor, it's essential to strike a balance between present gratification and future security.

One effective strategy is to implement the "50/30/20 rule" when allocating extra income. This rule suggests that you divide your additional funds as follows: 50% towards your savings goals, 30% towards discretionary spending or lifestyle upgrades, and 20% towards paying off debt or building an emergency fund.

By directing half of your extra income towards savings, you'll be making significant strides towards your financial objectives. Whether you're saving for a down payment on a house, funding your child's education, or building a nest egg for retirement, these additional contributions can add up quickly over time.

When it comes to windfalls, such as an inheritance, a tax refund, or a gift, it's crucial to approach them with a strategic mindset. While it's okay to splurge a little and celebrate your good fortune, consider allocating a significant portion of the windfall towards your savings goals.

For example, if you receive a $5,000 tax refund, you might choose to allocate $3,000 towards your retirement account, $1,000 towards your emergency fund, and $1,000 towards a family vacation. By striking this balance, you'll be enjoying the present while also securing your financial future.

It's important to remember that windfalls are often one-time events, so it's wise to make the most of them when they occur. By prioritizing your savings goals and resisting the urge to spend the entire amount, you'll be setting yourself up for long-term financial success.

In addition to saving windfalls, consider ways to increase your income on a more regular basis. This might involve negotiating a raise at work, taking on a side hustle, or investing in your education and skills to qualify for higher-paying positions.

By combining expense reduction strategies with income maximization techniques, you'll be able to supercharge your savings and reach your financial goals faster. Remember, every extra dollar you save today has the potential to grow and compound over time, creating a more secure and prosperous future for you and your loved ones.

Subsection 3.3: Taking Advantage of Employer-Sponsored Savings Plans

One of the most powerful tools for boosting your savings is right at your fingertips: employer-sponsored savings plans. Many companies offer retirement savings plans, such as 401(k)s, which provide employees with an opportunity to save for their future while enjoying valuable tax benefits and employer contributions.

When you participate in a 401(k) plan, you can choose to have a portion of your paycheck automatically deducted and invested in the plan before taxes are taken out. This means you're reducing your taxable income while consistently saving for retirement. For example, if you earn $50,000 per year and contribute $5,000 to your 401(k), you'll only pay taxes on $45,000 of income, lowering your tax bill for the year.

But the benefits don't stop there. Many employers offer matching contributions, which means they'll contribute additional money to your 401(k) based on how much you save. A common matching structure is 50% of your contributions, up to a certain percentage of your salary. So, if you contribute 6% of your salary and your employer matches 50%, they'll add an extra 3% to your account. This is essentially free money that can significantly boost your savings over time.

To illustrate the power of employer matching, let's consider an example. Suppose you earn $60,000 per year and contribute 6% of your salary ($3,600) to your 401(k). If your employer matches 50% of your contributions up to 6% of your salary, they'll add an extra $1,800 to your account annually. Over 30 years, assuming a 7% annual return, your 401(k) balance could grow to over $567,000, even though you only contributed

$108,000 yourself. That's the magic of employer matching and compound interest working together.

It's important to note that employer-sponsored plans often have different vesting schedules for employer contributions. Vesting refers to your ownership of the funds in your account. Some companies may require you to work for a certain number of years before you fully own the employer contributions. Be sure to understand your plan's vesting schedule and consider it when making career decisions.

In addition to traditional 401(k)s, some employers offer Roth 401(k)s. With a Roth 401(k), your contributions are made with after-tax dollars, but your withdrawals in retirement are tax-free. This can be advantageous if you expect to be in a higher tax bracket in retirement than you are now.

If your employer offers a 401(k) or similar plan, take the time to understand how it works and make the most of this valuable savings opportunity. Contribute as much as you can afford, especially if your employer offers matching contributions. By doing so, you'll be harnessing the power of tax benefits, employer contributions, and compound interest to supercharge your savings and secure a more comfortable retirement.

Subsection 3.4: Exploring High-Yield Savings Accounts and Certificates of Deposit

When it comes to saving money, not all bank accounts are created equal. While traditional savings accounts offer a safe place to store your funds, their interest rates are often disappointingly low. Fortunately, there are two savings vehicles that can help you grow your money faster: high-yield savings accounts and certificates of deposit (CDs).

High-yield savings accounts are exactly what they sound like – savings accounts that offer higher interest rates than their traditional counterparts. These accounts are typically offered by online banks or credit unions, which have lower overhead costs than brick-and-mortar institutions and can pass those savings on to their customers in the form of higher interest rates.

The interest rates on high-yield savings accounts can vary depending on the institution and the current economic climate, but they are often significantly higher than those offered by traditional banks. For example, while a traditional savings account might offer an annual percentage yield (APY) of 0.01%, a high-yield savings account could offer an APY of 1.50% or more.

To put this into perspective, let's consider an example. Suppose you have $10,000 to save and you put it into a traditional savings account with an APY of 0.01%. After one year, your balance would grow to $10,001. However, if you put that same $10,000 into a high-yield savings account with an APY of 1.50%, your balance would grow to $10,150 after one year – a difference of $149.

While $149 may not seem like a lot, the power of compound interest means that this difference can add up significantly over time. If you left that $10,000 in the high-yield savings account for 10 years, assuming the interest rate remained constant, your balance would grow to $11,605 – a total of $1,605 in interest earned.

Another savings vehicle that can offer higher interest rates than traditional savings accounts is a certificate of deposit, or CD. A CD is a type of savings account that requires you to leave your money untouched for a set period of time, typically ranging from a few months to several years. In exchange for this commitment, CDs often offer higher interest rates than traditional savings accounts.

The interest rates on CDs can vary depending on the term length and the financial institution offering them. Generally, the longer the term, the higher the interest rate. For example, a 1-year CD might offer an APY of 1.75%, while a 5-year CD could offer an APY of 2.25%.

It's important to note that CDs typically come with penalties for early withdrawal, meaning that if you need to access your funds before the term is up, you may have to pay a fee. This is why it's crucial to only invest money in a CD that you know you won't need for the duration of the term.

When considering a CD, it's also important to pay attention to the interest rate type. Some CDs offer fixed rates, meaning the interest rate will remain the same throughout the term. Others offer variable rates, which means the interest rate could fluctuate based on market conditions.

In addition to traditional CDs, some financial institutions offer specialty CDs with unique features. For example, some banks offer bump-up CDs, which allow you to "bump up" your interest rate once during the term if rates increase. Others offer no-penalty CDs, which allow you to withdraw your funds early without incurring a penalty.

When choosing between a high-yield savings account and a CD, it's important to consider your financial goals and timeline. If you need easy access to your funds and want the flexibility to make withdrawals at any time, a high-yield savings account may be the better choice. However, if you have a lump sum of money that you know you won't need for a set period of time, a CD could offer a higher return.

Regardless of which savings vehicle you choose, the key is to shop around and compare interest rates from multiple financial institutions. Don't be afraid to look beyond traditional banks and consider online banks, credit unions, and other alternative options. By doing your research and choosing an account with a competitive interest rate, you can make your money work harder for you and reach your savings goals faster.

Summary: Empowering Your Financial Journey

Congratulations on taking a significant step towards financial empowerment by exploring strategies to increase your savings. Throughout this section, we've uncovered a wealth of practical methods to boost your savings rate and make your money work harder for you.

From reducing expenses and cutting unnecessary costs to maximizing your income and making the most of windfalls, you now have a toolbox of techniques to supercharge your savings. By implementing these strategies and making saving a priority, you'll be amazed at how quickly your nest egg can grow.

We've also explored the power of employer-sponsored savings plans, such as 401(k)s, which offer valuable tax benefits and the potential for employer matching contributions. By taking full advantage of these plans and understanding how they work, you can harness the magic of compound interest and set yourself up for a more secure financial future.

Furthermore, we've delved into the world of high-yield savings accounts and certificates of deposit, which can help your money grow faster than traditional savings accounts. By shopping around and choosing accounts with competitive interest rates, you can make your savings work smarter, not just harder.

As you embark on this transformative journey towards financial security and prosperity, remember that every step counts. Each dollar saved, each expense reduced, and each opportunity seized brings you closer to your goals. By staying committed, focused, and proactive, you'll be well on your way to building a strong financial foundation that will support you throughout your life.

So, take a moment to reflect on the strategies you've learned and consider how you can start implementing them today. Whether it's cutting back on unnecessary expenses, negotiating a raise, or opening a high-yield savings account, every action you take is a step towards a brighter financial future.

Remember, the path to financial success is not always easy, but it is always worth it. With the knowledge and tools you've gained from this section, you have the power to shape your financial destiny and create the life you've always dreamed of.

As you continue on this exciting journey, keep learning, stay curious, and never stop believing in yourself. The future is yours to create, and with a solid savings strategy in place, there's no limit to what you can achieve. So, go forth with confidence, embrace the power of saving, and watch your financial dreams take flight.

Section 4: Building an Emergency Fund

Imagine this: You're going about your life, working hard to make ends meet, when suddenly, the unexpected strikes. Maybe it's a medical emergency, a car repair, or a job loss. Whatever the case, you find yourself facing a financial crisis that threatens to derail your carefully laid plans. This is where an emergency fund comes in. An emergency fund is like a lifeline, a safety net that catches you when life throws you a curveball.

But what exactly is an emergency fund, and why is it so important? In this section, we'll dive deep into the concept of building a financial safety net. We'll explore the definition of an emergency fund, its purpose, and how it can help you weather life's storms. You'll learn how to determine the right size for your emergency fund based on your unique circumstances and financial goals.

We'll also discuss the practical aspects of setting up and maintaining an emergency fund. From choosing the right account to house your savings to developing strategies for replenishing your fund after an emergency, we'll cover it all. By the end of this section, you'll have a clear understanding of why an emergency fund is a crucial component of your overall financial plan and how to go about building one that gives you peace of mind and financial security.

So, whether you're just starting your financial journey or looking to strengthen your existing safety net, this section is for you. Get ready to take control of your financial future and build the emergency fund that will help you navigate life's unexpected challenges with confidence and resilience.

Subsection 4.1: Defining an Emergency Fund and Its Purpose

An emergency fund is a crucial component of a solid financial foundation, serving as a safety net during unexpected life events that can strain your finances. It is a readily accessible sum of money, typically stored in a savings account, that covers essential expenses when you face a financial setback, such as a job loss, medical emergency, or major car repair.

The primary purpose of an emergency fund is to provide financial stability and peace of mind during challenging times. Without an emergency fund, you may be forced to rely on credit cards, loans, or even retirement savings to cover unexpected costs, which can lead to high-interest debt or derail your long-term financial goals. By having an emergency fund, you create a buffer between yourself and financial hardship, allowing you to navigate difficult situations without compromising your financial well-being.

An emergency fund is not intended for discretionary spending or planned expenses, such as vacations or home renovations. Instead, it should be reserved for genuine emergencies that cannot be anticipated or avoided. By clearly defining the purpose of your emergency fund and setting strict guidelines for its use, you can ensure that the money is available when you need it most.

Building an emergency fund takes time and discipline, but it is a critical step in securing your financial future. It provides a foundation of stability and resilience, enabling you to weather life's storms without falling into financial distress. In the following subsections, we will explore how to determine the appropriate size of your emergency fund, choose the right account to house it, and develop strategies for maintaining and replenishing your fund over time.

Subsection 4.2: Determining the Appropriate Size of Your Emergency Fund

When it comes to building an emergency fund, one of the most common questions people ask is, "How much should I save?" The answer to this question is not one-size-fits-all, as the appropriate size of your emergency fund depends on a variety of factors unique to your financial situation and lifestyle.

A general rule of thumb is to save enough to cover three to six months' worth of living expenses. This means that if you lose your income or face a major unexpected expense, you'll have a cushion to fall back on while you get back on your feet. However, this is just a starting point, and the actual amount you should save may be higher or lower depending on your circumstances.

One key factor to consider is the stability of your income. If you have a steady, reliable paycheck, you may be able to get by with a smaller emergency fund. On the other hand, if you're self-employed, work on commission, or have a variable income, you may need to save more to account for potential dry spells.

Another important consideration is your lifestyle and financial obligations. If you have a mortgage, car payments, or other significant expenses, you'll need a larger emergency fund to ensure you can keep up with these commitments during a financial setback. Similarly, if you have dependents or a family to support, you'll want to have a more substantial safety net.

It's also wise to think about your health and potential medical expenses. If you have a chronic condition or are at a higher risk for health issues, you may want to save more to cover potential medical bills or time off work.

When determining the size of your emergency fund, it can be helpful to create a budget and track your expenses for a few months. This will give you a clear picture of your essential monthly costs, such as rent/mortgage, utilities, food, and insurance. Multiply this total by the number of months you want to cover (e.g., three to six months) to arrive at your emergency fund target.

Keep in mind that building an emergency fund is a gradual process, and it's okay to start small. Even setting aside a few hundred dollars each month can add up over time. As you reach your initial goal, you can reassess and adjust your target based on any changes in your financial situation.

Ultimately, the right size for your emergency fund is the amount that gives you peace of mind and a sense of financial security. By taking the time to assess your unique circumstances and saving accordingly, you'll be better prepared to weather life's unexpected challenges without derailing your long-term financial goals.

Subsection 4.3: Choosing the Right Account for Your Emergency Fund

When it comes to building an emergency fund, choosing the right account to house your savings is crucial. Not all savings accounts are created equal, and selecting the appropriate one can make a significant difference in how quickly your fund grows and how easily you can access the money when you need it.

The ideal account for your emergency fund should have several key characteristics. First and foremost, it should be easily accessible. In the event of an unexpected expense or financial setback, you'll want to be able to withdraw your money quickly and without penalty. This means that accounts with long holding periods or early withdrawal penalties, such as certificates of deposit (CDs) or retirement accounts, are not the best choice for an emergency fund.

Instead, consider opening a high-yield savings account or a money market account. These accounts typically offer higher interest rates than traditional savings accounts, allowing your emergency fund to grow faster over time. They also provide easy access to your money, often with no minimum balance requirements or withdrawal restrictions.

Another important factor to consider is the stability and reputation of the financial institution where you open your account. Look for banks or credit unions that are well-established, federally insured, and have a track record of financial stability. This will ensure that your emergency fund is safe and secure, even in the face of economic uncertainty.

When comparing different account options, pay attention to the interest rates, fees, and minimum balance requirements. Some accounts may offer higher interest rates but require a larger minimum balance or charge monthly maintenance fees. Consider your own financial situation and choose an account that aligns with your needs and goals.

It's also a good idea to keep your emergency fund separate from your everyday checking and savings accounts. This will help you avoid the temptation to dip into your emergency savings for non-emergency expenses and ensure that the money is readily available when you need it most.

Once you've chosen the right account for your emergency fund, set up automatic transfers from your checking account to your emergency savings each month. This will help you build your fund consistently over time without having to remember to make manual transfers.

By taking the time to select the appropriate account for your emergency fund, you'll be better positioned to weather life's financial storms and maintain a sense of security and peace of mind. Remember, the key is to choose an account that combines easy access, competitive interest rates, and financial stability, so you can focus on building your safety net and achieving your long-term financial goals.

Subsection 4.4: Maintaining and Replenishing Your Emergency Fund

Congratulations! You've taken the crucial step of building your emergency fund, creating a financial safety net that can help you weather life's unexpected challenges. However, your work doesn't end there. To ensure that your emergency fund remains a reliable source of support, it's essential to regularly review and replenish it.

Think of your emergency fund as a dynamic resource that requires ongoing attention and care. Just as you wouldn't neglect your physical health after reaching a fitness goal, you shouldn't neglect your financial health once you've established your emergency fund.

One key aspect of maintaining your emergency fund is regularly reviewing your financial situation and adjusting your savings target as needed. As your life circumstances change, such as getting married, having children, or buying a home, your emergency fund needs may also evolve. Periodically reassess your living expenses and update your emergency fund target to ensure that it still provides an adequate cushion.

Another crucial element of emergency fund maintenance is replenishing the fund after you've had to use it. It's important to remember that the purpose of an emergency fund is to be spent during financial crises. If you find yourself in a situation where you need to tap into your emergency savings, don't feel guilty or discouraged. Instead, focus on rebuilding your fund as soon as possible.

To replenish your emergency fund, consider treating it as a priority in your budget. As you recover from the financial setback, allocate a portion of your income each month to rebuilding your savings. You may need to temporarily adjust your spending habits or find ways to boost your income to accelerate the process.

One helpful strategy for maintaining and replenishing your emergency fund is to automate your savings contributions. Set up automatic transfers from your checking account to your emergency fund each month, so you consistently save without having to think about it. This approach helps make saving a habit and ensures that your emergency fund remains a priority even when life gets busy.

It's also wise to periodically review the account where you keep your emergency fund. As your savings grow, you may find better options with higher interest rates or more favorable terms. Don't be afraid to shop around and move your emergency fund to a different account if it means earning more interest or enjoying greater accessibility.

Finally, remember that maintaining and replenishing your emergency fund is an ongoing process, not a one-time task. By regularly reviewing your financial situation, adjusting your savings target, and replenishing your fund after use, you'll ensure that your safety net remains strong and reliable over time.

In conclusion, building an emergency fund is a significant milestone in your financial journey, but it's just the beginning. By understanding the importance of regularly reviewing and replenishing your fund, you'll be better equipped to handle life's unexpected challenges and maintain financial stability in the face of adversity. With a well-maintained emergency fund, you can face the future with confidence, knowing that you have a solid foundation to support you through any storm.

Summary: Securing Your Financial Future with an Emergency Fund

In this section, we've explored the critical role that an emergency fund plays in securing your financial future and providing peace of mind in the face of life's unexpected challenges. By understanding the purpose of an emergency fund, determining the appropriate size based on your unique circumstances, choosing the right account to house your savings, and developing strategies for maintaining and replenishing your fund, you'll be well-equipped to build a robust financial safety net.

Remember, building an emergency fund is not a one-time task, but an ongoing process that requires commitment, discipline, and regular review. As you continue on your financial journey, make sure to prioritize your emergency fund, treating it as a non-negotiable aspect of your overall financial plan.

The knowledge and insights you've gained from this section will serve as a solid foundation for your financial security, empowering you to face life's uncertainties with confidence and resilience. By taking proactive steps to build and maintain your emergency fund, you're not only protecting yourself and your loved ones from financial hardship but also creating opportunities for long-term financial growth and success.

As you move forward, keep the lessons of this section close to your heart, and remember that your emergency fund is a powerful tool in your financial arsenal. With a well-stocked emergency fund by your side, you'll be ready to weather any storm and emerge stronger, more confident, and better prepared for whatever the future may bring.

So, take a moment to celebrate the progress you've made and the knowledge you've gained. Embrace the power of your emergency fund, and let it serve as a constant reminder of your commitment to financial security and well-being. The future is bright, and with your emergency fund firmly in place, you're ready to seize every opportunity and overcome any obstacle that comes your way.

Section 5: Balancing Saving with Other Financial Priorities

Saving money is a crucial aspect of financial stability, but it's not the only financial priority you'll face in life. As you work towards building your savings and emergency fund, you'll also encounter other competing financial goals that demand your attention and resources. These may include paying off debt, investing for the future, or saving for retirement while also meeting short-term objectives. Balancing these priorities can be a delicate act, requiring careful planning and decision-making.

In this section, we'll explore the challenges of allocating your money effectively across these various financial priorities. We'll discuss the trade-offs and considerations involved in deciding how much to save versus how much to put towards other goals, such as debt repayment or investment. You'll learn strategies for finding the right balance that allows you to make progress on multiple fronts while still maintaining a strong foundation of savings.

By understanding how to navigate these competing financial priorities, you'll be better equipped to make informed decisions about your money and create a comprehensive financial plan that supports your short-term and long-term goals. Whether you're just starting to save or you're further along in your financial journey, this section will provide valuable insights and guidance for balancing saving with other important financial objectives.

Subsection 5.1: Saving vs. Paying Off Debt

One of the most common financial dilemmas people face is whether to prioritize saving money or paying off debt. Both are important goals, but when resources are limited, it can be challenging to decide which one should take precedence. The answer to this question depends on various factors, such as the type of debt, interest rates, and your overall financial situation.

When it comes to high-interest debt, such as credit card balances, it's generally advisable to focus on paying them off as quickly as possible. The reason for this is simple: the interest you pay on these debts can quickly accumulate, making it harder to break free from the debt cycle. By prioritizing debt repayment, you can save money on interest charges in the long run and free up more cash flow for saving and investing.

However, it's essential not to neglect saving entirely while paying off debt. Having an emergency fund is crucial for managing unexpected expenses without resorting to more debt. A good rule of thumb is to save at least three to six months' worth of living expenses in a liquid, easily accessible account. This way, you'll have a financial cushion to fall back on if you face a job loss, medical emergency, or any other unforeseen event.

One strategy for balancing saving and debt repayment is the 50/30/20 rule. This approach suggests allocating 50% of your income towards essential expenses (like housing, food, and transportation), 30% towards discretionary spending (entertainment, dining out, etc.), and 20% towards financial goals (saving and debt repayment). By following this guideline, you can ensure that you're making progress on both fronts while still covering your basic needs and enjoying some discretionary spending.

Another approach is to focus on paying off debt while simultaneously contributing a smaller amount to your savings. For example, you might allocate 80% of your available funds towards debt repayment and 20% towards saving. As you pay off each debt, you can redirect those payments towards saving, gradually increasing your savings rate over time.

When deciding between saving and debt repayment, it's also important to consider the potential returns on your money. If you have low-interest debt, such as a mortgage or student loan, it might make more sense to prioritize saving and investing, especially if you can earn a higher return on your investments than the interest you're paying on the debt. This is known as arbitrage, and it can be a smart way to grow your wealth while still managing your debt obligations.

Ultimately, the key to balancing saving and debt repayment is to create a personalized plan that takes into account your unique financial situation and goals. By assessing your debts, interest rates, and income, you can develop a strategy that allows you to make progress on both fronts and work towards long-term financial stability. Remember, it's not always an either/or choice – with careful planning and discipline, you can successfully navigate the challenges of saving and debt repayment and achieve your financial objectives.

Subsection 5.2: Saving vs. Investing

When it comes to managing your money, two important concepts often come up: saving and investing. While both involve setting aside money for the future, they serve different purposes and involve different strategies. Understanding the differences between saving and investing is crucial for making informed decisions about your financial priorities and achieving your short-term and long-term goals.

Saving is the act of putting money aside for future use, typically in a low-risk, easily accessible account such as a savings account or a certificate of deposit (CD). The primary goal of saving is to preserve your money and maintain its value over time. When you save, you prioritize safety and liquidity over potential growth. Savings are generally used for short-term goals, such as building an emergency fund, saving for a down payment on a house, or planning for a vacation. The returns on savings are usually modest, often in the form of interest earned on the account balance.

On the other hand, investing involves putting your money into assets with the expectation of generating a return or profit over time. When you invest, you purchase assets such as stocks, bonds, mutual funds, or real estate with the goal of growing your wealth. Investing involves taking on more risk than saving, as the value of your investments can fluctuate based on market conditions. However, this increased risk also comes with the potential for higher returns over the long term. Investing is typically used for long-term goals, such as saving for retirement, funding a child's education, or building a diversified portfolio.

One key difference between saving and investing is the time horizon. Saving is generally focused on the short term, with the expectation that you may need to access your money within a few months or years. Investing, on the other hand, is a long-term strategy, with the understanding that you may not need to tap into your investments for several years or even decades. This longer time horizon allows your investments to weather short-term market fluctuations and benefit from compound growth over time.

Another important distinction is the level of risk involved. Savings are considered low-risk because the value of your money is generally stable and protected, often up to certain limits, by government-backed insurance programs such as the Federal Deposit Insurance Corporation (FDIC) in the United States. In contrast, investments carry varying degrees of risk, depending on the type of asset and market conditions. While diversification can help mitigate some of this risk, there is always the potential for loss when investing.

When deciding whether to prioritize saving or investing, it's essential to consider your financial goals, risk tolerance, and time horizon. A general rule of thumb is to ensure that you have a solid foundation of savings, including an emergency fund, before focusing on investing. This approach allows you to handle unexpected expenses without having to tap into your investments prematurely.

Once you have a sufficient savings cushion, you can start allocating more of your money towards investing for long-term growth. A common strategy is to create a diversified investment portfolio that includes a mix of assets, such as stocks, bonds, and real estate, tailored to your risk tolerance and financial objectives. As you progress in your financial journey, you may adjust the balance between saving and investing based on your changing needs and goals.

It's worth noting that saving and investing are not mutually exclusive. In fact, a well-rounded financial plan often includes both. For example, you might contribute to a retirement account, such as a 401(k) or IRA, which allows you to invest for the long term while also benefiting from tax advantages and employer contributions. At the same time, you can maintain a separate savings account for short-term goals and emergencies.

In summary, understanding the differences between saving and investing is crucial for making informed decisions about your financial priorities. Saving focuses on preserving your money for short-term needs, while investing aims to grow your wealth over the long term. By finding the right balance between the two based on your goals, risk tolerance, and time horizon, you can create a comprehensive financial plan that supports your short-term and long-term objectives.

Subsection 5.3: Saving for Retirement While Meeting Short-Term Goals

Saving for retirement is one of the most important long-term financial goals, but it can be challenging to balance this priority with short-term objectives. Many people find themselves torn between the need to save for the future and the desire to enjoy life in the present. However, with careful planning and the right strategies, it is possible to make progress on both fronts and achieve a healthy balance between short-term and long-term financial success.

One key to balancing retirement savings with short-term goals is to start early and make saving a habit. The earlier you begin setting aside money for retirement, the more time your investments have to grow through the power of compound interest. Even small contributions made consistently over time can add up to significant savings later in life. By making retirement saving a regular part of your financial routine, you can ensure that you're making steady progress towards your long-term goals while still having room in your budget for short-term priorities.

Another important strategy is to take advantage of employer-sponsored retirement plans, such as 401(k)s or pensions. Many employers offer matching contributions, which can significantly boost your retirement savings over time. For example, if your employer matches 50% of your contributions up to 6% of your salary, that's essentially a 50% return on your investment before any market gains. By contributing enough to take full advantage of employer matching, you can supercharge your retirement savings while still leaving room in your budget for other goals.

In addition to employer-sponsored plans, consider opening an individual retirement account (IRA) to further enhance your retirement savings. Traditional IRAs offer tax deductions on contributions, while Roth IRAs provide tax-free withdrawals in retirement. Depending on your income and other factors, one type of IRA may be more advantageous than the other. By diversifying your retirement savings across different account types, you can maximize your tax benefits and create a more robust savings strategy.

When it comes to balancing retirement savings with short-term goals, it's important to prioritize and make trade-offs as needed. For example, if you're saving for a down payment on a house, you may need to temporarily reduce your retirement contributions to free up more cash for your home purchase. However, it's crucial to have a plan for getting back on track with your retirement savings once you've met your short-term goal. One way to do this is to set up automatic increases in your retirement contributions each year, so that you're gradually ramping up your savings over time.

Another way to balance short-term and long-term goals is to create a separate savings account for each objective. By segregating your savings into different buckets, you can ensure that you're making progress on multiple fronts without sacrificing one goal for another. For example, you might have one account for your emergency fund, another for your retirement savings, and a third for your short-term goals like travel or home improvements. By automating your savings and allocating funds to each account based on your priorities, you can create a comprehensive savings strategy that supports all of your financial objectives.

It's also important to be flexible and adaptable as your financial situation changes over time. Life events like marriage, having children, or changing careers can all impact your short-term and long-term financial goals. By regularly reviewing your savings strategy and making adjustments as needed, you can ensure that you're staying on track and making progress towards your objectives. This may involve increasing your retirement contributions during periods of higher income, or scaling back on short-term goals during times of financial stress.

Ultimately, the key to balancing retirement savings with short-term goals is to have a clear plan and stay committed to your objectives. By setting realistic goals, automating your savings, and making trade-offs as needed, you can create a comprehensive financial strategy that supports your long-term and short-term success. Remember, saving for retirement is a marathon, not a sprint – by starting early, staying consistent, and remaining adaptable, you can achieve a secure and comfortable retirement while still enjoying life along the way.

Summary: Balancing Your Financial Priorities for Long-Term Success

Balancing saving with other financial priorities is a crucial skill for achieving long-term financial success. Throughout this section, we've explored the challenges and strategies involved in allocating your money effectively across competing goals, such as paying off debt, investing for the future, and saving for retirement while also meeting short-term objectives.

By understanding the trade-offs and considerations involved in these decisions, you can develop a comprehensive financial plan that allows you to make progress on multiple fronts simultaneously. Whether you're focusing on paying down high-interest debt, building an emergency fund, or investing for long-term growth, the key is to find a balance that works for your unique situation and goals.

Remember, there's no one-size-fits-all approach to managing your financial priorities. What matters most is that you take the time to assess your needs, create a clear plan, and stay committed to your objectives. By doing so, you'll be well on your way to achieving the financial stability and security you desire.

As you continue on your financial journey, keep in mind the lessons learned in this section. Prioritize your goals, make informed trade-offs, and remain adaptable as your circumstances change over time. By staying focused, disciplined, and proactive, you can successfully navigate the challenges of balancing saving with other financial priorities and achieve the long-term success you deserve.

So, take a moment to reflect on the insights gained from this section and consider how you can apply them to your own financial life. Whether you're just starting to save or you're further along in your journey, the strategies and principles outlined here can help you make the most of your money and build a brighter financial future. With the right mindset, tools, and determination, you have the power to take control of your finances and create the life you've always dreamed of.

Chapter Summary: Securing Your Financial Foundation Through Saving and Emergency Funds

In this chapter, we've explored the critical role that saving money and building an emergency fund play in achieving financial stability and security. By understanding the power of compound interest, developing a saving mindset, and implementing practical strategies to boost your savings, you can take control of your financial future and work towards your short-term and long-term goals.

We've also discussed the importance of having a dedicated emergency fund to protect you from unexpected expenses and financial setbacks. By determining the appropriate size of your emergency fund, choosing the right account to house it, and regularly maintaining and replenishing it, you can create a strong financial safety net that provides peace of mind and resilience in the face of life's uncertainties.

Throughout the chapter, we've emphasized the need to balance saving with other financial priorities, such as paying off debt, investing for the future, and saving for retirement. By taking a holistic approach to your finances and making informed decisions about how to allocate your money, you can build a solid foundation for long-term financial success.

Remember, saving money and building an emergency fund is not a one-time event, but rather an ongoing process that requires discipline, commitment, and a willingness to adapt to changing circumstances. By embracing the strategies and mindset outlined in this chapter, you can cultivate healthy financial habits that will serve you well throughout your life, empowering you to achieve your dreams and live with greater financial freedom and security.

Chapter 6: Understanding Credit and Managing Debt

In the world of personal finance, credit and debt are two sides of the same coin. Credit, when used responsibly, can be a powerful tool for achieving your financial goals, such as buying a home, starting a business, or financing your education. However, when mismanaged, credit can quickly turn into a burden of debt that can take years to overcome.

In this chapter, we'll dive deep into the world of credit and debt management. We'll start by exploring what credit is, how it works, and why it's important to build and maintain a good credit history. You'll learn about the different types of credit available, such as revolving credit and installment loans, and how they can impact your financial health.

Next, we'll discuss credit scores and reports, the key indicators of your creditworthiness. You'll discover what factors influence your credit score, such as payment history and credit utilization, and how to monitor and improve your score over time. We'll also explore the role of credit reporting agencies and how to interpret your credit report.

With a solid understanding of credit, we'll move on to the topic of responsible credit usage. You'll learn best practices for using credit wisely, such as keeping your balances low, making timely payments, and avoiding common pitfalls. We'll also discuss how to protect yourself against credit fraud and identity theft.

Despite our best efforts, sometimes debt can accumulate and become overwhelming. In this chapter, we'll provide you with practical strategies for managing and paying off debt, including assessing your debt situation, creating a repayment plan, and exploring options like debt consolidation and negotiation with creditors. You'll learn about popular debt repayment methods, such as the debt snowball and avalanche approaches, and how to stay motivated throughout your debt-free journey.

We'll also address special considerations for student loans and mortgages, two of the most common types of debt. You'll gain insights into navigating the student loan landscape, understanding repayment options, and managing your student debt effectively. We'll also discuss the process of obtaining a mortgage and the key factors to consider when becoming a homeowner.

Finally, we'll explore the topic of rebuilding and maintaining good credit. Whether you've experienced financial setbacks or simply want to establish a strong credit profile, you'll learn strategies for recovering from negative credit events and adopting best practices for long-term credit health. We'll also highlight the numerous benefits of having good credit, from securing better loan terms to opening up new financial opportunities.

By the end of this chapter, you'll have a comprehensive understanding of credit and debt management. Armed with this knowledge, you'll be empowered to make informed decisions about your credit usage, take control of your debt, and build a solid foundation for your financial future. So, let's dive in and start your journey towards mastering credit and conquering debt!

Section 1: Introduction to Credit

Picture this: you're standing at the crossroads of your financial journey, and before you lies a powerful tool that can either pave the way to your dreams or lead you down a treacherous path. This tool is credit, and it's essential to understand its fundamentals and the role it plays in your personal finance. In a world where instant gratification is just a swipe away, it's easy to fall into the trap of overusing credit without fully grasping its implications. But fear not, because in this section, we'll demystify the concept of credit and equip you with the knowledge you need to wield it wisely.

Credit is more than just a means to an end; it's a reflection of your financial reputation. It's the key that unlocks doors to opportunities, from renting your first apartment to securing a mortgage for your dream home. Your credit score, a numerical representation of your creditworthiness, is the gatekeeper that lenders consult before deciding whether to grant you credit and at what terms. The higher your credit score, the more favorable the conditions you'll be offered.

But credit is a double-edged sword. When used responsibly, it can help you achieve your financial goals and build a strong credit history. However, when misused or misunderstood, credit can quickly spiral into a cycle of debt that can take years to escape. That's why it's crucial to grasp the fundamentals of credit and develop a healthy relationship with it from the start.

In this section, we'll explore the different types of credit, from revolving credit like credit cards to installment loans such as car payments and mortgages. We'll delve into the factors that influence your credit score and provide practical tips on how to establish and maintain a stellar credit history. By the end of this section, you'll have a solid foundation in the world of credit and be well on your way to making informed financial decisions that will serve you well in the long run.

So, let's embark on this journey together and uncover the secrets to mastering credit and taking control of your financial destiny. Your future self will thank you for the knowledge and wisdom you're about to gain.

Subsection 1.1: Defining Credit and How It Works

At its core, credit is the ability to borrow money or access goods and services with the understanding that you'll pay for them in the future. It's a financial agreement between a lender and a borrower, based on trust and the borrower's promise to repay the lender according to the terms of the agreement. When you use credit, you're essentially using someone else's money to make a purchase or secure a loan, and you're obligated to pay it back, usually with interest.

Credit plays a crucial role in the modern financial system, enabling individuals and businesses to access funds they may not have on hand. It allows people to buy homes, cars, and other expensive items they might not be able to afford upfront. Businesses use credit to finance operations, expand, and invest in new opportunities. Governments also rely on credit to fund projects and services.

In the world of personal finance, there are several common types of credit, including credit cards, mortgages, auto loans, and personal loans. Each type of credit has its own terms, interest rates, and repayment schedules. For example, credit cards allow you to borrow money up to a certain limit and pay it back over time, with interest charged on the unpaid balance. Mortgages, on the other hand, are long-term loans used to purchase real estate, with the property serving as collateral.

When you apply for credit, lenders assess your creditworthiness—your ability to repay the borrowed money. They consider factors such as your credit score, income, debt-to-income ratio, and credit history. A higher credit score and a solid financial track record generally make it easier to secure credit and obtain favorable terms, such as lower interest rates.

As you use credit and make payments, your credit history is recorded by credit bureaus, which compile this information into credit reports. These reports are used to calculate your credit score, a three-digit number that represents your creditworthiness. Maintaining a good credit score is essential, as it can impact your ability to secure future credit, rent an apartment, or even land a job.

While credit can be a valuable financial tool, it's important to use it responsibly. Overextending yourself or failing to make payments can lead to debt, damaged credit, and financial stress. By understanding how credit works and using it wisely, you can harness its power to achieve your financial goals and build a strong foundation for your future.

Subsection 1.2: Types of Credit: Revolving vs. Installment

When it comes to borrowing money, not all credit is created equal. There are two main types of credit: revolving credit and installment credit. Understanding the differences between these two forms of credit is crucial for managing your finances effectively and making informed decisions about borrowing.

Revolving credit is a type of credit that allows you to borrow money up to a predetermined limit, known as your credit limit. Credit cards are the most common example of revolving credit. With a credit card, you can make purchases and borrow money up to your credit limit, and you're required to make a minimum payment each month. If you carry a balance from month to month, you'll be charged interest on the outstanding amount. The key feature of revolving credit is that as you pay down your balance, you can borrow again up to your credit limit without having to reapply for credit.

One advantage of revolving credit is its flexibility. You can borrow as much or as little as you need, up to your credit limit, and you only pay interest on the amount you borrow. This makes revolving credit ideal for short-term expenses or emergencies. However, the interest rates on revolving credit tend to be higher than those on installment loans, and carrying high balances can negatively impact your credit score.

Installment credit, on the other hand, involves borrowing a fixed amount of money and repaying it in regular, equal payments over a set period of time. Examples of installment credit include mortgages, auto loans, and personal loans. With installment credit, you know exactly how much you need to pay each month and when the loan will be paid off, making budgeting and financial planning more straightforward.

One benefit of installment credit is that it often comes with lower interest rates compared to revolving credit, particularly if you have a good credit score. This makes installment loans a good choice for larger, long-term expenses such as buying a home or a car. Additionally, having a mix of both revolving and installment credit on your credit report can positively impact your credit score, as it demonstrates your ability to manage different types of credit responsibly.

When considering revolving vs. installment credit, it's essential to evaluate your financial needs and goals. Revolving credit can be a useful tool for managing short-term expenses and building credit, but it requires discipline to avoid overspending and accumulating high-interest debt. Installment credit is often better suited for larger, long-term purchases and can help you establish a positive credit history if you make your payments on time.

Ultimately, the key to using both revolving and installment credit wisely is to borrow only what you can afford to repay, make your payments on time, and monitor your credit regularly. By understanding the differences between these two types of credit and using them strategically, you can build a strong credit profile and achieve your financial objectives.

Subsection 1.3: The Importance of Credit in Building Financial Stability

In the grand scheme of personal finance, credit plays a vital role in establishing and maintaining financial stability. It's not just about borrowing money; credit is a powerful tool that can open doors to opportunities and help you weather life's unexpected storms. A strong credit profile is the foundation upon which you can build a secure financial future, and it's essential to understand why.

First and foremost, good credit can save you money in the long run. When you have a high credit score, lenders view you as a responsible and trustworthy borrower. This perception translates into lower interest rates on loans and credit cards, meaning you'll pay less in interest charges over time. For example, when applying for a mortgage, even a small difference in interest rates can save you thousands of dollars over the life of the loan. By maintaining a strong credit score, you can minimize the cost of borrowing and keep more money in your pocket.

Moreover, a solid credit history can provide you with financial flexibility and security. Life is full of surprises, both good and bad. Whether you need to replace a broken appliance, cover an unexpected medical expense, or seize a once-in-a-lifetime investment opportunity, having access to credit can help you navigate these situations with greater ease. With a strong credit profile, you'll have more options available to you when you need them most, allowing you to make decisions based on what's best for your financial well-being.

In addition to providing access to affordable credit, a good credit score can also impact your ability to secure essential services. Many landlords, utility companies, and even employers use credit checks as part of their decision-making process. A strong credit history can make it easier to rent an apartment, set up utility accounts, and potentially even land your dream job. On the flip side, a poor credit score can limit your options and make these experiences more challenging and expensive.

Building and maintaining good credit is also a crucial component of long-term financial planning. Your credit score is a reflection of your financial habits and responsibility over time. By consistently making payments on time, keeping credit card balances low, and managing your debt responsibly, you demonstrate to lenders that you are a reliable borrower. This positive credit behavior not only helps you access credit when you need it but also sets the stage for future financial milestones, such as buying a home or starting a business.

Furthermore, having a strong credit foundation can provide peace of mind and reduce financial stress. When you know you have a solid credit profile, you can face life's challenges with greater confidence and resilience. You'll have the tools and resources necessary to handle unexpected expenses, take advantage of opportunities, and plan for the future. This financial stability can have a ripple effect on your overall well-being, allowing you to focus on other important aspects of your life, such as your career, relationships, and personal growth.

In conclusion, credit is a critical component of building and maintaining financial stability. It's not just a number; it's a reflection of your financial health and a key that unlocks doors to opportunities. By understanding the importance of credit and taking steps to build and maintain a strong credit profile, you can create a solid foundation for your financial future. With the knowledge and tools to use credit wisely, you'll be well-equipped to navigate life's twists and turns with confidence and security.

Summary: Harnessing the Power of Credit for Your Financial Journey

In this section, we've explored the fundamental concepts of credit and its significance in personal finance. We've seen how credit can be a powerful tool for achieving your financial goals, whether it's buying a home, starting a business, or managing unexpected expenses. By understanding the different types of credit, such as revolving and installment credit, you can make informed decisions about how to use credit strategically to meet your needs.

We've also discussed the importance of building and maintaining a strong credit profile. Your credit score is a reflection of your financial responsibility and creditworthiness, and it can have a profound impact on your ability to access affordable credit, secure essential services, and even land your dream job. By consistently making payments on time, keeping credit balances low, and managing your debt wisely, you can establish a solid credit foundation that will serve you well throughout your financial journey.

As we've seen, credit is not just about borrowing money; it's a tool for building financial stability and resilience. With a strong credit profile, you'll have the flexibility and security to navigate life's challenges and opportunities with greater confidence and ease. You'll be better equipped to handle unexpected expenses, take advantage of valuable opportunities, and plan for a brighter financial future.

Of course, using credit responsibly requires discipline, knowledge, and a commitment to your long-term financial well-being. By understanding the principles outlined in this section and applying them to your own life, you can harness the power of credit to achieve your goals and build a strong financial foundation.

As we move forward in this book, we'll delve deeper into the practical strategies and tools you can use to manage credit effectively, from building a positive credit history to navigating the challenges of debt. With the knowledge and insights gained from this section, you'll be well-prepared to embark on a successful credit journey and take control of your financial destiny.

Section 2: Credit Scores and Reports

Picture this: you're about to make a major financial decision, like buying a car or applying for a mortgage. You've done your research, saved up some money, and feel confident in your ability to take on this new responsibility. But then, you're hit with a surprise – your credit score isn't quite what you thought it was, and suddenly, your plans are thrown into uncertainty.

This is a scenario that many people face at some point in their lives, and it highlights the crucial role that credit scores and reports play in our financial well-being. Your credit score is essentially a numerical representation of your creditworthiness, based on your history of managing credit and debt. It's a key factor that lenders, landlords, and even employers consider when making decisions about whether to approve your applications or offer you favorable terms.

But what exactly goes into your credit score, and how can you ensure that it accurately reflects your financial responsibility? In this section, we'll dive deep into the world of credit scores and reports, demystifying the factors that influence them and providing you with practical strategies for monitoring and improving your credit standing.

We'll start by exploring what credit scores are and how they're calculated, including the role of the three major credit reporting agencies in maintaining your credit history. From there, we'll identify the key factors that can impact your credit score, both positively and negatively, such as payment history, credit utilization, and length of credit history.

Armed with this knowledge, you'll be empowered to take control of your credit profile and make informed decisions about your financial future. Whether you're just starting to build your credit or working to recover from past setbacks, the insights and strategies covered in this section will provide you with a roadmap for success.

So, let's embark on this journey together and unlock the secrets to achieving and maintaining a strong credit score – one that opens doors to opportunities and helps you reach your financial goals with confidence.

Subsection 2.1: Understanding Credit Scores

Your credit score is a three-digit number that represents your creditworthiness, or how likely you are to repay debts on time. It's a crucial factor that lenders, creditors, and even landlords and employers consider when making decisions about your financial reliability. But how is this seemingly simple number calculated, and what does it really mean for your financial life?

At its core, your credit score is based on the information contained in your credit report, which is a detailed record of your credit history maintained by the three major credit bureaus: Equifax, Experian, and TransUnion. These agencies collect data from various sources, including banks, credit card companies, and other lenders, to create a comprehensive picture of your credit behavior over time.

The most widely used credit scoring model is the FICO score, developed by the Fair Isaac Corporation. FICO scores range from 300 to 850, with higher scores indicating better creditworthiness. The exact formula for calculating FICO scores is proprietary, but we do know that it takes into account several key factors:

1. Payment history (35% of score): This looks at whether you've made payments on time, including credit cards, loans, and other bills.
2. Credit utilization (30% of score): This is the amount of credit you're using compared to your credit limits, also known as your credit utilization ratio. Generally, it's best to keep this ratio below 30%.
3. Length of credit history (15% of score): This considers how long you've had credit accounts open and the average age of your accounts.

4. Credit mix (10% of score): This looks at the different types of credit you have, such as credit cards, installment loans, and mortgages. Having a diverse mix of credit can be beneficial.
5. New credit inquiries (10% of score): This takes into account the number of hard inquiries on your credit report, which occur when you apply for new credit. Too many inquiries in a short period can be seen as a red flag.

It's important to note that FICO scores are not the only credit scoring model out there. VantageScore, developed by the three credit bureaus, is another popular model that uses slightly different criteria and ranges from 501 to 990. However, the underlying principles of credit scoring remain the same: demonstrating responsible credit behavior over time is key to achieving and maintaining a good credit score.

By understanding the factors that go into your credit score, you can take proactive steps to improve and protect it. In the following subsections, we'll explore how to monitor your credit reports, interpret your credit scores, and take action to build and maintain a strong credit profile that opens doors to financial opportunities.

Subsection 2.2: The Major Credit Reporting Agencies

In the United States, there are three main credit reporting agencies, also known as credit bureaus, that play a crucial role in collecting, maintaining, and disseminating information about individuals' credit histories. These agencies are Equifax, Experian, and TransUnion. Each of these companies gathers data from various sources, including banks, credit card companies, and other lenders, to create comprehensive credit reports for millions of consumers.

Credit reporting agencies serve as intermediaries between consumers and lenders, providing the latter with the information they need to make informed decisions about creditworthiness. When you apply for a loan, credit card, or any other form of credit, the lender will typically request your credit report from one or more of these agencies to assess your risk as a borrower. The information contained in your credit report, along with other factors like your income and employment history, helps lenders determine whether to approve your application and at what terms.

But credit reporting agencies don't just collect and provide information – they also have a responsibility to ensure that the data they maintain is accurate, up-to-date, and secure. Under the Fair Credit Reporting Act (FCRA), these agencies must follow strict guidelines for handling consumer data, including responding to disputes and correcting errors in a timely manner. Consumers have the right to request their credit reports from each of the three agencies once per year, free of charge, through the official website AnnualCreditReport.com.

It's important to note that while Equifax, Experian, and TransUnion all collect similar types of information, they may not have identical data on every consumer. This is because not all lenders report to all three agencies, and some may report to only one or two. As a result, it's a good idea to review your credit reports from all three agencies regularly to ensure accuracy and completeness.

Understanding the role of credit reporting agencies is essential for anyone looking to build and maintain a strong credit profile. By monitoring your credit reports, disputing errors, and practicing responsible credit behaviors, you can work with these agencies to ensure that your credit history accurately reflects your creditworthiness and opens doors to financial opportunities.

Subsection 2.3: Factors That Affect Your Credit Score

Your credit score is a dynamic number that can fluctuate over time, influenced by a variety of factors that reflect your credit behavior and history. Understanding these key factors is essential for anyone looking to build, maintain, or improve their credit standing. By knowing what affects your credit score, you can make informed decisions and take proactive steps to ensure that your score accurately reflects your creditworthiness.

One of the most significant factors that impact your credit score is your payment history. This includes your record of paying bills on time, including credit cards, loans, and other financial obligations. Late payments, missed payments, and collections can all have a negative effect on your credit score, as they indicate a higher risk to lenders. On the other hand, consistently making payments on time can help you establish a positive payment history and improve your credit score over time.

Another crucial factor is your credit utilization, which refers to the amount of credit you are using compared to your credit limits. This is often expressed as a percentage, known as your credit utilization ratio. For example, if you have a credit card with a $10,000 limit and a balance of $3,000, your credit utilization ratio would be 30%. Generally, it's recommended to keep your credit utilization below 30%, as high utilization can be seen as a red flag by lenders and may lower your credit score.

The length of your credit history is also an important consideration. This includes the age of your oldest credit account, the average age of all your accounts, and the frequency with which you open new accounts. A longer credit history with a mix of well-managed accounts can demonstrate your experience and responsibility with credit, which can positively impact your score. However, opening too many new accounts in a short period can be seen as a risk factor and may temporarily lower your score.

The types of credit you have, also known as your credit mix, can also play a role in your credit score. Having a diverse mix of credit accounts, such as credit cards, installment loans, and mortgages, can show lenders that you can manage different types of credit responsibly. However, it's important to note that you should not open new accounts solely for the sake of improving your credit mix, as this can backfire if you take on more debt than you can handle.

Finally, the number of hard inquiries on your credit report can also affect your credit score. Hard inquiries occur when you apply for new credit, and lenders request your credit report to assess your creditworthiness. While a few hard inquiries are not likely to have a significant impact, too many in a short period can be seen as a sign of financial distress or excessive credit-seeking behavior, which may lower your score.

By understanding these key factors that influence your credit score, you can take control of your credit profile and make informed decisions to build and maintain a strong credit history. In the following subsections, we will explore practical strategies for monitoring your credit reports, interpreting your credit scores, and taking action to address any issues that may be holding you back from achieving your financial goals.

Subsection 2.4: Monitoring and Improving Your Credit Score

Your credit score is not a static number; it's a dynamic reflection of your ongoing credit behavior and financial health. As such, regularly monitoring and taking proactive steps to improve your credit score is essential for maintaining a strong credit profile and achieving your financial goals.

One of the most important habits you can develop is checking your credit reports regularly. As mentioned earlier, you are entitled to one free credit report from each of the three major credit bureaus annually through AnnualCreditReport.com. By reviewing your credit reports, you can ensure that all the information is accurate and up-to-date, and identify any potential errors or fraudulent activity that may be impacting your credit score.

If you do find errors on your credit report, such as incorrect account information or unauthorized inquiries, it's crucial to dispute them promptly. You can file a dispute directly with the credit bureau online, by mail, or by phone. The bureau is required to investigate your claim and remove any inaccurate information, which can help improve your credit score.

In addition to monitoring your credit reports, there are several strategies you can employ to actively improve your credit score over time. One of the most effective ways is to consistently make all your payments on time. Late payments can have a significant negative impact on your credit score, so setting up automatic payments or reminders can help ensure that you never miss a due date.

Another key strategy is to keep your credit utilization low. As mentioned earlier, it's generally recommended to keep your credit utilization ratio below 30%. This means that if you have a credit card with a $10,000 limit, you should aim to keep your balance below $3,000. If you find yourself with high balances, work on paying them down and consider strategies like debt consolidation or balance transfers to help manage your credit utilization.

Over time, building a long and diverse credit history can also help improve your credit score. This means keeping old credit accounts open, even if you don't use them frequently, and maintaining a mix of different types of credit, such as credit cards, installment loans, and mortgages. However, be cautious about opening too many new accounts at once, as this can temporarily lower your score and be seen as a risk factor by lenders.

Finally, if you're struggling to improve your credit score on your own, consider seeking help from a reputable credit counseling agency or financial advisor. These professionals can provide personalized advice and support to help you develop a plan for managing your credit and achieving your financial goals.

By regularly monitoring your credit reports, disputing errors, and implementing strategies to improve your credit behavior, you can take control of your credit score and open doors to better financial opportunities. Remember, building and maintaining a strong credit score is a journey, not a destination, and every positive step you take can have a lasting impact on your financial well-being.

Summary: Mastering Your Credit Profile for Financial Success

In this section, we've taken a deep dive into the world of credit scores and reports, uncovering the key factors that shape your creditworthiness and financial reputation. By understanding how credit scores are calculated and the role of credit reporting agencies, you're now equipped with the knowledge to take control of your credit profile and make informed decisions about your financial future.

We've explored the significance of payment history, credit utilization, length of credit history, credit mix, and new credit inquiries in determining your credit score. Armed with this information, you can prioritize the actions that will have the most significant impact on improving and maintaining a strong credit standing.

But knowledge alone isn't enough – it's crucial to put these insights into practice. By monitoring your credit reports regularly, disputing errors, and implementing strategies to build and maintain a positive credit history, you can open doors to better financial opportunities and achieve your goals with confidence.

Remember, your credit score is not a static number but a dynamic reflection of your ongoing financial behavior. Every positive step you take, whether it's making payments on time, keeping credit utilization low, or building a diverse credit mix, can have a lasting impact on your creditworthiness.

As you continue your journey through this book, keep these credit score insights in mind. They form the foundation for making informed choices about borrowing, investing, and managing your financial life. In the coming sections, we'll build upon this knowledge, exploring practical strategies for managing debt, optimizing your credit usage, and leveraging your credit profile to achieve your dreams.

So, take a moment to reflect on the power of your credit score and the steps you can take to master it. With dedication, discipline, and the right knowledge, you can transform your credit profile from a source of stress to a tool for financial empowerment. The path to financial success is within your reach – it all starts with understanding and harnessing the potential of your credit score.

Section 3: Responsible Credit Usage

Picture this: you're standing at the checkout counter, ready to make a purchase, when the cashier asks, "Will that be cash or credit?" It's a question we've all heard countless times, but have you ever stopped to consider the power and responsibility that comes with choosing credit? In a world where instant gratification is just a swipe away, it's easy to fall into the trap of overusing or misusing credit. But fear not, because in this section, we'll explore the best practices for using credit wisely and avoiding common pitfalls that can lead to financial stress and strain.

Imagine credit as a double-edged sword. When wielded skillfully, it can be a valuable tool for building your financial future, helping you establish a strong credit history, and even earning rewards along the way. However, when used recklessly, credit can quickly become a burden, leading to mounting debt, damaged credit scores, and a cycle of financial struggle. The key to mastering credit lies in understanding its power and learning to use it responsibly.

Throughout this section, we'll dive into the essential strategies for establishing credit responsibly, managing credit card balances and payments, and steering clear of credit pitfalls that can derail your financial journey. We'll explore real-life examples of individuals who have successfully navigated the world of credit, as well as cautionary tales of those who have fallen victim to its allure. By the end of this section, you'll be equipped with the knowledge and tools necessary to harness the power of credit and make it work for you, rather than against you.

So, whether you're a credit novice just starting to build your credit history or a seasoned user looking to refine your approach, this section is designed to empower you with the insights and strategies you need to use credit responsibly and confidently. Let's embark on this journey together and discover how to make credit a valuable ally in your financial toolbox.

Subsection 3.1: Establishing Credit Responsibly

Establishing credit is a crucial step in building a strong financial foundation, but it's essential to approach it with caution and responsibility. Many people, especially young adults, are eager to start their credit journey but may not fully understand the implications of their actions. It's like being handed the keys to a powerful vehicle without proper training – the results can be disastrous if not handled with care.

The first step in establishing credit responsibly is to educate yourself about the basics of credit. This includes understanding what credit is, how it works, and the different types of credit available. It's also important to familiarize yourself with key terms such as credit scores, credit reports, and interest rates. By gaining a solid understanding of these concepts, you'll be better equipped to make informed decisions when it comes to your own credit.

One of the most common ways to start building credit is by applying for a credit card. However, it's crucial to choose the right card for your needs and financial situation. Look for cards with low interest rates, no annual fees, and rewards programs that align with your spending habits. It's also wise to start with a low credit limit to avoid the temptation of overspending.

When using your credit card, treat it as if you're spending your own money. Only charge what you can afford to pay off in full each month, and make sure to pay your bills on time. Late payments can have a significant negative impact on your credit score, so it's essential to prioritize timely payments. Consider setting up automatic payments or reminders to ensure you never miss a due date.

Another way to establish credit responsibly is by becoming an authorized user on someone else's credit card account, such as a parent or spouse with a strong credit history. This allows you to "piggyback" on their good credit and start building your own credit history without the full responsibility of managing the account yourself. However, it's important to choose someone you trust and who has a track record of responsible credit use.

In addition to credit cards, there are other types of credit you can use to build your credit history. These include installment loans, such as student loans or car loans, and retail credit accounts. When taking on these types of credit, it's important to borrow only what you need and can afford to repay. Make sure to read the terms and conditions carefully, and understand the interest rates and repayment schedules before signing on the dotted line.

As you establish credit, it's also crucial to monitor your credit reports regularly. You're entitled to one free credit report from each of the three major credit bureaus annually, so take advantage of this opportunity to review your credit history for accuracy and any potential signs of fraud or identity theft. If you notice any errors or discrepancies, dispute them promptly with the credit bureau and the creditor involved.

Remember, establishing credit responsibly is a marathon, not a sprint. It takes time, patience, and discipline to build a strong credit history. By starting slowly, using credit wisely, and monitoring your progress, you'll be well on your way to achieving your financial goals and creating a solid foundation for your future.

Subsection 3.2: Managing Credit Card Balances and Payments

Picture this: you're sitting at your kitchen table, surrounded by a stack of credit card statements, each one bearing a balance that seems to have grown since the last time you looked. It's a familiar scene for many people, and it's one that can quickly lead to feelings of overwhelm and financial stress. But what if we told you that there's a way to break free from the cycle of credit card debt and take control of your financial future? In this subsection, we'll explore proven techniques for managing credit card balances and making timely payments, so you can enjoy the benefits of credit without the burden of debt.

One of the most important things to understand about credit card balances is that they can quickly spiral out of control if left unchecked. It's easy to fall into the trap of making only the minimum payment each month, but doing so can result in years of debt and thousands of dollars in interest charges. To avoid this fate, it's essential to develop a plan for paying down your balances and keeping them low over time.

The first step in managing your credit card balances is to take a honest look at your spending habits. Are you using your credit cards to make purchases that you can't afford to pay off right away? Are you relying on credit to cover everyday expenses or emergencies? By identifying the root causes of your credit card debt, you can start to make changes that will help you get back on track.

One effective strategy for managing credit card balances is to create a budget that includes a dedicated line item for debt repayment. By setting aside a specific amount of money each month to put toward your credit card balances, you can make steady progress toward paying them off. It's also important to prioritize your debts, focusing on the cards with the highest interest rates first, as these will cost you the most in the long run.

Another key aspect of managing credit card balances is making timely payments. Late payments can result in fees, higher interest rates, and damage to your credit score, so it's crucial to stay on top of your due dates. One helpful strategy is to set up automatic payments through your bank or credit card issuer, ensuring that your payments are made on time each month. You can also consider changing your payment due dates to align with your paycheck or other income, making it easier to budget and avoid missed payments.

In addition to making timely payments, it's also important to pay more than the minimum amount due each month. While it may be tempting to make only the minimum payment and free up cash for other expenses, doing so will keep you in debt for longer and cost you more in interest over time. Instead, aim to pay as much as you can afford each month, even if it means making sacrifices in other areas of your budget.

If you're struggling to make payments or get your balances under control, don't be afraid to reach out for help. Many credit card issuers offer hardship programs or payment plans for customers experiencing financial difficulties. You can also consider working with a credit counselor or financial advisor to develop a personalized plan for managing your debt and improving your financial health.

Remember, managing credit card balances and making timely payments is an ongoing process, not a one-time fix. By staying vigilant, developing healthy financial habits, and being proactive about your debt, you can take control of your credit and enjoy the many benefits it has to offer. With the right mindset and tools, you can transform your relationship with credit and build a strong foundation for your financial future.

Subsection 3.3: Avoiding Credit Pitfalls and Protecting Against Fraud

In the world of credit, it's not just about knowing what to do – it's also crucial to understand what not to do. Credit pitfalls and fraud can quickly derail your financial progress and leave you with a damaged credit score and a mountain of debt. In this subsection, we'll explore the common credit mistakes to avoid and the steps you can take to safeguard yourself against credit fraud.

One of the most prevalent credit pitfalls is overspending. It's easy to get caught up in the convenience and instant gratification of credit cards, but it's essential to remember that every swipe comes with a price. To avoid falling into the overspending trap, create a budget and stick to it. Before making a purchase, ask yourself if it's a necessity or a want, and consider whether you can afford to pay off the balance in full when the statement arrives. By being mindful of your spending habits and living within your means, you can avoid the slippery slope of credit card debt.

Another common credit mistake is applying for too many credit cards or loans in a short period. Each time you apply for credit, the lender will perform a hard inquiry on your credit report, which can temporarily lower your credit score. Additionally, having too many credit accounts can make it challenging to keep track of payments and balances, increasing the risk of missed payments and default. To avoid this pitfall, be selective about the credit you apply for and only apply for what you truly need.

Late payments are another major credit pitfall to avoid. Payment history is the most significant factor in determining your credit score, so even one missed payment can have a negative impact. To ensure you never miss a payment, set up automatic payments or reminders, and make sure you have enough funds in your account to cover the bills. If you're struggling to make ends meet, reach out to your creditors to discuss potential hardship programs or payment plans before falling behind.

In addition to avoiding credit pitfalls, it's also crucial to protect yourself against credit fraud. Identity thieves and scammers are always on the lookout for opportunities to steal your personal information and use it to open fraudulent accounts or make unauthorized purchases. To safeguard yourself, be vigilant about protecting your sensitive information, such as your Social Security number, credit card numbers, and login credentials.

One effective way to protect against credit fraud is to regularly monitor your credit reports and financial statements. Review your credit reports from all three major credit bureaus at least once a year, and check your bank and credit card statements monthly for any suspicious activity. If you notice any unauthorized transactions or accounts, report them immediately to your financial institution and the credit bureaus.

Another important step in protecting against credit fraud is to be cautious about sharing your personal information online or over the phone. Scammers often pose as legitimate companies or government agencies to trick you into revealing sensitive data. Be wary of unsolicited emails, calls, or texts asking for your personal information, and never click on links or download attachments from unknown sources. If you're unsure about the legitimacy of a request, contact the company or agency directly using a verified phone number or email address.

Finally, consider using additional security measures to protect your credit, such as fraud alerts and credit freezes. A fraud alert notifies creditors that they should take extra steps to verify your identity before granting credit in your name, while a credit freeze prevents new accounts from being opened altogether. These tools can provide an extra layer of protection against credit fraud and give you peace of mind.

Remember, avoiding credit pitfalls and protecting against fraud is an ongoing process that requires vigilance and proactive steps. By being mindful of your credit habits, monitoring your accounts regularly, and taking steps to safeguard your personal information, you can enjoy the benefits of credit without falling victim to its potential dangers. With the right knowledge and tools, you can build a strong, healthy credit profile that will serve you well for years to come.

Summary: Mastering Credit for a Brighter Financial Future

Throughout this section, we've explored the essential strategies and best practices for using credit responsibly and avoiding the common pitfalls that can lead to financial strain. By understanding the power of credit and learning to wield it wisely, you can transform this valuable tool into a catalyst for achieving your financial goals and building a strong foundation for your future.

We've discussed the importance of establishing credit responsibly, starting with a solid understanding of credit basics and making informed decisions when choosing credit products. By treating credit as a privilege and using it judiciously, you can build a positive credit history that will open doors to future opportunities and financial success.

Managing credit card balances and making timely payments are crucial skills that can help you avoid the debt trap and maintain a healthy credit profile. By creating a budget, prioritizing debt repayment, and developing disciplined spending habits, you can take control of your credit and enjoy its benefits without the burden of overwhelming debt.

We've also highlighted the common credit pitfalls to avoid, such as overspending, applying for too much credit, and falling behind on payments. By staying vigilant and proactive, you can navigate the credit landscape with confidence and steer clear of the mistakes that can derail your financial progress.

Moreover, we've emphasized the importance of protecting yourself against credit fraud and identity theft. By monitoring your credit reports, safeguarding your personal information, and using additional security measures, you can minimize the risk of falling victim to these insidious threats and maintain a clean credit record.

As you move forward on your financial journey, remember that responsible credit usage is an ongoing process that requires commitment, discipline, and a willingness to learn and adapt. By embracing the principles and strategies outlined in this section, you can harness the power of credit to achieve your dreams, build wealth, and create a brighter financial future for yourself and your loved ones.

So, take a moment to reflect on the insights you've gained and the steps you can take to apply them in your own life. Whether you're just starting to build your credit history or looking to refine your approach, the knowledge and tools you've acquired will serve you well on the path to financial success. With responsible credit usage as your guide, you can confidently navigate the world of credit and unlock the many opportunities it has to offer.

Section 4: Managing and Paying Off Debt

Debt can be a heavy burden, weighing down your financial freedom and hindering your ability to achieve your goals. Whether it's credit card balances, student loans, or personal loans, the pressure of debt can be overwhelming and stressful. However, with the right strategies and mindset, you can take control of your debt and work towards a brighter financial future.

In this section, we'll explore effective techniques for managing and eliminating debt. We'll start by assessing your current debt situation, helping you gain a clear understanding of what you owe and to whom. From there, we'll dive into proven debt repayment strategies, such as the debt snowball and debt avalanche methods, which can help you prioritize your debts and make steady progress towards paying them off.

But what if your debt feels insurmountable? We'll also discuss options for negotiating with creditors and seeking debt relief when necessary. You'll learn how to communicate effectively with lenders, explore potential debt consolidation or settlement programs, and understand the pros and cons of each approach.

Throughout your debt repayment journey, staying motivated and accountable is crucial. We'll share tips and techniques for setting realistic goals, tracking your progress, and celebrating your successes along the way. By breaking down your debt into manageable chunks and maintaining a positive attitude, you'll be better equipped to stay the course and reach your ultimate goal of becoming debt-free.

Remember, managing and paying off debt is a process that requires patience, discipline, and persistence. But with the knowledge and tools you'll gain in this section, you'll be well on your way to reclaiming your financial freedom and building a more secure future for yourself and your loved ones. So, let's dive in and start tackling your debt head-on!

Subsection 4.1: Assessing Your Debt Situation

Before you can effectively tackle your debt, it's crucial to have a clear understanding of your current debt obligations. This process involves taking a thorough inventory of all your debts, including credit card balances, student loans, personal loans, and any other outstanding balances. By assessing your debt situation, you'll gain a comprehensive picture of what you owe, to whom, and at what interest rates.

Start by gathering all your debt-related documents, such as credit card statements, loan agreements, and billing statements. Make a list of each debt, including the creditor's name, the total amount owed, the interest rate, and the minimum monthly payment. This exercise will help you organize your debts and provide a foundation for creating a repayment plan.

Next, prioritize your debts based on factors such as interest rates and the potential consequences of defaulting. High-interest debts, such as credit card balances, should generally be prioritized over lower-interest debts like student loans. Additionally, consider the impact of not paying certain debts, such as the risk of losing your home or facing legal action.

Once you have a clear understanding of your debts, it's time to create a debt repayment plan. Start by calculating your total monthly debt payments and comparing them to your income. If your debt payments consume a significant portion of your income, you may need to explore options for increasing your income or reducing your expenses to free up more money for debt repayment.

Consider using budgeting tools, such as spreadsheets or mobile apps, to track your income, expenses, and debt payments. These tools can help you visualize your financial situation and identify areas where you can cut back on spending to allocate more money towards debt repayment.

When creating your debt repayment plan, set realistic goals and timelines for paying off each debt. Break down your total debt into smaller, manageable chunks and celebrate your progress along the way. Remember that paying off debt is a marathon, not a sprint, and it requires patience, discipline, and perseverance.

In addition to creating a repayment plan, explore options for lowering your interest rates or consolidating your debts. You may be able to negotiate with creditors for lower rates, transfer high-interest balances to a lower-interest credit card, or consolidate multiple debts into a single, more manageable payment.

By thoroughly assessing your debt situation and creating a comprehensive repayment plan, you'll be well-equipped to take control of your debt and work towards a brighter financial future. Remember, the journey to becoming debt-free may be challenging, but with the right tools, mindset, and support, it is achievable.

Subsection 4.2: Debt Repayment Strategies: Snowball vs. Avalanche

When it comes to paying off debt, two popular strategies have emerged: the debt snowball method and the debt avalanche method. Both approaches have their merits and can be effective in helping you become debt-free, but they prioritize debts differently and may appeal to different individuals based on their personal preferences and motivations.

The debt snowball method, popularized by personal finance expert Dave Ramsey, focuses on paying off debts in order of smallest to largest balance, regardless of interest rates. The idea behind this approach is to build momentum and motivation by achieving quick wins. By tackling the smallest debts first, you experience the satisfaction of eliminating individual debts more frequently, which can help keep you motivated and committed to the repayment process.

To implement the debt snowball method, start by listing all your debts from smallest to largest balance. Continue making minimum payments on all debts, but allocate any extra funds towards paying off the smallest debt first. Once that debt is eliminated, roll over the payment you were making on it to the next smallest debt, and so on. As you progress, your payments will "snowball," gaining momentum and size until all debts are paid off.

On the other hand, the debt avalanche method prioritizes debts based on interest rates, targeting the debt with the highest interest rate first. This approach is mathematically optimal, as it minimizes the total interest paid over the course of the debt repayment journey. By focusing on high-interest debts, you can save money in the long run and potentially become debt-free faster.

To apply the debt avalanche method, list your debts from highest to lowest interest rate. Make minimum payments on all debts, but direct any extra funds towards the debt with the highest interest rate. Once that debt is paid off, move on to the next highest interest rate debt, and continue the process until all debts are eliminated.

While the debt avalanche method may be the most cost-effective approach, it can be psychologically challenging for some individuals. Paying off high-interest debts first may take longer, especially if they have larger balances, which can be discouraging and demotivating. The debt snowball method, although not mathematically optimal, provides a sense of accomplishment and progress that can help maintain motivation.

Ultimately, the choice between the debt snowball and debt avalanche methods depends on your personal preferences, financial situation, and psychological needs. If you thrive on quick wins and need the motivation boost of eliminating smaller debts rapidly, the debt snowball method may be the best fit for you. However, if you are more focused on minimizing overall interest payments and are comfortable with delayed gratification, the debt avalanche method may be the preferred approach.

Regardless of which method you choose, the key is to stay consistent, disciplined, and committed to the repayment process. Create a budget, track your progress, and celebrate your milestones along the way. Remember that becoming debt-free is a journey, and by employing a systematic and focused approach, you can achieve your goal and take control of your financial future.

Subsection 4.3: Negotiating with Creditors and Seeking Debt Relief

When faced with overwhelming debt, it may feel like there's no way out. However, there are options available to help you manage your debt and find relief. One such option is negotiating with your creditors. By communicating openly and honestly with your lenders, you may be able to work out alternative payment plans, reduce interest rates, or even settle your debts for less than the full amount owed.

Before reaching out to your creditors, it's essential to assess your financial situation and gather all relevant information, such as your income, expenses, and a list of your debts. This will help you determine what you can realistically afford to pay and provide a starting point for negotiations.

When contacting your creditors, be proactive and honest about your financial challenges. Explain your situation calmly and clearly, expressing your desire to find a mutually beneficial solution. Many creditors are willing to work with borrowers who show a genuine commitment to repaying their debts, as it's often more cost-effective for them than pursuing collection actions or writing off the debt entirely.

During the negotiation process, be prepared to discuss various options, such as:

1. Payment plans: Propose a structured repayment plan that fits your budget, allowing you to make smaller, more manageable payments over a longer period.
2. Interest rate reduction: Request a lower interest rate on your outstanding balances, which can help you pay off your debts more quickly and save money on interest charges.
3. Debt settlement: In some cases, creditors may be willing to accept a lump sum payment that is less than the full amount owed, known as a debt settlement. This can be a good option if you have access to funds, such as savings or a settlement from a lawsuit, but be aware that settled debts may have tax implications and can negatively impact your credit score.

If you're unable to reach an agreement with your creditors or if your debt situation is particularly complex, consider seeking assistance from a reputable debt relief program or credit counseling agency. These organizations can help you explore your options, create a personalized debt management plan, and negotiate with creditors on your behalf.

Debt relief programs, such as debt consolidation loans or debt management plans, can simplify your repayment process by combining multiple debts into a single, more manageable payment. These programs may also offer lower interest rates or waived fees, making it easier to pay off your debts over time.

However, it's crucial to research and choose a reputable debt relief program or credit counseling agency. Some unscrupulous companies may make promises they can't keep, charge high fees, or even engage in fraudulent practices. Look for organizations that are accredited by recognized industry associations, such as the National Foundation for Credit Counseling (NFCC) or the Financial Counseling Association of America (FCAA).

Remember, negotiating with creditors and seeking debt relief is not a quick fix, and it may take time and effort to find the right solution for your unique situation. However, by taking proactive steps, communicating openly with your creditors, and seeking professional guidance when needed, you can work towards a more stable and debt-free financial future.

Subsection 4.4: Staying Motivated and Accountable in Debt Repayment

Paying off debt can be a long and challenging journey, and it's not uncommon to experience moments of frustration, discouragement, or temptation along the way. Staying motivated and accountable throughout the debt repayment process is crucial to achieving your goal of becoming debt-free. In this subsection, we'll explore various strategies and tips to help you maintain your motivation and stay on track.

One of the most effective ways to stay motivated is to set clear, achievable goals and celebrate your progress along the way. Break down your overall debt repayment goal into smaller, manageable milestones, such as paying off a specific credit card or reducing your total debt by a certain percentage. As you reach each milestone, take a moment to acknowledge your accomplishment and reward yourself in a meaningful, yet budget-friendly way. This could be as simple as treating yourself to a favorite homemade meal or enjoying a movie night with loved ones. Celebrating your progress helps reinforce the positive habits you've developed and keeps you focused on the bigger picture.

Another key to staying motivated is to visualize your debt-free future. Take some time to imagine what your life will look like once you've successfully paid off your debts. Will you have more financial freedom to pursue your passions, travel, or invest in your future? Will you experience a sense of relief and pride in your accomplishment? Create a vivid mental picture of your debt-free life and use it as a source of inspiration when faced with challenges or temptations. You can even create a vision board or write down your goals and aspirations to serve as a tangible reminder of what you're working towards.

Accountability is another essential component of successful debt repayment. Surround yourself with supportive individuals who understand your goals and can offer encouragement and guidance when needed. Consider sharing your debt repayment journey with a trusted friend, family member, or partner who can help keep you accountable and celebrate your progress. You can also join online communities or support groups focused on debt repayment, where you can connect with others facing similar challenges, share tips and strategies, and find motivation in their success stories.

Tracking your progress is also crucial for maintaining accountability and motivation. Use budgeting tools, such as spreadsheets or mobile apps, to monitor your income, expenses, and debt payments. Regularly review your progress and adjust your budget as needed to ensure you're staying on track. Visual aids, such as debt repayment charts or graphs, can help you see the bigger picture and appreciate how far you've come, even when progress feels slow.

In addition to these strategies, it's essential to practice self-care and maintain a positive mindset throughout your debt repayment journey. Engage in activities that bring you joy and help you manage stress, such as exercise, meditation, or hobbies. Surround yourself with positive affirmations and reminders of your strength and resilience. Remember that setbacks and challenges are a normal part of the process, and don't let them derail your progress. Instead, use them as opportunities to learn, grow, and recommit to your goals.

Finally, don't be afraid to seek professional help if you need additional support or guidance. Financial coaches, counselors, or therapists can provide valuable insights, tools, and strategies to help you stay motivated, accountable, and on track. They can also help you address any underlying emotional or psychological barriers that may be hindering your progress.

By implementing these strategies and maintaining a focused, positive mindset, you can stay motivated and accountable throughout your debt repayment journey. Remember, becoming debt-free is a process that requires patience, perseverance, and self-compassion. Celebrate your victories, learn from your setbacks, and keep your eyes on the prize – a brighter, more secure financial future.

Summary: Taking Control of Your Debt and Building a Brighter Financial Future

Managing and paying off debt is a critical step in achieving financial freedom and security. By assessing your debt situation, creating a comprehensive repayment plan, and employing proven strategies like the debt snowball or debt avalanche methods, you can take control of your debt and make steady progress towards eliminating it.

Throughout this section, we've explored the importance of understanding your debt obligations, prioritizing your debts based on interest rates or balances, and creating a budget that allows you to allocate more money towards debt repayment. We've also discussed the options available when dealing with overwhelming debt, such as negotiating with creditors and seeking assistance from reputable debt relief programs or credit counseling agencies.

However, the journey to becoming debt-free is not just about the numbers and strategies; it's also about maintaining the right mindset and staying motivated. By setting clear goals, celebrating your progress, and surrounding yourself with a supportive network, you can stay accountable and committed to your debt repayment journey, even in the face of challenges and setbacks.

Remember, managing and paying off debt is a process that requires patience, discipline, and perseverance. It's not always easy, but the rewards of financial freedom and peace of mind are well worth the effort. By applying the knowledge and tools gained in this section, you can break free from the burden of debt and build a brighter, more secure financial future for yourself and your loved ones.

As you move forward on your debt repayment journey, keep in mind that you are not alone. Countless others have successfully navigated the path to debt freedom, and their stories can serve as a source of inspiration and motivation. Embrace the challenges, learn from your experiences, and never lose sight of your ultimate goal – a life unburdened by debt and filled with endless possibilities.

In the next section, we'll explore the unique considerations and strategies for managing student loan debt and navigating the mortgage process, as these types of debt often require special attention and planning. Armed with the foundation of knowledge and skills you've gained so far, you'll be well-prepared to tackle these specific debt challenges and continue your journey towards financial independence.

Section 5: Special Considerations for Student Loans and Mortgages

For many individuals, student loans and mortgages represent two of the most significant financial commitments they will make in their lifetime. These types of debt are unique in their nature and impact on personal finances, requiring careful consideration and strategic management. Whether you are a recent graduate grappling with the burden of student loan repayment or a prospective homeowner navigating the complex world of mortgage financing, understanding the intricacies of these financial obligations is crucial to your long-term financial well-being.

In this section, we will delve into the specific challenges and opportunities associated with student loans and mortgages. We will explore the various types of student loans available, including federal and private options, and discuss the key factors to consider when selecting a repayment plan that aligns with your financial goals and capabilities. Additionally, we will provide practical strategies for managing student loan debt effectively, such as consolidation, refinancing, and loan forgiveness programs.

Turning our attention to mortgages, we will guide you through the process of becoming a homeowner, from assessing your readiness and creditworthiness to understanding the different types of mortgage products and their associated costs. We will highlight the importance of shopping around for the best rates and terms, as well as the critical role of budgeting and financial planning in ensuring a successful homeownership experience.

By the end of this section, you will be equipped with the knowledge and tools necessary to make informed decisions about student loans and mortgages, empowering you to navigate these unique financial challenges with confidence and achieve your long-term financial aspirations.

Subsection 5.1: Understanding Student Loan Options and Repayment Plans

For many students, obtaining a college education would be impossible without the assistance of student loans. However, navigating the various types of student loans and repayment options can be overwhelming, especially for those who are new to the world of financial aid. Understanding the differences between loan types and the repayment plans available is crucial for making informed decisions that will impact your financial future.

When it comes to student loans, there are two main categories: federal loans and private loans. Federal student loans are funded by the government and typically offer more favorable terms and repayment options compared to private loans. These loans include Direct Subsidized

Loans, Direct Unsubsidized Loans, Direct PLUS Loans, and Direct Consolidation Loans. Each type of federal loan has its own eligibility requirements, interest rates, and borrowing limits.

On the other hand, private student loans are offered by banks, credit unions, and other financial institutions. These loans often have higher interest rates and less flexible repayment terms compared to federal loans. However, they can be a useful option for students who have exhausted their federal loan options and still need additional funding to cover educational expenses.

Once you have obtained student loans, it's essential to understand the various repayment plans available. For federal loans, there are several repayment options designed to fit different financial situations and goals. The Standard Repayment Plan is the default option, which involves fixed monthly payments over a 10-year period. However, if you need more flexibility, you may consider other plans such as the Graduated Repayment Plan, which starts with lower payments that increase over time, or the Extended Repayment Plan, which allows you to extend your repayment term up to 25 years.

Additionally, there are income-driven repayment plans for federal loans, such as Income-Based Repayment (IBR), Pay As You Earn (PAYE), Revised Pay As You Earn (REPAYE), and Income-Contingent Repayment (ICR). These plans calculate your monthly payments based on your income and family size, which can be particularly helpful if you are facing financial hardship or have a low income compared to your debt load.

It's important to note that while income-driven repayment plans can provide relief in the short term, they may result in paying more interest over the life of the loan. Furthermore, these plans may have tax implications for any forgiven loan balances at the end of the repayment term.

When choosing a repayment plan, consider factors such as your current financial situation, long-term career goals, and the total cost of the loan over time. Don't hesitate to reach out to your loan servicer or a financial advisor for guidance in selecting the best repayment option for your unique circumstances.

By understanding the different types of student loans and repayment plans available, you can make informed decisions that will help you manage your debt effectively and work towards a stable financial future.

Subsection 5.2: Strategies for Managing and Paying Off Student Loans

Managing and paying off student loan debt can be a daunting task, especially when you're just starting your career and facing other financial obligations. However, with the right strategies and a proactive approach, you can effectively manage your student loans and work towards becoming debt-free.

One of the first steps in managing your student loans is to create a budget that accounts for your loan payments alongside your other expenses. By having a clear picture of your income and expenditures, you can ensure that you're allocating enough money each month to cover your student loan payments while still meeting your other financial needs.

If you're struggling to make your monthly payments, consider exploring income-driven repayment plans for your federal loans. These plans, such as IBR, PAYE, REPAYE, and ICR, can adjust your monthly payments based on your income and family size, making them more manageable. Keep in mind, however, that these plans may extend your repayment term and result in paying more interest over time.

Another strategy for managing student loan debt is to prioritize paying off high-interest loans first. If you have multiple loans with varying interest rates, focus on allocating extra funds towards the loans with the highest rates while still making the minimum payments on your other loans. This approach, known as the debt avalanche method, can help you save on interest and pay off your loans more quickly.

If you have federal loans, you may also be eligible for loan forgiveness programs based on your career or employer. For example, the Public Service Loan Forgiveness (PSLF) program offers loan forgiveness after 120 qualifying payments for individuals working full-time in government organizations or non-profit organizations. Other loan forgiveness programs exist for teachers, nurses, and other specific professions.

Consolidation and refinancing are two other options to consider when managing student loan debt. Consolidation allows you to combine multiple federal loans into a single loan with a fixed interest rate, which can simplify your repayment process. Refinancing, on the other hand, involves taking out a new loan with a private lender to pay off your existing loans, potentially securing a lower interest rate or more favorable repayment terms. However, keep in mind that refinancing federal loans with a private lender means losing access to federal loan benefits, such as income-driven repayment plans and loan forgiveness programs.

In addition to these strategies, there are several practical steps you can take to accelerate your student loan repayment:

1. Make biweekly payments instead of monthly payments, which can result in an extra payment each year and help you pay off your loans faster.
2. Apply any windfalls, such as tax refunds, bonuses, or gifts, directly to your student loan principal to reduce the overall interest you'll pay.
3. Consider taking on a side hustle or freelance work to generate extra income that you can put towards your student loans.
4. Cut back on discretionary expenses and redirect that money towards your loan payments.
5. Communicate with your loan servicer if you're facing financial hardship or have questions about your repayment options.

Remember, paying off student loan debt is a marathon, not a sprint. By staying organized, proactive, and committed to your repayment plan, you can successfully manage your student loans and work towards a debt-free future. Don't hesitate to seek guidance from financial professionals or student loan counselors if you need additional support or advice along the way.

Subsection 5.3: Navigating the Mortgage Process and Homeownership

For many individuals, purchasing a home is one of the most significant financial decisions they will make in their lifetime. A crucial aspect of this process is obtaining a mortgage, which is a loan specifically designed to help finance the purchase of a property. Navigating the mortgage process and understanding the responsibilities of homeownership are essential steps in achieving the dream of owning a home.

Before embarking on the mortgage process, it's important to assess your readiness for homeownership. This involves evaluating your financial stability, including your income, savings, and credit score. A solid credit history and a stable income are key factors that lenders consider when determining your eligibility for a mortgage and the terms they will offer you.

Once you have determined that you are ready to pursue homeownership, the next step is to research and compare different mortgage options. There are several types of mortgages available, each with its own characteristics and benefits. Some common mortgage types include fixed-rate mortgages, where the interest rate remains constant throughout the loan term, and adjustable-rate mortgages (ARMs), where the interest rate can fluctuate based on market conditions. Other options, such as government-backed loans like FHA or VA loans, may offer more flexible qualification requirements or lower down payment options.

When comparing mortgage options, it's crucial to consider factors beyond just the interest rate. Pay attention to the loan term, which is the length of time you have to repay the mortgage, as well as any associated fees, such as origination fees or closing costs. These elements can significantly impact the overall cost of your mortgage and your monthly payments.

Before applying for a mortgage, it's advisable to obtain a pre-approval from a lender. A pre-approval involves providing the lender with your financial information, such as income, assets, and credit score, to determine how much they are willing to lend you. This step can help you establish a realistic budget for your home purchase and demonstrate to sellers that you are a serious and qualified buyer.

Once you have found a property that meets your needs and budget, you can proceed with the mortgage application process. This typically involves submitting a formal application, along with supporting documentation such as proof of income, employment history, and assets. The lender will then conduct a thorough review of your application and credit history to make a final decision on your loan approval and terms.

If your mortgage application is approved, the next step is to prepare for closing. This is the final stage of the mortgage process, where you sign the loan documents and officially become a homeowner. Before closing, review all the paperwork carefully and ask questions about anything you don't understand. You will also need to provide proof of homeowner's insurance and pay any required closing costs or down payment funds.

As a new homeowner, it's essential to understand the ongoing responsibilities that come with owning a property. This includes making timely mortgage payments, paying property taxes and insurance, and budgeting for home maintenance and repairs. Developing a financial plan that accounts for these expenses can help ensure a successful and sustainable homeownership experience.

In addition to the financial aspects, homeownership also involves taking care of your property and being a responsible member of your community. This may include tasks such as maintaining your home's exterior, participating in neighborhood events, and being mindful of local ordinances and regulations.

Navigating the mortgage process and becoming a homeowner can be complex and overwhelming at times, but with proper preparation, research, and guidance, it can also be a rewarding and fulfilling experience. Don't hesitate to seek advice from professionals, such as real estate agents, mortgage brokers, or financial advisors, who can provide valuable insights and support throughout the process.

By understanding the key considerations and steps involved in obtaining a mortgage and embracing the responsibilities of homeownership, you can make informed decisions and achieve the long-term benefits of owning your own home.

Summary: Navigating the Path to Financial Freedom through Student Loans and Mortgages

Student loans and mortgages are two significant financial commitments that can greatly impact an individual's long-term financial well-being. By understanding the intricacies of these obligations and developing effective strategies to manage them, you can take control of your financial future and work towards achieving your goals.

Throughout this section, we have explored the various types of student loans and repayment options available, empowering you to make informed decisions that align with your unique circumstances. We have also delved into the practical strategies for managing and paying off student loan debt, such as creating a budget, exploring income-driven repayment plans, and considering loan forgiveness programs.

Furthermore, we have navigated the complex world of mortgage financing, guiding you through the process of becoming a homeowner. From assessing your readiness and creditworthiness to understanding the different types of mortgage products and their associated costs, you now have the knowledge and tools necessary to make informed decisions about homeownership.

As you embark on your journey to financial freedom, remember that managing student loans and mortgages is not a one-size-fits-all approach. It requires careful consideration, proactive planning, and a commitment to your long-term financial goals. By staying informed, seeking guidance when needed, and remaining dedicated to your repayment plan, you can successfully navigate these unique financial challenges and build a solid foundation for your future.

The path to financial freedom is not always easy, but with the right mindset, strategies, and support, you have the power to overcome obstacles and achieve your dreams. Embrace the lessons learned in this section and apply them to your own life, knowing that every step you take towards managing your student loans and mortgages is a step closer to securing a brighter financial future.

Section 6: Rebuilding and Maintaining Good Credit

Imagine you've hit a rough patch in your financial journey, and your credit has taken a hit. Maybe you've missed a few payments, or perhaps you've had to deal with a significant setback like a job loss or a medical emergency. Whatever the reason, your credit score has dropped, and you're worried about how it will impact your future financial opportunities. The good news is that rebuilding your credit and maintaining a strong credit profile is possible, and this section will show you how.

Rebuilding your credit after a setback can feel like an uphill battle, but with the right strategies and a consistent approach, you can get back on track. It's important to remember that your credit score is not a permanent mark against you, but rather a snapshot of your current financial situation. By taking proactive steps to address any negative items on your credit report and establishing positive credit habits, you can gradually improve your credit score over time.

But rebuilding your credit is only half the battle. Once you've worked hard to improve your credit score, you'll want to maintain that progress and avoid falling back into old habits that could jeopardize your financial future. This section will provide you with practical tips and strategies for maintaining a strong credit profile, even in the face of life's unexpected challenges.

Whether you're just starting to rebuild your credit or you're looking to maintain the progress you've already made, the information in this section will be invaluable. We'll cover everything from addressing negative items on your credit report to establishing positive credit habits that will serve you well for years to come. By the end of this section, you'll have the knowledge and tools you need to take control of your credit and build a strong foundation for your financial future.

Subsection 6.1: Recovering from Credit Setbacks and Negative Events

Life is full of unexpected twists and turns, and sometimes these events can have a negative impact on your credit. Whether it's a job loss, a medical emergency, or a period of overspending, financial setbacks can leave you feeling overwhelmed and unsure of how to recover. However, it's important to remember that credit setbacks are not permanent, and with the right strategies and mindset, you can rebuild your credit and get back on track.

The first step in recovering from credit setbacks is to assess the damage. This means obtaining a copy of your credit report from each of the three major credit bureaus (Equifax, Experian, and TransUnion) and reviewing it carefully for errors or negative items. If you find any inaccuracies, dispute them with the credit bureau and the creditor immediately. This can help to remove any negative items that are not truly reflective of your credit history.

Next, create a plan to address any outstanding debts or delinquent accounts. This may involve reaching out to creditors to negotiate payment plans or settlements, consolidating debts through a personal loan or balance transfer credit card, or seeking the assistance of a credit counseling agency. The key is to take action and start making progress, even if it's small at first.

As you work to pay down your debts and bring your accounts current, it's also important to start building positive credit history. This can be done by opening a secured credit card or becoming an authorized user on someone else's credit card account. These options allow you to demonstrate responsible credit use and start establishing a track record of on-time payments, which can help to improve your credit score over time.

Another important aspect of recovering from credit setbacks is to address the underlying issues that led to the financial difficulties in the first place. This may involve creating a budget to better manage your expenses, seeking additional sources of income, or addressing any underlying medical or personal issues that may have contributed to the setback. By taking a holistic approach and addressing both the symptoms and the root causes of your credit issues, you can set yourself up for long-term success.

Throughout the credit recovery process, it's important to stay focused on your goals and maintain a positive attitude. Rebuilding credit takes time and effort, but with persistence and dedication, it is possible to overcome even the most significant setbacks. Celebrate your progress along the way, and don't be afraid to seek support from friends, family, or professionals if needed.

In conclusion, recovering from credit setbacks and negative events is a challenging but achievable goal. By assessing the damage, creating a plan to address outstanding debts, building positive credit history, and addressing underlying issues, you can take control of your financial future and emerge stronger and more resilient than ever before.

Subsection 6.2: Best Practices for Maintaining Good Credit

Congratulations on taking the steps to rebuild your credit! Your hard work and dedication have paid off, and you're now on the path to a healthier financial future. However, the journey doesn't end here. Maintaining good credit requires ongoing effort and commitment, but the rewards are well worth it.

One of the most important things you can do to maintain good credit is to consistently make on-time payments for all of your bills and debts. Late payments can quickly undo the progress you've made and negatively impact your credit score. Set up automatic payments or reminders to ensure that you never miss a due date.

Another key factor in maintaining good credit is keeping your credit utilization low. This means avoiding maxing out your credit cards or using a large portion of your available credit. Aim to keep your credit utilization below 30%, and ideally even lower. If you do need to make a large purchase, consider spreading it out over several months or using a personal loan instead of relying solely on credit cards.

Regularly monitoring your credit reports is also essential for maintaining good credit. By keeping a close eye on your credit reports, you can quickly identify any errors or fraudulent activity and take action to address them. You're entitled to one free credit report from each of the three major credit bureaus annually, so take advantage of this opportunity to stay informed about your credit health.

When it comes to applying for new credit, it's important to be strategic and selective. Applying for too many credit accounts in a short period can raise red flags for lenders and potentially lower your credit score. Only apply for credit when necessary, and shop around to find the best terms and rates.

In addition to these best practices, there are several habits you can adopt to support your ongoing credit health. For example, consider setting up emergency savings to avoid relying on credit in case of unexpected expenses. Regularly review your budget and spending habits to ensure that you're living within your means and not accumulating unnecessary debt.

If you do find yourself facing financial challenges or struggling to make payments, don't hesitate to reach out for help. Many creditors offer hardship programs or are willing to work with you to find a solution. Seeking the guidance of a credit counselor or financial advisor can also provide valuable support and resources.

Remember, maintaining good credit is a lifelong journey, but the benefits are numerous. From qualifying for better interest rates and loan terms to having a stronger financial foundation for your future goals, the efforts you put in now will pay dividends for years to come. By staying committed to these best practices and making informed financial decisions, you can enjoy the peace of mind and opportunities that come with a healthy credit profile.

Subsection 6.3: The Long-Term Benefits of Good Credit

Achieving and maintaining a strong credit history is not just about short-term gains; it's a long-term investment in your financial future. The benefits of good credit extend far beyond the immediate advantages of qualifying for better loan terms or lower interest rates. In fact, the positive impact of a healthy credit profile can be felt for years, even decades, to come.

One of the most significant long-term benefits of good credit is the potential for significant savings over the course of your lifetime. When you have a strong credit score, you're more likely to qualify for the most competitive interest rates on mortgages, car loans, and other forms of credit. Even a small difference in interest rates can translate to thousands of dollars saved over the life of a loan. For example, consider two individuals who take out a 30-year mortgage for $200,000. The person with excellent credit may qualify for a 3.5% interest rate, while the person with average credit may only qualify for a 4.5% rate. Over the course of the loan, the person with excellent credit would save over $40,000 in interest payments compared to the person with average credit. These savings can be redirected towards other financial goals, such as saving for retirement or investing in education.

In addition to the financial savings, good credit can also open up a world of opportunities that may otherwise be unavailable. Many employers now consider credit history as part of their background check process, particularly for positions that involve handling money or sensitive information. A strong credit profile can demonstrate responsibility, trustworthiness, and financial stability, making you a more attractive candidate for employment. Similarly, landlords often review credit reports when evaluating potential tenants, and a solid credit history can improve your chances of securing your desired rental property.

Good credit can also provide a safety net during times of financial uncertainty or emergency. If you face an unexpected job loss, medical emergency, or other financial setback, having a strong credit profile can make it easier to access credit or loans to bridge the gap until you regain financial stability. This can be particularly important if you don't have a substantial emergency fund or savings to fall back on.

Furthermore, maintaining good credit can contribute to a greater sense of financial empowerment and peace of mind. When you have a strong credit history, you have more control over your financial destiny. You're not beholden to high-interest lenders or predatory financial products, and you have the freedom to make choices that align with your long-term financial goals. This sense of empowerment can reduce financial stress and anxiety, allowing you to focus on building a fulfilling life.

It's important to note that the benefits of good credit are not just limited to your individual financial well-being; they can also have a positive impact on your family and loved ones. By modeling responsible credit behavior and maintaining a strong credit profile, you set a positive example for your children and future generations. You also create a more stable financial foundation for your family, which can provide greater security and opportunities for growth.

In conclusion, the long-term benefits of good credit are vast and far-reaching. From significant financial savings to expanded opportunities and greater peace of mind, a strong credit history is a valuable asset that can serve you well throughout your life. By prioritizing credit health and making informed financial decisions, you invest in a brighter, more secure financial future for yourself and your loved ones. The efforts you put in today to build and maintain good credit will pay dividends for years to come, providing a solid foundation for your financial success and well-being.

Summary: Empowering Your Financial Future through Responsible Credit Management

Rebuilding and maintaining good credit is a journey that requires dedication, patience, and a proactive approach. By understanding the strategies and best practices outlined in this section, you are now equipped with the knowledge and tools needed to take control of your credit health and pave the way for a brighter financial future.

Remember, whether you are recovering from credit setbacks or working to maintain a strong credit profile, the key is to stay committed to responsible credit management. Consistently making on-time payments, keeping credit utilization low, monitoring your credit reports regularly, and being strategic about new credit applications are all essential habits that will support your ongoing credit success.

As you embrace these practices and make informed financial decisions, you will begin to experience the numerous long-term benefits that come with a healthy credit profile. From significant savings on interest rates to expanded opportunities in employment and housing, the positive impact of good credit can be felt in nearly every aspect of your life.

Moreover, by prioritizing credit health, you are not only investing in your own financial well-being but also setting a powerful example for your loved ones. Your commitment to responsible credit management can inspire and empower future generations to take control of their own financial destinies.

As you continue on your credit journey, remember that setbacks and challenges are a normal part of the process. What matters most is how you respond to these obstacles and use them as opportunities for growth and learning. With the right mindset and the strategies you have learned, you have the power to overcome any credit hurdles and emerge stronger and more financially resilient.

So, embrace your role as the architect of your financial future, and let your credit health be a testament to your dedication, discipline, and vision. By rebuilding and maintaining good credit, you are opening the door to a world of possibilities and creating a solid foundation for long-term financial success. Stay the course, celebrate your progress, and look forward to a future filled with financial empowerment and prosperity.

Chapter Summary: Mastering Credit and Debt for Financial Freedom

Throughout this chapter, we've explored the crucial role that credit plays in your financial life and the importance of managing debt effectively. By understanding the fundamentals of credit, credit scores, and credit reports, you can make informed decisions and build a strong financial foundation.

We've discussed the different types of credit, the factors that influence your credit score, and strategies for monitoring and improving your credit profile. By using credit responsibly, establishing a positive payment history, and keeping your credit utilization low, you can demonstrate your creditworthiness and open up valuable financial opportunities.

However, we've also addressed the challenges of managing debt and the potential pitfalls to avoid. Whether you're dealing with credit card balances, student loans, or a mortgage, it's essential to have a clear plan for repaying your obligations and staying on top of your payments. By implementing proven debt repayment strategies, such as the debt snowball or debt avalanche methods, and seeking assistance when needed, you can take control of your debt and work towards financial freedom.

Remember, your credit and debt management practices have long-lasting effects on your financial well-being. By consistently making smart choices, staying disciplined, and seeking education and support, you can overcome financial challenges and achieve your goals. Whether you're rebuilding your credit after setbacks or striving to maintain a strong credit profile, the knowledge and strategies you've gained in this chapter will serve as valuable tools on your journey to financial success.

As you move forward, keep these lessons in mind and continue to prioritize responsible credit usage and proactive debt management. With dedication and perseverance, you can master your credit and debt, unlocking a world of financial possibilities and securing a brighter financial future.

Chapter 7: Investing for the Future: Stocks, Bonds, and Beyond

Investing is a crucial aspect of building long-term wealth and securing your financial future. Whether you're just starting your investment journey or looking to expand your portfolio, understanding the various investment options available is essential. In this chapter, we'll explore the world of investing, focusing on stocks, bonds, and other investment vehicles that can help you grow your money over time.

Investing can seem intimidating at first, with countless options and strategies to consider. However, by gaining a solid understanding of the fundamentals and developing a well-thought-out plan, you can navigate the investment landscape with confidence. We'll demystify the concepts of risk and return, highlighting how different investments offer varying levels of potential growth and stability.

Throughout this chapter, we'll dive into the characteristics and benefits of stocks, which represent ownership in companies, and bonds, which involve lending money to governments or corporations. You'll learn how to evaluate and select individual stocks and bonds, as well as how to diversify your portfolio to manage risk effectively.

But investing goes beyond just stocks and bonds. We'll also introduce you to mutual funds and exchange-traded funds (ETFs), which pool money from multiple investors to purchase a diverse range of assets. These investment vehicles can provide easy access to a well-diversified portfolio, even with a relatively small amount of capital.

Real estate is another important asset class to consider, and we'll explore the opportunities available through direct property ownership and real estate investment trusts (REITs). Additionally, we'll touch on alternative investments such as commodities, currencies, and cryptocurrencies, discussing their unique characteristics and the roles they can play in a comprehensive investment strategy.

Creating a diversified investment portfolio is a key aspect of successful investing. We'll guide you through the process of determining your investment goals, assessing your risk tolerance, and allocating your assets accordingly. You'll learn how to construct a portfolio that aligns with your financial objectives and how to rebalance it periodically to maintain the desired level of risk and return.

By the end of this chapter, you'll have a solid foundation in the world of investing and the tools to start building a portfolio that can help you achieve your long-term financial goals. Whether you're saving for retirement, a child's education, or other major milestones, investing wisely can make a significant difference in your ability to reach those targets. So, let's dive in and explore the exciting opportunities that await you in the realm of stocks, bonds, and beyond.

Section 1: Introduction to Investing

Imagine a world where your money works for you, growing and multiplying while you sleep. A world where you're not just earning a paycheck, but building a foundation for a financially secure future. Welcome to the world of investing.

For many people, the concept of investing can seem daunting, filled with complex jargon and intimidating numbers. But at its core, investing is simply a way to put your money to work, allowing it to grow over time and potentially provide you with greater financial freedom.

In this section, we'll demystify the basics of investing and explore how it can play a crucial role in building your wealth. We'll dive into the fundamental concepts that every investor should understand, such as the relationship between risk and return, the power of compounding, and the importance of starting early.

Whether you're a complete novice or have some experience with investing, this section will provide you with a solid foundation to build upon. We'll explore the various investment vehicles available, from stocks and bonds to mutual funds and real estate, and help you understand how they work together to create a diversified portfolio.

But investing isn't just about numbers and charts. It's about creating a better future for yourself and your loved ones. It's about turning your dreams into reality, whether that means retiring comfortably, sending your children to college, or leaving a lasting legacy.

So, let's embark on this journey together. In the following pages, we'll arm you with the knowledge and tools you need to become a confident, successful investor. We'll show you how to navigate the ups and downs of the market, make informed decisions, and stay focused on your long-term goals.

By the end of this section, you'll see investing in a whole new light. You'll understand that it's not just for the wealthy or the Wall Street elite, but for anyone who wants to take control of their financial destiny. Are you ready to unlock the power of investing? Let's get started.

Subsection 1.1: What is Investing and Why It Matters

Investing, at its core, is the act of allocating resources, usually money, with the expectation of generating an income or profit. It is the process of putting your money to work for you, with the goal of growing your wealth over time. When you invest, you are essentially purchasing assets that you believe will increase in value, provide income, or both.

The concept of investing is often associated with the stock market, where individuals buy shares of companies with the hope that the value of those shares will appreciate. However, investing encompasses a much broader range of assets, including bonds, real estate, commodities, and even your own education or business.

So, why does investing matter? The answer lies in the power of compound returns. When you invest your money, you have the potential to earn returns on your initial investment, which can then be reinvested to generate even more returns. Over time, this compounding effect can lead to significant growth in your wealth.

Consider this simple example: if you invest $1,000 and earn a 7% annual return, after 10 years, your investment would grow to $1,967. After 20 years, it would grow to $3,870. And after 30 years, it would be worth $7,612. Now, imagine if you invested $1,000 every year for those 30 years. Your total investment would be $30,000, but thanks to the power of compounding, your portfolio would be worth $94,460.

Investing is also crucial for outpacing inflation. Inflation is the rate at which the general level of prices for goods and services is rising, and subsequently, purchasing power is falling. If your money is sitting in a savings account earning minimal interest, its value is actually decreasing over time due to inflation. By investing in assets that have the potential to generate higher returns, you can help protect your purchasing power and grow your wealth in real terms.

Moreover, investing is a key component of achieving your financial goals, whether that's buying a house, funding your children's education, or securing a comfortable retirement. By starting to invest early and consistently, you give your money more time to grow and compound, increasing your chances of reaching those goals.

In summary, investing is the process of putting your money to work to earn more money. It matters because it enables you to grow your wealth, outpace inflation, and achieve your financial objectives. Understanding and embracing investing is a crucial step in taking control of your financial future and building long-term prosperity.

Subsection 1.2: The Relationship Between Risk and Return

In the world of investing, the relationship between risk and return is a fundamental concept that every investor must understand. At its core, this principle suggests that the potential return on an investment is directly proportional to the level of risk involved. In other words, the higher the risk, the higher the potential return, and conversely, the lower the risk, the lower the potential return.

To illustrate this concept, let's consider two investment options: a government bond and a stock in a new technology company. The government bond is generally considered a low-risk investment because the likelihood of the government defaulting on its debt is relatively low. As a result, the potential return on a government bond is typically modest. On the other hand, the stock in the new technology company is considered a higher-risk investment because the company's future success is uncertain. However, if the company does succeed, the potential return on the stock could be substantial.

The relationship between risk and return is rooted in the idea that investors must be compensated for taking on additional risk. If all investments offered the same return regardless of risk, there would be no incentive for investors to take on higher-risk investments. The risk-return trade-off is a balancing act that investors must navigate, deciding how much risk they are willing to accept in pursuit of potentially higher returns.

One way to quantify risk is through the concept of volatility, which measures how much an investment's price fluctuates over time. Investments with higher volatility, such as stocks, are generally considered riskier because their prices can change dramatically in a short period. On the other hand, investments with lower volatility, such as bonds, are generally considered less risky because their prices tend to be more stable.

It's important to note that the relationship between risk and return is not always linear. In some cases, an investment may offer a high potential return without a correspondingly high level of risk. These situations are often referred to as "mispriced opportunities" and can be difficult to identify. Additionally, the perception of risk can vary from investor to investor, depending on factors such as individual risk tolerance, investment goals, and time horizon.

Understanding the relationship between risk and return is crucial for developing a well-rounded investment strategy. By carefully considering the risk-return trade-off, investors can construct portfolios that align with their individual goals and risk tolerance. This may involve creating a diversified portfolio that includes a mix of low-risk and high-risk investments, or focusing on specific asset classes that offer the desired balance of risk and return.

Ultimately, the key to navigating the risk-return relationship is to make informed decisions based on a thorough understanding of the underlying investments and one's own financial situation. By doing so, investors can work towards achieving their financial goals while managing the inherent risks involved in investing.

Subsection 1.3: The Power of Compounding and Time in the Market

Imagine you have a choice between receiving a million dollars today or a single penny that doubles in value every day for 30 days. Which would you choose? While the million dollars might seem like the obvious choice, the power of compounding would actually make the penny the far more lucrative option. By the end of the 30 days, that penny would have grown to over $5 million.

This simple example illustrates the incredible potential of compounding, a concept that lies at the heart of successful investing. Compounding occurs when the returns earned on an investment are reinvested, generating additional returns on those returns. Over time, this process can lead to exponential growth, turning even small initial investments into substantial sums.

The magic of compounding lies in its ability to harness the power of time. The longer your money is invested, the more time it has to grow and compound upon itself. This is why starting to invest early, even with small amounts, can make a significant difference in the long run.

Consider two investors, Alice and Bob, both aged 25. Alice begins investing $200 per month and continues doing so until she retires at age 65. Bob, on the other hand, waits until he's 35 to start investing, but contributes $400 per month to catch up. Assuming an annual return of 7%, Alice will have accumulated over $524,000 by retirement, while Bob will have only around $490,000, despite contributing more each month. The extra ten years Alice had in the market allowed her money to compound for a longer period, resulting in a significantly larger nest egg.

The power of compounding is further amplified by the frequency of compounding. The more often returns are compounded, the faster the growth. This is why investments that compound daily, such as many savings accounts, tend to grow faster than those that compound annually, all other factors being equal.

It's important to note that compounding is not just limited to traditional investments like stocks and bonds. It can be applied to any area of your financial life where you can earn a return on your money, such as high-yield savings accounts, real estate investments, or even your own business ventures.

However, to truly harness the power of compounding, it's crucial to remain invested for the long term. Time in the market, rather than timing the market, is what allows compounding to work its magic. Attempting to buy and sell investments based on short-term market fluctuations can be a risky strategy that undermines the benefits of compounding.

Moreover, the power of compounding extends beyond just financial returns. It can also be applied to knowledge, skills, and habits. By consistently investing time and effort into learning and self-improvement, you can compound your personal and professional growth, leading to greater success and fulfillment over time.

In conclusion, understanding and leveraging the power of compounding is a fundamental aspect of successful investing and financial planning. By starting early, investing consistently, and allowing time to work in your favor, you can harness the incredible potential of compounding to grow your wealth and achieve your long-term financial goals. As the famous quote by Albert Einstein goes, "Compound interest is the eighth wonder of the world. He who understands it, earns it; he who doesn't, pays it."

Summary: Unlocking the Power of Investing for Your Financial Future

In this introductory section, we've explored the fundamental concepts of investing and how it can play a crucial role in building your wealth over time. We've seen that investing is not just about numbers and charts, but about creating a better future for yourself and your loved ones.

By understanding the relationship between risk and return, you can make informed decisions about how to allocate your resources and construct a diversified portfolio that aligns with your goals and risk tolerance. And by harnessing the power of compounding and time in the market, you can watch your investments grow exponentially, turning even small initial amounts into significant sums.

But investing is not a one-time event; it's a lifelong journey. As you continue through this book, you'll gain the knowledge and tools you need to navigate the ups and downs of the market, make sound investment choices, and stay focused on your long-term objectives. Whether you're saving for retirement, funding your children's education, or pursuing other financial goals, investing can help you get there.

So, as we move forward, remember that investing is not just for the wealthy or the Wall Street elite. It's for anyone who wants to take control of their financial destiny and build a brighter tomorrow. With the right mindset, strategies, and discipline, you too can unlock the incredible potential of investing and chart a course towards financial freedom.

As the legendary investor Warren Buffett once said, "Someone's sitting in the shade today because someone planted a tree a long time ago." By embracing the power of investing and taking action today, you can plant the seeds of your own financial success and enjoy the fruits of your labor for years to come. So, let's continue this journey together and discover how you can make investing work for you.

Section 2: Types of Investment Vehicles

Picture this: you're standing at the entrance of a vast, bustling marketplace, filled with a dizzying array of stalls and vendors, each offering a unique product or service. This is the world of investment vehicles, where countless opportunities await, ready to help you grow your wealth and secure your financial future. But with so many options to choose from, it's easy to feel overwhelmed and unsure of where to begin.

Fear not, intrepid investor, for in this section, we'll take you on a guided tour of the most common types of investment vehicles available to individual investors like yourself. From the tried-and-true classics like stocks and bonds to the more exotic offerings like real estate investment trusts and cryptocurrencies, we'll explore the ins and outs of each option, giving you the knowledge and confidence to make informed decisions about where to put your hard-earned money.

As we embark on this journey, remember that no single investment vehicle is inherently better than another. Each comes with its own set of risks and rewards, and the key to successful investing lies in understanding how these pieces fit together to create a diversified portfolio tailored to your unique goals and circumstances. So, whether you're a seasoned investor looking to expand your horizons or a newcomer to the world of finance, this section will provide you with the tools and insights you need to navigate the marketplace with ease and build a solid foundation for your financial future.

Subsection 2.1: Stocks: Equity Ownership in Companies

Picture yourself as a budding entrepreneur, eager to start your own business. You have a brilliant idea, a solid business plan, and the drive to make it happen. But there's one thing missing: the capital to turn your vision into reality. That's where stocks come in.

When a company decides to go public, it offers shares of ownership in the form of stocks to investors. By purchasing these stocks, you become a part-owner of the company, entitled to a portion of its profits and growth. It's like becoming a silent partner in the business, without the day-to-day responsibilities of running it.

But how do stocks function as an investment? Let's say you buy 100 shares of a company's stock at $10 per share, for a total investment of $1,000. If the company performs well and its stock price rises to $15 per share, your investment is now worth $1,500. You've just earned a 50% return on your investment, simply by holding onto those shares.

Of course, the stock market is not without its risks. Just as a company's success can lead to a rise in its stock price, poor performance or external factors can cause the price to drop. If that same company's stock falls to $5 per share, your investment would be worth only $500, resulting in a 50% loss.

Despite the risks, stocks remain one of the most popular investment vehicles, and for a good reason. Over the long term, stocks have historically outperformed other investments, such as bonds and savings accounts. By investing in a diverse portfolio of stocks across various sectors and industries, you can potentially maximize your returns while minimizing your risk.

But how do you choose which stocks to invest in? This is where research and due diligence come into play. By analyzing a company's financial health, growth potential, and competitive landscape, you can make informed decisions about whether its stock is a good fit for your investment strategy.

In the following subsections, we'll explore other types of investment vehicles, each with its own unique characteristics and potential for growth. But for now, remember this: when you invest in stocks, you're not just buying a piece of paper; you're becoming a part of a company's story and its potential for success.

Subsection 2.2: Bonds: Lending Money to Governments and Corporations

Imagine you have a friend who comes to you with a proposition. They're starting a business and need some money to get it off the ground. They promise to pay you back in full, with interest, over a set period of time. In essence, you'd be lending them money and earning a return on your investment. This is the basic concept behind bonds.

Bonds are a type of investment vehicle that allows governments and corporations to borrow money from investors. When you purchase a bond, you're essentially lending money to the issuer, who promises to pay you back the face value of the bond, along with regular interest payments, over a specified term.

One of the key characteristics of bonds is their predictability. Unlike stocks, which can be volatile and subject to market fluctuations, bonds offer a fixed rate of return. This makes them an attractive option for investors who prefer a more stable and reliable income stream.

Bonds come in various types, each with its own unique features and risk profile. Government bonds, for example, are issued by national governments and are generally considered one of the safest investments, as they're backed by the full faith and credit of the issuing country. In the United States, these include Treasury bonds, notes, and bills.

Corporate bonds, on the other hand, are issued by companies looking to raise capital for various purposes, such as expansion, research and development, or debt refinancing. These bonds typically offer higher interest rates than government bonds, as they carry more risk. The creditworthiness of the issuing company plays a significant role in determining the interest rate and the overall risk of the bond.

Another important factor to consider when investing in bonds is the bond's maturity date. This is the date on which the issuer must repay the face value of the bond to the investor. Bonds with longer maturities generally offer higher interest rates, as investors are compensated for tying up their money for a more extended period.

It's also worth noting that bonds can be bought and sold on the secondary market, just like stocks. This means that bond prices can fluctuate based on various factors, such as changes in interest rates, the issuer's creditworthiness, and overall market conditions. When interest rates rise, bond prices typically fall, and vice versa.

In summary, bonds are a vital component of a well-diversified investment portfolio, offering a predictable income stream and potentially lower risk compared to stocks. By understanding the characteristics and types of bonds available, you can make informed decisions about whether and how to incorporate them into your investment strategy.

Subsection 2.3: Mutual Funds and Exchange-Traded Funds (ETFs)

Picture yourself at a grand buffet, filled with a vast array of delectable dishes from around the world. Each dish represents a unique investment opportunity, with its own distinct flavors and characteristics. While you might be tempted to sample every offering, you quickly realize that filling your plate with a little bit of everything is the best way to ensure a satisfying and well-rounded meal. This, in essence, is the philosophy behind mutual funds and exchange-traded funds (ETFs).

Mutual funds and ETFs are investment vehicles that pool money from many investors to purchase a diverse collection of stocks, bonds, or other securities. By buying shares in these funds, you effectively gain exposure to a wide range of investments without having to purchase each one individually. This diversification helps to spread risk and potentially smooth out the ups and downs of the market.

Mutual funds are professionally managed by fund managers who actively make decisions about which securities to buy and sell within the fund's portfolio. Investors purchase shares directly from the fund company, and the price of each share, known as the net asset value (NAV), is calculated at the end of each trading day based on the value of the fund's underlying assets.

ETFs, on the other hand, are traded on stock exchanges, just like individual stocks. This means that investors can buy and sell shares of an ETF throughout the trading day at prices that fluctuate based on market demand. Many ETFs are designed to track the performance of a specific index, such as the S&P 500, by holding a basket of securities that mirrors the composition of the index.

One of the primary advantages of mutual funds and ETFs is their accessibility to individual investors. With relatively low minimum investment requirements and the ability to purchase fractional shares, these investment vehicles make it easy for anyone to start building a diversified portfolio. Additionally, the professional management and broad diversification offered by these funds can be particularly appealing to those who lack the time, expertise, or inclination to actively manage their own investments.

However, it's essential to understand that not all mutual funds and ETFs are created equal. Factors such as the fund's investment strategy, management team, and expense ratio can significantly impact its performance and overall returns. Expense ratios, in particular, represent the annual fees charged by the fund to cover operating costs and can eat into your investment returns over time.

When selecting mutual funds or ETFs for your portfolio, it's crucial to conduct thorough research and due diligence. Consider factors such as the fund's historical performance, investment philosophy, and risk profile, and ensure that they align with your own financial goals and risk tolerance. Additionally, be mindful of the potential impact of fees and taxes on your returns, and seek out funds with competitive expense ratios and tax efficiency.

In summary, mutual funds and ETFs offer individual investors a convenient and accessible way to build a diversified investment portfolio. By pooling money from many investors and spreading it across a wide range of securities, these investment vehicles can help to manage risk and potentially enhance returns over the long term. As with any investment, however, it's essential to approach mutual funds and ETFs with a clear understanding of their characteristics, risks, and potential benefits, and to make informed decisions based on your unique financial situation and goals.

Subsection 2.4: Real Estate and Real Estate Investment Trusts (REITs)

Picture yourself strolling through a bustling city street, surrounded by towering skyscrapers, quaint coffee shops, and trendy boutiques. Each of these properties, from the grand office buildings to the charming storefronts, represents a unique investment opportunity in the world of real estate.

Real estate investing involves the purchase, ownership, management, and sale of properties for the purpose of generating income or capital appreciation. This can include residential properties, such as single-family homes or apartment buildings, as well as commercial properties, like office buildings, retail spaces, or warehouses.

One of the primary advantages of real estate investing is the potential for both steady cash flow and long-term appreciation. When you own a rental property, for example, you can generate a consistent stream of income from tenants while also benefiting from the potential increase in the property's value over time.

However, investing in physical real estate can also come with significant challenges. Buying and managing properties directly requires a substantial upfront investment, as well as ongoing responsibilities like property maintenance, tenant management, and navigating local regulations. Additionally, real estate investments can be illiquid, meaning that it may take time to sell a property and access your invested capital.

Enter Real Estate Investment Trusts, or REITs. These investment vehicles provide a way for individual investors to gain exposure to the real estate market without the need to directly own and manage properties.

REITs are companies that own and operate income-generating real estate properties. They can specialize in various sectors, such as residential, commercial, or industrial properties, and may focus on specific geographic regions. By purchasing shares in a REIT, investors can effectively become part-owners of the company's real estate portfolio, entitled to a portion of the income generated by the properties.

One of the key benefits of REITs is their accessibility. Shares of publicly-traded REITs can be bought and sold on stock exchanges, just like individual stocks, making it easy for investors to add real estate exposure to their portfolios. Additionally, REITs are required by law to distribute at least 90% of their taxable income to shareholders in the form of dividends, providing a potential source of regular income for investors.

REITs also offer the advantages of professional management and diversification. REIT managers are responsible for the day-to-day operations and strategic decision-making involved in running the company's properties, relieving investors of these responsibilities. Furthermore, by investing in a REIT, you gain exposure to a diverse portfolio of properties, helping to spread risk and potentially smooth out the impact of any single property's performance.

When considering an investment in REITs, it's essential to conduct thorough research and due diligence. Factors to consider include the REIT's management team, financial health, growth prospects, and dividend yield. Additionally, be aware that REIT performance can be influenced by broader economic conditions, such as changes in interest rates or fluctuations in the real estate market.

In summary, real estate investing offers the potential for both income and long-term appreciation, but also comes with significant challenges and responsibilities. REITs provide a more accessible and diversified way for individual investors to gain exposure to the real estate market, offering the benefits of professional management and potential dividend income. As with any investment, however, it's crucial to approach REITs with a clear understanding of their characteristics, risks, and potential rewards, and to make informed decisions based on your unique financial goals and circumstances.

Subsection 2.5: Alternative Investments: Commodities, Currencies, and Cryptocurrencies

Picture yourself as an intrepid explorer, venturing beyond the well-trodden paths of traditional investments and into the uncharted territories of alternative assets. In this realm, you'll encounter a fascinating array of opportunities, each with its own unique characteristics and potential for growth. From the tangible allure of commodities to the global dance of currencies and the digital frontier of cryptocurrencies, alternative investments offer a way to diversify your portfolio and tap into new sources of return.

Commodities are physical goods that are interchangeable with other goods of the same type, such as gold, oil, or agricultural products. These assets have been traded for centuries, with their prices determined by supply and demand dynamics in global markets. Investing in commodities can provide a hedge against inflation, as their prices often rise in response to increasing economic activity and a weakening currency. Additionally, commodities can offer diversification benefits, as their performance is often uncorrelated with that of stocks and bonds.

One way to invest in commodities is through futures contracts, which are agreements to buy or sell a specific amount of a commodity at a predetermined price and date in the future. These contracts are traded on exchanges, allowing investors to gain exposure to commodity price movements without physically owning the underlying assets. Another option is to invest in exchange-traded funds (ETFs) or mutual funds that focus on commodities, providing a more accessible and diversified way to participate in this market.

Currencies, on the other hand, represent the money used in different countries around the world. The foreign exchange (forex) market is the largest financial market globally, with trillions of dollars in daily trading volume. Investors can participate in this market by buying and selling currencies in pairs, aiming to profit from fluctuations in exchange rates. Factors that influence currency prices include interest rates, economic growth, political stability, and global trade flows.

Investing in currencies can provide diversification benefits, as their performance is often driven by different factors than those affecting stocks and bonds. However, the forex market is also known for its high volatility and leverage, which can amplify both gains and losses. As with any investment, it's crucial to understand the risks involved and to approach currency trading with caution and a well-defined strategy.

In recent years, cryptocurrencies have emerged as a new frontier in alternative investments. These digital assets, such as Bitcoin and Ethereum, use cryptography and blockchain technology to secure transactions and control the creation of new units. Cryptocurrencies operate independently of central banks and governments, offering the potential for decentralized, peer-to-peer transactions and a hedge against traditional financial systems.

Investing in cryptocurrencies can be a high-risk, high-reward proposition. These assets are known for their extreme volatility, with prices often experiencing significant swings in short periods. Additionally, the regulatory landscape for cryptocurrencies is still evolving, with different countries taking varying approaches to their legal status and taxation. As with any speculative investment, it's essential to conduct thorough research, understand the technology behind cryptocurrencies, and only invest what you can afford to lose.

In summary, alternative investments such as commodities, currencies, and cryptocurrencies offer unique opportunities for diversification and potential growth. However, these assets also come with their own set of risks and challenges, requiring careful consideration and a well-informed approach. By understanding the characteristics and dynamics of these markets, investors can make more informed decisions about whether and how to incorporate alternative investments into their overall financial strategy.

Summary: Navigating the Investment Landscape

Throughout this section, we've explored the diverse and fascinating world of investment vehicles, each offering unique opportunities for growth and financial success. From the tried-and-true classics like stocks and bonds to the more innovative options like REITs and cryptocurrencies, the modern investor has a wealth of choices at their fingertips.

As we've seen, each investment vehicle comes with its own set of characteristics, risks, and potential rewards. Stocks offer the chance to own a piece of a company and participate in its growth, while bonds provide a more predictable income stream and potential stability. Mutual funds and ETFs allow investors to access a diversified portfolio with professional management, while real estate and REITs provide exposure to the dynamic world of property ownership and rental income. And for those seeking to venture off the beaten path, alternative investments like commodities, currencies, and cryptocurrencies offer the potential for high returns, albeit with higher risks.

But perhaps the most important takeaway from this section is that no single investment vehicle is inherently better than another. The key to successful investing lies in understanding how these various options fit together to create a well-rounded, diversified portfolio that aligns with your unique financial goals, risk tolerance, and personal circumstances.

By taking the time to educate yourself about the different types of investment vehicles available, you've taken a crucial first step towards building a solid foundation for your financial future. Armed with this knowledge, you can now approach the investment landscape with confidence, ready to make informed decisions and seize the opportunities that lie ahead.

Remember, investing is not just about chasing returns or beating the market. It's about creating a roadmap for your financial journey, one that takes into account your short-term needs and long-term aspirations. With a clear understanding of the tools at your disposal and a commitment to ongoing learning and growth, you can navigate the investment landscape with purpose and conviction, charting a course towards a brighter, more prosperous future.

So, as we move forward in this book, keep an open mind and a curious spirit. Embrace the diversity of the investment world, and never stop exploring the possibilities that lie within it. With dedication, discipline, and a willingness to adapt and grow, you can harness the power of these investment vehicles to build the financial life you've always dreamed of.

Section 3: Building a Diversified Investment Portfolio

Imagine a world where your financial future is secure, where your investments are working hard for you, and where you can sleep soundly at night knowing that your portfolio is built to withstand the ups and downs of the market. This is the power of a well-diversified investment portfolio.

In the previous sections, we explored the various investment vehicles available to you, from stocks and bonds to mutual funds and real estate. But how do you put these pieces together to create a portfolio that is tailored to your unique goals, risk tolerance, and time horizon?

The answer lies in diversification. Just as a chef carefully selects a variety of ingredients to create a delicious meal, you must carefully select a mix of investments to create a portfolio that is both resilient and capable of delivering the returns you need to achieve your financial objectives.

But diversification is more than just picking a random assortment of investments. It requires a strategic approach, one that takes into account the complex interplay of risk and return, the ever-changing economic landscape, and your personal financial situation.

In this section, we will take a deep dive into the art and science of building a diversified investment portfolio. We will explore the key principles of diversification, the role of asset allocation, and the importance of regularly rebalancing your portfolio to stay on track.

Whether you are a seasoned investor or just starting out on your investment journey, the insights and strategies you will gain in this section will empower you to make informed decisions and take control of your financial future. So let's roll up our sleeves and get started on building a portfolio that will stand the test of time.

Subsection 3.1: The Importance of Diversification

In the world of investing, there is one golden rule that stands above all others: diversification. It is the key to managing risk and ensuring the long-term stability of your investment portfolio. But what exactly is diversification, and why is it so important?

At its core, diversification is the practice of spreading your investments across a variety of asset classes, sectors, and geographic regions. The idea is simple: by not putting all your eggs in one basket, you reduce your exposure to any single point of failure. If one investment performs poorly, the others can help to cushion the blow and keep your overall portfolio on track.

Think of it like a game of roulette. If you were to bet all your money on a single number, your chances of winning would be slim. But if you were to spread your bets across multiple numbers, your chances of coming out ahead would be much higher. The same principle applies to investing.

Of course, diversification is not a magic bullet. It cannot eliminate risk entirely, and it does not guarantee a profit. But it does help to mitigate the impact of market volatility and unexpected events. By holding a mix of stocks, bonds, real estate, and other assets, you can create a portfolio that is better equipped to weather the storms of the market.

One of the key benefits of diversification is that it allows you to tailor your portfolio to your specific goals and risk tolerance. If you are a young investor with a long time horizon, you may be able to afford to take on more risk in pursuit of higher returns. But if you are nearing retirement, you may want to focus on preserving your capital and generating a steady income stream.

Diversification also helps to reduce the impact of individual investment decisions. Even the most skilled investors can make mistakes or fall prey to emotional biases. By spreading your investments across a range of assets, you can minimize the impact of any single decision and ensure that your portfolio is not overly dependent on the success of any one company or sector.

But perhaps the most compelling reason to diversify is the simple fact that the future is uncertain. No one can predict with certainty which investments will perform well in the years ahead. By diversifying, you can position yourself to benefit from a range of potential outcomes and reduce your exposure to any single point of failure.

In the end, diversification is not a guarantee of success, but it is a powerful tool for managing risk and achieving your long-term financial goals. As you build your investment portfolio, make sure to keep this key principle in mind and seek out a wide range of assets that can help you navigate the ever-changing landscape of the market.

Subsection 3.2: Asset Allocation: Balancing Risk and Return

Picture yourself as a tightrope walker, carefully balancing on a thin wire high above the ground. The key to your success lies in maintaining a delicate equilibrium between the forces pulling you in different directions. In the world of investing, this balancing act is known as asset allocation.

Asset allocation is the process of dividing your investment portfolio among different asset classes, such as stocks, bonds, and cash, in a way that aligns with your financial goals, risk tolerance, and time horizon. It is the foundation upon which a well-diversified portfolio is built, and it plays a crucial role in determining the risk and return characteristics of your investments.

At its core, asset allocation is about managing risk. Each asset class carries its own unique set of risks and rewards. Stocks, for example, have the potential for high returns but also come with greater volatility and the risk of losing money in the short term. Bonds, on the other hand, offer more stable returns but may not keep pace with inflation over the long run.

By spreading your investments across different asset classes, you can create a portfolio that strikes a balance between risk and return. The right mix of assets will depend on your individual circumstances and goals. A young investor with a long time horizon may be able to afford a higher allocation to stocks, while someone nearing retirement may want to focus on preserving capital with a larger allocation to bonds.

But asset allocation is not a one-time decision. As your life circumstances change and market conditions evolve, your ideal asset mix may need to be adjusted. This is where the concept of rebalancing comes into play. Rebalancing involves periodically selling assets that have become overweighted in your portfolio and buying those that have become underweighted, in order to maintain your desired asset allocation.

For example, let's say you start with a portfolio that is 60% stocks and 40% bonds. If the stock market experiences a significant gain, your portfolio may become skewed towards stocks, with a 70/30 split. By rebalancing, you would sell some of your stocks and buy more bonds to bring your portfolio back to the original 60/40 allocation.

Rebalancing not only helps to manage risk but also forces you to sell high and buy low, a key principle of successful investing. It can be emotionally challenging to sell investments that have performed well, but rebalancing ensures that you are not overly exposed to any single asset class and that your portfolio remains aligned with your goals.

Of course, asset allocation is not a guarantee of investment success. No matter how carefully you construct your portfolio, there will always be some level of risk involved. But by thoughtfully allocating your assets and regularly rebalancing, you can create a portfolio that is better positioned to weather the ups and downs of the market and deliver the returns you need to achieve your financial objectives.

In the end, asset allocation is both an art and a science. It requires a deep understanding of the characteristics and behavior of different asset classes, as well as an honest assessment of your own risk tolerance and goals. But with the right approach and a commitment to regular rebalancing, asset allocation can be a powerful tool for building a diversified, resilient investment portfolio that will serve you well for years to come.

Subsection 3.3: Determining Your Investment Goals and Risk Tolerance

Investing is not a one-size-fits-all endeavor. Each individual has unique financial circumstances, aspirations, and emotional responses to market fluctuations. Before embarking on your investment journey, it is crucial to take a step back and define your personal investment goals and assess your risk tolerance. These two factors will serve as the compass guiding your investment decisions, ensuring that your portfolio aligns with your needs and preferences.

Let's begin by exploring the concept of investment goals. These are the financial objectives you aim to achieve through your investments, such as saving for retirement, buying a home, funding your children's education, or building wealth for future generations. Your investment goals will depend on your age, income, family situation, and personal values. For example, a young professional just starting their career may prioritize saving for a down payment on a house, while a couple nearing retirement may focus on generating a stable income stream to support their lifestyle.

To determine your investment goals, start by envisioning your ideal financial future. What do you want your life to look like in 5, 10, or 20 years? What milestones do you hope to achieve along the way? Once you have a clear picture of your long-term objectives, break them down into specific, measurable, achievable, relevant, and time-bound (SMART) goals. This process will help you quantify your targets and create a roadmap for your investment strategy.

Next, let's discuss risk tolerance, which refers to your emotional and financial ability to withstand market volatility and potential losses. Some investors are comfortable with the idea of taking on higher risk in pursuit of greater returns, while others prefer a more conservative approach that prioritizes capital preservation. Your risk tolerance is influenced by factors such as your personality, investment experience, time horizon, and financial stability.

To assess your risk tolerance, consider how you would react to different market scenarios. How would you feel if your portfolio lost 10%, 20%, or even 30% of its value in a short period? Would you be tempted to sell your investments in a panic, or would you have the discipline to stay the course and ride out the storm? Be honest with yourself about your emotional capacity to handle market downturns, as this will help you determine the appropriate level of risk for your portfolio.

It's important to note that your risk tolerance may change over time as your life circumstances evolve. For example, as you approach retirement, you may become more risk-averse and prioritize capital preservation over growth. Regularly reassessing your risk tolerance and adjusting your portfolio accordingly is an essential part of the investment process.

Once you have defined your investment goals and assessed your risk tolerance, you can begin to construct a portfolio that aligns with these parameters. This process involves selecting a mix of assets that balances your desire for returns with your ability to tolerate risk. A well-diversified portfolio should include a range of asset classes, such as stocks, bonds, real estate, and cash, in proportions that reflect your individual goals and risk profile.

For example, an investor with a high risk tolerance and a long time horizon may allocate a larger portion of their portfolio to stocks, which offer the potential for higher returns but also come with greater volatility. On the other hand, an investor with a lower risk tolerance and a shorter time horizon may prioritize bonds and cash, which provide more stable returns and help preserve capital.

In addition to asset allocation, your investment goals and risk tolerance will also influence your choice of specific investments within each asset class. For example, an investor with a high risk tolerance may gravitate towards small-cap stocks or emerging market funds, while a more conservative investor may prefer blue-chip stocks or government bonds.

Determining your investment goals and risk tolerance is a critical step in building a successful investment portfolio. By taking the time to define your objectives and assess your emotional capacity for risk, you can create a personalized investment strategy that supports your financial aspirations while allowing you to sleep soundly at night. Remember, investing is a journey, not a destination, and your goals and risk tolerance may evolve along the way. By regularly reviewing and adjusting your portfolio, you can ensure that your investments remain aligned with your unique needs and preferences.

Subsection 3.4: Rebalancing Your Portfolio Periodically

Imagine you've carefully crafted a delicious, nutritious meal, perfectly balanced with the right proportions of proteins, carbohydrates, and fats. But as time passes, you find yourself adding a little extra sauce here, a sprinkle of cheese there, and before you know it, your once-balanced meal has become a bit too heavy on the cheese and light on the veggies. The same can happen with your investment portfolio if you don't take the time to periodically rebalance it.

Rebalancing is the process of adjusting your portfolio's asset allocation back to its original target percentages. Over time, as different assets in your portfolio experience varying rates of growth or decline, the proportions of your holdings can drift away from your intended allocation. For example, if stocks have performed particularly well, they may now make up a larger percentage of your portfolio than you initially planned, potentially exposing you to more risk than you're comfortable with.

Think of rebalancing as a way to maintain the health and vitality of your investment portfolio. Just as you might adjust your diet or exercise routine to stay in shape, rebalancing helps keep your portfolio in line with your goals and risk tolerance. By selling assets that have become overweighted and buying those that have become underweighted, you effectively "trim the fat" and restore balance to your portfolio.

But why is this balance so important? Remember, your asset allocation is designed to strike a specific balance between risk and potential return, based on your individual financial goals and risk tolerance. When your portfolio drifts away from this allocation, it can have significant consequences. An overallocation to stocks, for instance, could leave you vulnerable to larger losses during market downturns, while an underallocation to stocks could mean missing out on potential growth opportunities.

Rebalancing also helps enforce the age-old investment adage of "buying low and selling high." By selling assets that have become overweighted (and thus, more expensive relative to your other holdings), and buying those that have become underweighted (and thus, cheaper), you're effectively locking in gains and taking advantage of potential bargains.

So, how often should you rebalance your portfolio? The answer depends on several factors, including your investment goals, risk tolerance, and the overall market conditions. Some investors choose to rebalance on a regular schedule, such as once a year or every quarter, while others prefer to rebalance only when their asset allocation has drifted beyond a certain threshold, such as 5% or 10% from their target percentages.

There's no one-size-fits-all approach to rebalancing, but it's generally a good idea to review your portfolio at least annually and make adjustments as needed. Keep in mind that rebalancing does involve selling and buying assets, which can trigger taxes and transaction costs, so it's essential to consider these factors when deciding how often to rebalance.

In some cases, you may be able to set up automatic rebalancing through your investment platform or brokerage, which can help take the emotion and guesswork out of the process. However, it's still important to review your portfolio regularly and make sure your asset allocation remains aligned with your overall financial plan.

Rebalancing may not be the most exciting part of investing, but it's a crucial step in maintaining a healthy, diversified portfolio that can weather the ups and downs of the market. By periodically trimming the excesses and restoring balance to your holdings, you can help ensure that your investments continue to work hard for you, no matter what the future may bring. So don't neglect this important aspect of portfolio management – your financial well-being may depend on it.

Summary: Constructing a Resilient Portfolio for Long-Term Financial Success

Congratulations on taking a significant step towards securing your financial future by learning how to build a well-diversified investment portfolio. Throughout this section, we have explored the key principles and strategies that underpin successful portfolio construction, from understanding the importance of diversification to mastering the art of asset allocation and regular rebalancing.

By spreading your investments across a range of asset classes, sectors, and geographies, you can create a portfolio that is resilient to market fluctuations and optimized for long-term growth. Diversification is not about chasing the latest investment fads or trying to time the market; rather, it is a disciplined approach to managing risk and maximizing returns over time.

Central to this process is determining your unique investment goals and risk tolerance. By taking an honest look at your financial objectives, time horizon, and emotional capacity for market volatility, you can craft a portfolio that aligns with your individual needs and preferences. Remember, investing is a deeply personal journey, and what works for one investor may not be suitable for another.

But building a diversified portfolio is only the beginning. To ensure that your investments continue to work hard for you, it is essential to regularly monitor and rebalance your holdings. By periodically trimming the excesses and restoring balance to your portfolio, you can maintain its health and vitality, even as market conditions change and your own life circumstances evolve.

As you embark on the next stage of your investment journey, remember that the knowledge and skills you have gained in this section will serve you well for years to come. By embracing the principles of diversification, asset allocation, and rebalancing, you are laying the foundation for a lifetime of financial security and prosperity.

So, take a moment to reflect on how far you have come and the exciting opportunities that lie ahead. With a well-constructed, diversified portfolio at your side, you are well-equipped to navigate the complex world of investing and achieve your long-term financial goals. The future is bright, and your investment success story is just beginning.

Section 4: Investing Strategies and Approaches

Picture yourself as a traveler embarking on a journey through the vast landscape of investing. Just as there are many paths to reach a destination, there are numerous strategies and approaches to navigate the world of investments. In this section, we will explore the diverse philosophies and methods that investors employ to achieve their financial goals.

Investing is not a one-size-fits-all endeavor. Each investor brings a unique set of objectives, risk tolerance, and time horizon to the table. Some may prefer a hands-on approach, actively managing their portfolios and seeking to capitalize on market opportunities. Others may opt for a more passive strategy, focusing on long-term growth and minimizing the impact of short-term market fluctuations.

As we delve into the various investing strategies and approaches, we will uncover the underlying principles and rationale behind each one. From the age-old debate between active and passive investing to the nuances of value investing and growth investing, we will examine the key characteristics and potential benefits of these different paths.

Whether you are a novice investor just starting to dip your toes into the market or a seasoned pro looking to refine your strategies, understanding the array of investing approaches is crucial. By gaining insight into the different philosophies and techniques, you can make informed decisions about which strategies align with your personal financial goals and risk tolerance.

Throughout this section, we will provide practical examples and real-world applications to illustrate how these strategies can be implemented in your own investment journey. We will also discuss the importance of adapting your approach as market conditions and your personal circumstances evolve over time.

So, let us embark on this exploration of investing strategies and approaches, arming ourselves with the knowledge and tools to make sound investment decisions and work towards building a prosperous financial future.

Subsection 4.1: Active vs. Passive Investing

In the world of investing, there are two primary approaches that investors can take: active investing and passive investing. Each approach has its own unique characteristics, benefits, and drawbacks, and understanding the differences between them is crucial for making informed investment decisions.

Active investing involves a hands-on approach, where investors or fund managers actively buy and sell securities in an attempt to outperform the market. They rely on research, analysis, and their own judgment to identify undervalued or overvalued stocks, bonds, or other assets. Active investors believe that through careful selection and timing, they can generate returns that exceed the overall market performance.

One of the main advantages of active investing is the potential for higher returns. By capitalizing on market inefficiencies and identifying promising investment opportunities, active investors aim to beat the market and achieve superior results. However, this potential for higher returns comes with increased risk and volatility, as the success of active investing largely depends on the skill and expertise of the individual or team making the investment decisions.

On the other hand, passive investing takes a more hands-off approach, focusing on long-term growth and minimizing the impact of short-term market fluctuations. Passive investors typically invest in index funds or exchange-traded funds (ETFs) that track a particular market index, such as the S&P 500. By doing so, they aim to match the performance of the overall market rather than trying to outperform it.

The primary advantage of passive investing is its simplicity and cost-effectiveness. By investing in index funds or ETFs, passive investors can achieve broad market exposure with relatively low fees and minimal trading costs. Additionally, passive investing tends to be less time-consuming and emotionally demanding than active investing, as it does not require constant monitoring and decision-making.

However, the trade-off for the simplicity and cost-effectiveness of passive investing is the acceptance of market returns. Passive investors acknowledge that they will not outperform the market, but rather aim to capture the overall growth of the economy over the long term. They believe that trying to consistently beat the market is a challenging and often futile endeavor, and that a more reliable path to financial success is through steady, long-term investment in a diversified portfolio.

Ultimately, the choice between active and passive investing depends on an individual's investment goals, risk tolerance, and personal preferences.

Some investors may prefer the potential for higher returns and the thrill of actively managing their investments, while others may prioritize simplicity, cost-effectiveness, and a more hands-off approach. Many investors also choose to incorporate both active and passive strategies in their portfolios, seeking a balance between the two approaches.

As you explore the world of investing and consider which approach aligns with your financial objectives, it is essential to understand the fundamental differences between active and passive investing. By weighing the potential benefits and drawbacks of each approach, you can make informed decisions and develop an investment strategy that suits your unique needs and goals.

Subsection 4.2: Value Investing and Fundamental Analysis

Picture yourself as a detective, sifting through clues to uncover hidden treasures in the world of investing. This is the essence of value investing, a time-honored approach that seeks to identify undervalued companies with strong fundamentals and long-term growth potential.

At the heart of value investing lies the belief that the market often misprices securities, presenting opportunities for astute investors to buy stocks at a discount to their intrinsic value. By focusing on companies with solid financial health, stable earnings, and a durable competitive advantage, value investors aim to minimize risk while maximizing potential returns.

One of the key tools in the value investor's arsenal is fundamental analysis. This involves a thorough examination of a company's financial statements, including its balance sheet, income statement, and cash flow statement. By scrutinizing these documents, investors can gain insights into a company's revenue growth, profitability, debt levels, and cash generation abilities.

Fundamental analysis goes beyond the numbers, however. Value investors also assess qualitative factors such as the quality of a company's management team, its market position, and its ability to weather economic downturns. They look for companies with a clear competitive advantage, such as a strong brand, proprietary technology, or a loyal customer base.

One of the most famous proponents of value investing is Warren Buffett, the legendary investor and CEO of Berkshire Hathaway. Buffett's approach, which he learned from his mentor Benjamin Graham, focuses on identifying companies with a wide "economic moat" – a term that refers to a company's ability to maintain its competitive advantage over time.

To illustrate the power of value investing, let's consider a real-world example. In the early 2000s, the stock of a little-known company called Apple Inc. was trading at a price-to-earnings ratio of around 15, significantly lower than the market average. At the time, Apple was primarily known for its Mac computers, and many investors were skeptical about its growth prospects.

However, value investors who conducted fundamental analysis on Apple would have noticed several key strengths. The company had a loyal customer base, a strong brand, and a history of innovation. It also had a solid balance sheet, with minimal debt and ample cash reserves. By investing in Apple at a time when it was undervalued by the market, value investors could have reaped substantial rewards as the company's stock price soared over the subsequent years.

Of course, value investing is not without its challenges. It requires patience, discipline, and a willingness to go against the crowd. Value investors often have to wait for the market to recognize the intrinsic value of their investments, which can take years. They also have to be comfortable with holding a concentrated portfolio of carefully selected stocks, rather than diversifying broadly across the market.

Despite these challenges, value investing has proven to be a successful strategy over the long term. By focusing on the fundamental health and intrinsic value of companies, value investors can build wealth steadily and minimize the impact of market volatility.

As you explore the world of investing, consider the merits of value investing and fundamental analysis. By learning to identify undervalued companies with strong fundamentals, you can position yourself for long-term financial success while minimizing risk. Remember, investing is not about following the herd, but about having the courage to make informed decisions based on sound analysis and a long-term perspective.

Subsection 4.3: Growth Investing and Momentum Strategies

In the fast-paced world of investing, growth investing and momentum strategies have gained significant popularity among investors seeking to capitalize on the potential of rapidly expanding companies and market trends. These approaches stand in contrast to the more conservative value investing philosophy, as they prioritize future growth prospects and market sentiment over traditional valuation metrics.

At its core, growth investing focuses on identifying companies with strong potential for revenue and earnings growth, often driven by innovative products, services, or business models. Growth investors are willing to pay a premium for stocks that demonstrate robust growth rates, even if their current valuations appear high relative to traditional metrics like price-to-earnings ratios. They believe that the company's future growth will justify the higher price and lead to substantial returns over time.

One of the key characteristics of growth companies is their ability to disrupt industries and create new markets. These companies often operate in sectors such as technology, biotechnology, and e-commerce, where innovation and scalability are paramount. Growth investors seek out companies with a clear competitive advantage, a large addressable market, and a management team with a proven track record of execution.

To identify potential growth opportunities, investors employ a range of techniques, including fundamental analysis of financial statements, assessment of industry trends, and evaluation of a company's competitive position. They may also consider factors such as revenue growth rates, profit margins, and cash flow generation to gauge a company's ability to sustain its growth trajectory.

Momentum investing, on the other hand, is a strategy that seeks to capitalize on the continuance of existing market trends. Momentum investors believe that stocks that have performed well in the recent past are likely to continue their upward trajectory, while those that have underperformed are likely to continue lagging. They aim to buy stocks that are showing strong positive momentum and sell those that are exhibiting negative momentum.

The premise behind momentum investing is rooted in behavioral finance, which suggests that investors tend to underreact to new information and exhibit herd mentality. As a result, stocks that have recently outperformed may continue to attract buyers, driving prices higher, while underperforming stocks may face continued selling pressure. Momentum investors seek to exploit these market inefficiencies by riding the wave of positive sentiment and avoiding the downside of negative momentum.

To implement a momentum strategy, investors typically rely on technical analysis tools, such as moving averages, relative strength indices, and chart patterns, to identify stocks with strong momentum characteristics. They may also consider factors like trading volume, price volatility, and market sentiment indicators to assess the strength and sustainability of a stock's momentum.

While growth investing and momentum strategies have the potential to generate significant returns, they also come with their own set of risks and challenges. Growth companies, for example, may face intense competition, regulatory hurdles, or execution risks that could derail their growth prospects. Momentum investing, on the other hand, can be susceptible to sudden market reversals and may require nimble trading skills to navigate volatile market conditions.

Moreover, both growth and momentum investing often involve a higher degree of volatility compared to more conservative strategies like value investing. The prices of growth and momentum stocks can be more sensitive to market sentiment, earnings reports, and other short-term factors, leading to greater fluctuations in portfolio value.

To mitigate these risks, investors may employ a diversified approach that combines elements of growth, momentum, and other investing styles. By spreading investments across different sectors, market capitalizations, and geographies, investors can potentially smooth out the impact of individual stock or sector-specific risks.

As with any investment strategy, it is crucial for investors to conduct thorough research, maintain a long-term perspective, and regularly monitor and adjust their portfolios to align with their financial goals and risk tolerance. Growth investing and momentum strategies can be powerful tools for wealth creation, but they require discipline, patience, and a willingness to embrace the inherent uncertainties of the market.

In the ever-evolving landscape of investing, growth investing and momentum strategies offer exciting opportunities for those seeking to capitalize on the dynamism of the market. By understanding the principles behind these approaches and carefully navigating the associated risks, investors can position themselves to benefit from the potential of high-growth companies and the power of market momentum. As with any investment decision, however, it is essential to approach growth and momentum investing with a well-informed and disciplined mindset, always keeping sight of one's long-term financial objectives.

Subsection 4.4: Income Investing: Dividends and Interest

In the vast landscape of investing strategies, income investing emerges as a compelling approach for those seeking to generate a steady stream of cash flow from their investments. At its core, income investing focuses on building a portfolio of assets that provide regular income in the form of dividends or interest payments. This strategy appeals to investors who prioritize consistent, reliable returns over the potential for capital appreciation.

One of the primary vehicles for income investing is dividend-paying stocks. These are shares of companies that distribute a portion of their profits to shareholders on a regular basis, typically quarterly or annually. Dividend investors seek out established, financially stable companies with a history of consistent dividend payments and a strong likelihood of continued payouts in the future. By carefully selecting a diversified portfolio of dividend stocks, investors can create a reliable source of income that can supplement their regular earnings or support their lifestyle in retirement.

To illustrate the power of dividend investing, consider the following example. Imagine an investor who purchases 1,000 shares of a company that trades at $50 per share and pays an annual dividend of $2 per share. The initial investment would be $50,000, and the investor would receive $2,000 in dividends each year. If the company maintains its dividend payment and the stock price remains stable, the investor would earn a 4% annual return on their investment through dividends alone. Over time, if the company increases its dividend payments, the investor's income stream could grow without the need to sell their shares.

Another key component of income investing is bonds, which are debt securities issued by corporations or governments. When an investor purchases a bond, they are essentially lending money to the issuer in exchange for regular interest payments, known as coupon payments, and the return of the principal amount at maturity. Bonds offer a more predictable income stream compared to dividend stocks, as the interest payments are contractually obligated and the principal is returned on a set date.

Income investors often build a diversified bond portfolio across various sectors, credit ratings, and maturities to manage risk and optimize returns. For example, an investor might allocate a portion of their portfolio to high-quality corporate bonds with a lower yield but greater stability, while also including some higher-yielding, lower-quality bonds to boost overall returns. By carefully balancing risk and reward, income investors can construct a bond portfolio that aligns with their financial goals and risk tolerance.

While dividend stocks and bonds are the primary focus of income investing, there are other assets that can contribute to a diversified income portfolio. Real Estate Investment Trusts (REITs), for instance, are companies that own and manage income-generating real estate properties, such as apartment buildings, office complexes, or shopping centers. REITs are required by law to distribute at least 90% of their taxable income to shareholders in the form of dividends, making them an attractive option for income-seeking investors.

Moreover, income investors may also consider incorporating preferred stocks into their portfolios. Preferred stocks are a hybrid security that combines features of both stocks and bonds. They typically offer higher dividend yields than common stocks, and their dividends are paid out before common stock dividends. However, preferred stockholders generally do not have voting rights and may face more limited capital appreciation potential compared to common stockholders.

As with any investment strategy, income investing comes with its own set of risks and considerations. Dividend stocks, for example, are not immune to market volatility and may experience price fluctuations. Companies can also choose to reduce or eliminate their dividend payments if they face financial difficulties, which can impact an investor's income stream. Similarly, bonds are subject to interest rate risk, credit risk, and inflation risk, which can affect the value of the bonds and the purchasing power of the interest payments over time.

To mitigate these risks, income investors should focus on building a well-diversified portfolio across various sectors, industries, and asset classes. They should also conduct thorough research on the financial health and stability of the companies or issuers they invest in, paying close attention to factors such as dividend payout ratios, debt levels, and cash flow generation. Additionally, income investors should regularly monitor their portfolios and make adjustments as needed to ensure that their investments continue to align with their financial goals and risk tolerance.

In conclusion, income investing offers a compelling strategy for those seeking to generate a steady stream of cash flow from their investments. By focusing on dividend-paying stocks, bonds, and other income-generating assets, investors can build a diversified portfolio that provides regular income and supports their financial objectives. While income investing is not without risks, a well-constructed and carefully managed income portfolio can be a powerful tool for achieving long-term financial security and stability. As with any investment approach, it is essential for income investors to conduct thorough research, maintain a long-term perspective, and regularly review and adjust their portfolios to navigate the ever-changing market landscape.

Summary: Navigating the Investment Landscape with Confidence

As we conclude our exploration of investing strategies and approaches, it's essential to recognize that there is no one-size-fits-all solution when it comes to building a successful investment portfolio. Each approach, whether it's active or passive investing, value or growth investing, or income investing, has its own merits and challenges. The key is to understand your personal financial goals, risk tolerance, and investment timeline, and then align your strategy accordingly.

Throughout this section, we've delved into the fundamental principles and philosophies that underpin various investing approaches. We've examined the age-old debate between active and passive investing, highlighting the potential for higher returns with active management, as well as the simplicity and cost-effectiveness of passive investing. We've also explored the world of value investing, where investors seek to uncover hidden gems by focusing on companies with strong fundamentals and intrinsic value. On the other hand, we've seen how growth investing and momentum strategies aim to capitalize on the potential of rapidly expanding companies and market trends.

Moreover, we've discussed the importance of income investing for those seeking to generate a steady stream of cash flow from their investments. By focusing on dividend-paying stocks, bonds, and other income-generating assets, investors can build a diversified portfolio that provides regular income and supports their financial objectives.

As you reflect on the insights gained from this section, remember that successful investing is a journey, not a destination. It requires continuous learning, adaptability, and a willingness to embrace the inherent uncertainties of the market. By arming yourself with knowledge, maintaining a long-term perspective, and regularly reviewing and adjusting your portfolio, you can navigate the investment landscape with confidence and work towards achieving your financial goals.

So, take the lessons learned from this section and apply them to your own investment journey. Embrace the power of a well-informed and disciplined approach, and never stop learning and growing as an investor. With dedication, patience, and a sound investment strategy, you can unlock the potential of the market and build a prosperous financial future.

Section 5: Navigating Market Cycles and Economic Conditions

Picture this: you've carefully crafted your investment portfolio, diversifying your assets and aligning your strategies with your financial goals. But as you embark on your investing journey, you quickly realize that the road ahead is not always smooth. The economy ebbs and flows, and market cycles can bring both opportunities and challenges. Just like a sailor navigating choppy waters, you must learn to adapt to changing conditions and steer your portfolio towards long-term success.

In this section, we'll dive into the world of market cycles and economic conditions, equipping you with the knowledge and tools needed to make informed investment decisions in any environment. We'll explore the characteristics of bull and bear markets, and how these cycles can impact your investments. You'll learn to recognize key economic indicators and understand their influence on financial markets, giving you a deeper understanding of the forces at play.

But navigating market cycles and economic conditions isn't just about understanding the theory; it's about developing practical strategies to protect and grow your wealth. We'll discuss how to invest during times of uncertainty and volatility, helping you maintain a level head and avoid common pitfalls. By the end of this section, you'll have a roadmap for navigating the ever-changing landscape of investing, allowing you to confidently make decisions that align with your long-term financial objectives.

So, whether you're a seasoned investor or just starting out, this section will provide you with the insights and guidance needed to weather any storm and emerge stronger on the other side. Get ready to set sail on a journey of financial empowerment, as we explore the art and science of navigating market cycles and economic conditions.

Subsection 5.1: Bull Markets and Bear Markets

Picture a fierce bull, charging forward with unbridled optimism, and a lumbering bear, cautiously retreating into hibernation. These powerful animal metaphors have become ingrained in the language of investing, representing the two primary phases of market cycles: bull markets and bear markets.

In a bull market, investor confidence soars, and stock prices rise steadily, often exceeding previous highs. It's a time of optimism and growth, where the overall market sentiment is positive, and investors are eager to participate in the potential rewards. During bull markets, companies tend to expand, unemployment rates decrease, and the economy generally thrives. The term "bull market" is believed to have originated from the way a bull attacks, thrusting its horns upward, symbolizing the upward movement of stock prices.

On the other hand, a bear market is characterized by a persistent decline in stock prices, typically falling 20% or more from recent highs. During a bear market, investor confidence wanes, and pessimism prevails. Companies may struggle, leading to layoffs and reduced earnings. The overall market sentiment is negative, and many investors become risk-averse, often selling their holdings to minimize potential losses. The term "bear market" is derived from the way a bear attacks, swiping its paws downward, symbolizing the downward trend of stock prices.

It's crucial to understand that bull and bear markets are natural parts of the economic cycle, and they can have significant impacts on your investments. During bull markets, investors often see the value of their portfolios grow, as rising stock prices can lead to substantial gains. However, it's essential to remain cautious and avoid getting caught up in the euphoria, as bull markets can sometimes lead to overvaluation and speculative bubbles.

In contrast, bear markets can be challenging for investors, as the value of their holdings may decline. It's during these times that many investors face the temptation to sell their investments out of fear, locking in losses. However, history has shown that bear markets are often temporary, and patient investors who stay the course and maintain a long-term perspective can weather the storm and potentially benefit from the eventual market recovery.

Understanding the characteristics and potential impacts of bull and bear markets is essential for making informed investment decisions. By recognizing these cycles and adapting your strategies accordingly, you can navigate the ups and downs of the market with greater confidence and resilience. In the following subsections, we'll explore how to identify key economic indicators and develop practical strategies for investing through different market conditions.

Subsection 5.2: Economic Indicators and Their Influence on Markets

Picture yourself as a sailor navigating the vast ocean of the financial markets. Just as a sailor relies on various instruments and signals to guide their journey, investors must also pay attention to key economic indicators that can provide valuable insights into the health and direction of the economy. These indicators act as signposts, helping you make informed decisions about your investments and adjust your portfolio accordingly.

Economic indicators are statistical measures that reflect the state of the economy, and they can have a significant impact on financial markets. When these indicators show positive trends, such as strong economic growth, low unemployment, or rising consumer confidence, it often signals a favorable environment for investments. Conversely, when indicators point to economic slowdown, increasing inflation, or declining business activity, it may be a sign of potential challenges ahead.

One of the most closely watched economic indicators is the Gross Domestic Product (GDP), which measures the total value of goods and services produced within a country's borders. GDP growth is a key gauge of economic expansion, and when it is strong and consistent, it often bodes well for corporate earnings and stock market performance. However, if GDP growth slows down or contracts, it may indicate a weakening economy and potential headwinds for investments.

Another crucial indicator is the unemployment rate, which reflects the percentage of the labor force that is actively seeking work but unable to find employment. A low unemployment rate suggests a healthy labor market and a robust economy, which can support consumer spending and business growth. On the other hand, rising unemployment may signal economic distress and could lead to reduced consumer confidence and spending, affecting companies' bottom lines and stock prices.

Inflation is another economic indicator that can have a significant impact on financial markets. Inflation refers to the rate at which the general price level of goods and services increases over time. When inflation is low and stable, it can provide a favorable environment for businesses and consumers. However, if inflation rises too quickly or becomes unpredictable, it can erode the purchasing power of money and lead to higher borrowing costs, potentially affecting economic growth and investment returns.

In addition to these broad economic indicators, investors also pay close attention to more specific measures, such as consumer confidence indices, housing market data, manufacturing activity surveys, and retail sales figures. Each of these indicators provides a piece of the puzzle, contributing to a clearer picture of the overall economic landscape.

It's important to note that economic indicators don't exist in isolation; they are interconnected and can influence each other. For example, strong GDP growth and low unemployment may lead to higher consumer confidence, which in turn can boost spending and further support economic expansion. Similarly, rising inflation may prompt central banks to raise interest rates, which can affect borrowing costs and investment decisions across various sectors.

As an investor, staying attuned to economic indicators and their potential impact on financial markets is crucial for making informed decisions. However, it's equally important to maintain a long-term perspective and avoid knee-jerk reactions to short-term fluctuations. Economic indicators are just one piece of the puzzle, and they should be considered alongside other factors, such as company fundamentals, market trends, and your own financial goals and risk tolerance.

By understanding the relationship between economic indicators and financial markets, you can navigate the ever-changing landscape of investing with greater confidence and adaptability. In the next subsection, we'll explore practical strategies for investing during times of uncertainty and volatility, helping you stay the course and capitalize on opportunities in any economic environment.

Subsection 5.3: Investing During Times of Uncertainty and Volatility

Picture yourself as a sailor navigating a stormy sea, with waves crashing against your boat and winds howling in your ears. The journey is treacherous, and the path ahead is uncertain, but with the right strategies and a steady hand, you can weather the storm and emerge victorious. Similarly, investing during times of uncertainty and volatility can be a daunting task, but with the right mindset and approach, you can navigate these choppy waters and come out stronger on the other side.

Uncertainty and volatility are an inevitable part of the investing landscape. Whether it's geopolitical tensions, economic downturns, or unexpected events like a global pandemic, there will always be factors that can shake up the markets and leave investors feeling unsettled. However, it's important to remember that these periods of turbulence are often temporary, and those who stay the course and adapt their strategies can potentially reap the rewards in the long run.

One key strategy for investing during uncertain times is to maintain a long-term perspective. It's easy to get caught up in the day-to-day fluctuations of the market, especially when media headlines are screaming about the latest downturn or selloff. However, successful investors know that short-term volatility is a natural part of the market cycle, and that focusing on long-term goals and staying invested through the ups and downs can be a winning strategy. By keeping your eyes on the horizon and not getting swayed by temporary setbacks, you can ride out the storm and potentially benefit from the eventual recovery.

Another important aspect of investing during uncertainty is to maintain a well-diversified portfolio. Diversification is often referred to as the only free lunch in investing, and for good reason. By spreading your investments across different asset classes, sectors, and geographies, you can potentially mitigate the impact of any one particular event or downturn. For example, if the stock market is experiencing a correction, having a portion of your portfolio allocated to bonds or real estate can provide a buffer and help smooth out overall returns. By not putting all your eggs in one basket, you can reduce your exposure to risk and increase your chances of long-term success.

In addition to diversification, it's also important to have a clear understanding of your risk tolerance and investment goals. During times of uncertainty, it can be tempting to make impulsive decisions based on fear or emotion, such as selling off investments at a loss or chasing after the latest hot stock. However, these knee-jerk reactions can often do more harm than good, and can lead to missed opportunities or permanent losses. By having a well-defined investment plan and sticking to it, even in the face of volatility, you can avoid making rash decisions and stay focused on your long-term objectives.

Another strategy for navigating uncertain markets is to take advantage of dollar-cost averaging. This involves investing a fixed amount of money at regular intervals, regardless of market conditions. By consistently investing over time, you can potentially smooth out the impact of short-term price fluctuations and take advantage of the long-term growth potential of the market. This approach can be especially effective during volatile periods, as it allows you to buy more shares when prices are low and fewer shares when prices are high, potentially leading to a lower average cost per share over time.

It's also important to stay informed and educated about the markets and the broader economic environment. While it's not necessary to become a financial expert, having a basic understanding of key concepts like market cycles, economic indicators, and investment vehicles can help you make more informed decisions and avoid common pitfalls. By staying up-to-date on market news and analysis, and seeking out reliable sources of information and guidance, you can navigate uncertainty with greater confidence and clarity.

Finally, it's crucial to remember that investing is not a one-size-fits-all endeavor, and what works for one investor may not work for another. During times of uncertainty, it's important to assess your own unique circumstances, goals, and risk tolerance, and to adapt your strategies accordingly. Whether it's adjusting your asset allocation, rebalancing your portfolio, or seeking professional advice, being proactive and flexible can help you weather the storm and emerge stronger on the other side.

Investing during times of uncertainty and volatility can be a challenging and emotional experience, but with the right mindset, strategies, and support, it's possible to navigate these choppy waters and come out ahead. By maintaining a long-term perspective, diversifying your portfolio, staying true to your investment plan, and staying informed and adaptable, you can potentially turn uncertainty into opportunity and build lasting wealth over time. So, take a deep breath, steady your hand on the wheel, and remember that the storm will eventually pass, leaving you stronger and wiser for having weathered it.

Summary: Navigating the Tides of Change

As we conclude this section on navigating market cycles and economic conditions, let's take a moment to reflect on the key insights we've gained. Just like a sailor who has weathered a storm, you now have a deeper understanding of the forces that shape the investing landscape and the tools to chart your course through any market environment.

We've explored the ebb and flow of bull and bear markets, recognizing that these cycles are a natural part of the economic rhythm. By understanding the characteristics and potential impacts of these phases, you can make informed decisions and adapt your strategies to the prevailing market conditions. Remember, success in investing is not about timing the market perfectly, but about staying the course and maintaining a long-term perspective.

We've also delved into the world of economic indicators, those signposts that provide valuable insights into the health and direction of the economy. By staying attuned to these measures, from GDP growth and unemployment rates to inflation and consumer confidence, you can gain a clearer picture of the economic landscape and anticipate potential shifts in the market. However, it's crucial to remember that no single indicator tells the whole story, and that a holistic view is essential for making sound investment decisions.

Perhaps most importantly, we've explored practical strategies for investing during times of uncertainty and volatility. In a world that is constantly changing, the ability to navigate choppy waters is a critical skill for any investor. By maintaining a well-diversified portfolio, staying true to your investment plan, and embracing a long-term mindset, you can weather any storm and emerge stronger on the other side.

As you reflect on the insights gained from this section, remember that investing is not a destination, but a journey. The road ahead may be filled with twists and turns, but armed with the knowledge and strategies we've discussed, you have the power to navigate the tides of change with confidence and resilience.

So, as you set sail on the next leg of your investing journey, keep your eyes on the horizon and trust in the process. Embrace the challenges and opportunities that lie ahead, knowing that you have the tools and the mindset to succeed. The future is yours to shape, and with the right approach, you can turn uncertainty into opportunity and build lasting wealth in any market environment.

Section 6: Implementing Your Investment Plan

You've learned about the various investment vehicles available, the importance of diversification, and different investing strategies. Now, it's time to put that knowledge into action and take the crucial step of implementing your investment plan. Many people spend countless hours researching and crafting the perfect investment strategy, only to falter when it comes to execution. Don't let that be you.

Implementing your investment plan is where the rubber meets the road. It's the moment when you transform your ideas and intentions into tangible actions that can set you on the path to financial success. But getting started can be daunting, especially if you're new to investing. Where do you begin? How do you choose the right investment platform? What steps should you take to ensure you're making informed decisions?

In this section, we'll guide you through the process of bringing your investment plan to life. We'll discuss the practical considerations you need to keep in mind, such as selecting an appropriate brokerage, conducting thorough research, and monitoring your investments over time. We'll also explore the importance of seeking professional advice when necessary and how to find the right financial advisor for your needs.

Remember, investing is not a one-time event but a continuous journey. As you implement your plan, you'll need to stay engaged, adapt to changing market conditions, and make adjustments as your goals and circumstances evolve. But with the right mindset, tools, and support, you can navigate this journey with confidence and work towards building the financial future you envision.

So, let's dive in and explore the actionable steps you can take to turn your investment plan into a reality. By the end of this section, you'll have a clear roadmap for getting started and a framework for making informed investment decisions that align with your unique goals and risk tolerance. Are you ready to take control of your financial future? Let's get started.

Subsection 6.1: Choosing the Right Investment Platform and Brokerage

With your investment plan in hand, the next crucial step is to choose the right investment platform and brokerage that aligns with your needs and goals. The financial landscape is filled with a myriad of options, each offering different features, fees, and levels of support. Navigating this maze can be overwhelming, especially for new investors. However, taking the time to carefully consider your options and select the most suitable platform and brokerage can set you up for long-term success.

When evaluating investment platforms and brokerages, there are several key factors to keep in mind. First, consider the range of investment products and services offered. Do they provide access to the types of investments you're interested in, such as stocks, bonds, mutual funds, or exchange-traded funds (ETFs)? Some platforms may specialize in specific asset classes or offer unique investment opportunities, so ensure that the platform aligns with your investment strategy.

Next, take a close look at the fees and commissions associated with each platform. These costs can vary widely and can have a significant impact on your investment returns over time. Look for platforms with competitive pricing structures, such as low trading commissions, no account maintenance fees, and minimal or no fees for transferring funds. Keep in mind that some platforms may offer lower fees but provide fewer features or less personalized support, so strike a balance that works for you.

Ease of use and accessibility are also important considerations. The platform should have a user-friendly interface that allows you to easily navigate, research investments, and execute trades. Consider whether the platform offers mobile apps or web-based access, enabling you to manage your investments on the go. Additionally, look for platforms with robust educational resources, such as tutorials, webinars, and investment guides, which can help you make informed decisions and continuously improve your investing knowledge.

Customer support is another crucial factor when selecting an investment platform. You want a brokerage that offers responsive, knowledgeable, and helpful support when you need it. Look for platforms with multiple channels of communication, such as phone, email, and live chat, and consider the availability of support during trading hours. Reading reviews and testimonials from other investors can provide valuable insights into the quality of customer support provided by different platforms.

Finally, consider the reputation and security of the investment platform. Choose a brokerage that is well-established, regulated, and has a track record of protecting client assets. Look for platforms that offer robust security measures, such as two-factor authentication, encryption, and SIPC insurance, which protects your investments in case of brokerage failure.

Ultimately, the right investment platform and brokerage for you will depend on your unique needs, preferences, and investment goals. Take the time to research and compare different options, and don't hesitate to reach out to customer support with any questions or concerns. By selecting a platform that aligns with your investment plan and provides the support and resources you need, you'll be well-equipped to implement your strategy and work towards your financial objectives.

Subsection 6.2: Conducting Research and Due Diligence

Before making any investment decisions, it is crucial to conduct thorough research and due diligence. This process involves gathering and analyzing information about potential investments to assess their viability, risks, and potential returns. Neglecting this critical step can lead to uninformed decisions, increased exposure to risk, and potential financial losses.

When conducting research, it's essential to consult a variety of reliable sources to gain a comprehensive understanding of the investment opportunity. Start by reviewing the company's financial statements, such as income statements, balance sheets, and cash flow statements. These documents provide valuable insights into the company's financial health, profitability, and growth potential. Look for trends in revenue, expenses, and profits over time, and compare the company's performance to its competitors in the industry.

In addition to financial statements, research the company's management team, their track record, and their strategy for future growth. Evaluate the company's competitive advantages, market share, and potential risks or challenges it may face. Stay informed about the industry as a whole, including regulatory changes, technological advancements, and consumer trends that could impact the company's performance.

For investors considering mutual funds or exchange-traded funds (ETFs), research the fund's investment objective, portfolio composition, and historical performance. Review the fund's prospectus and fact sheet to understand its investment strategy, fees, and risks. Compare the fund's performance to its benchmark index and peer funds in the same category to assess its relative performance and potential value.

When researching individual stocks, analyze key financial metrics such as price-to-earnings ratio (P/E), price-to-book ratio (P/B), and dividend yield. These metrics can help you assess whether a stock is undervalued, overvalued, or fairly priced compared to its peers and the broader market. Additionally, consider the stock's liquidity, trading volume, and volatility to ensure it aligns with your investment goals and risk tolerance.

Beyond quantitative analysis, qualitative research is equally important. Stay informed about the company's news, press releases, and investor presentations to gauge its future prospects and potential risks. Monitor market sentiment, analyst opinions, and media coverage to identify any red flags or potential controversies that could impact the company's reputation and stock price.

It's also crucial to consider the credibility and reliability of the sources you consult during your research. Stick to reputable financial news outlets, well-established research firms, and official company reports. Be cautious of unsolicited investment advice, rumors, or "hot tips" from unverified sources, as these can often be misleading or manipulative.

Remember that due diligence is an ongoing process that extends beyond the initial investment decision. Regularly monitor your investments, stay informed about market developments, and reassess your portfolio's alignment with your goals and risk tolerance. By dedicating time and effort to thorough research and due diligence, you can make informed investment decisions, minimize potential risks, and increase your chances of long-term financial success.

Subsection 6.3: Monitoring Your Investments and Adjusting as Needed

Implementing your investment plan is not a set-it-and-forget-it endeavor. The financial markets are dynamic, and your personal circumstances may change over time. Therefore, it's crucial to regularly monitor your investments and make adjustments as needed to ensure that your portfolio remains aligned with your goals, risk tolerance, and overall financial situation.

Monitoring your investments involves keeping a close eye on their performance, assessing how they fare compared to relevant benchmarks, and identifying any potential issues or opportunities. This process should be done regularly, such as quarterly or semi-annually, depending on the nature of your investments and your personal preferences.

When monitoring your investments, pay attention to key metrics such as returns, volatility, and asset allocation. Compare the performance of your individual investments to their respective benchmarks or industry averages to gauge whether they are meeting your expectations. If an investment consistently underperforms or experiences significant volatility, it may be a sign to reevaluate its place in your portfolio.

In addition to performance, consider how your investments align with your overall asset allocation strategy. Over time, market movements can cause your portfolio to drift away from your intended allocation, potentially exposing you to more risk than you're comfortable with. For example, if your target allocation is 60% stocks and 40% bonds, but a strong stock market performance has shifted your allocation to 70% stocks, you may need to rebalance your portfolio by selling some stocks and buying more bonds to restore your desired allocation.

Rebalancing is an essential aspect of monitoring your investments and maintaining a well-diversified portfolio. By periodically selling assets that have become overweighted and buying those that have become underweighted, you can help manage risk and potentially enhance long-term returns. Many experts recommend rebalancing your portfolio at least once a year or whenever your asset allocation deviates from your target by a certain threshold, such as 5% or 10%.

Another important reason to monitor your investments is to ensure that they continue to align with your financial goals and risk tolerance. As you move through different stages of life, your investment objectives and risk appetite may change. For example, as you approach retirement, you may want to shift your portfolio towards more conservative investments to preserve your wealth and generate income. Regularly assessing your investments in light of your evolving needs can help you make timely adjustments and stay on track towards your long-term financial objectives.

When making adjustments to your portfolio, it's important to consider the potential tax implications of selling investments, especially in taxable accounts. Selling investments that have appreciated in value may trigger capital gains taxes, which can impact your overall returns. However, tax considerations should not be the sole driver of your investment decisions. Sometimes, it may be necessary to sell an investment and incur a tax liability if it no longer aligns with your goals or if there are better opportunities elsewhere.

Monitoring your investments and making adjustments as needed requires discipline, objectivity, and a long-term perspective. It's essential to avoid making impulsive decisions based on short-term market fluctuations or emotions. Stick to your investment plan, but be willing to adapt when necessary based on sound analysis and guidance from trusted financial professionals.

In summary, regularly monitoring your investments and making strategic adjustments are critical components of implementing a successful investment plan. By staying vigilant, disciplined, and focused on your long-term objectives, you can navigate the ever-changing financial landscape and work towards building a robust and resilient investment portfolio that supports your financial well-being.

Subsection 6.4: Seeking Professional Advice When Necessary

While it's essential to take an active role in managing your investments and financial future, there may be times when seeking professional advice is necessary and beneficial. Navigating the complex world of investing can be overwhelming, especially for those who lack the time, knowledge, or experience to make informed decisions on their own. In such cases, working with a qualified financial professional can provide valuable guidance, support, and peace of mind.

One of the primary reasons to seek professional advice is when you're faced with a major financial decision or life event. This could include starting a new job, getting married, having a child, or approaching retirement. These milestones often involve significant financial considerations, such as adjusting your investment strategy, updating your insurance coverage, or creating a comprehensive financial plan. A financial advisor can help you assess your options, identify potential risks and opportunities, and develop a tailored plan that aligns with your goals and circumstances.

Another situation where professional advice can be invaluable is when you're unsure about your investment strategy or feel that your portfolio is underperforming. A skilled financial advisor can review your current investments, assess your risk tolerance, and recommend adjustments or new opportunities that may better suit your needs. They can also help you understand the potential implications of different investment choices, such as the impact of fees, taxes, and market volatility on your returns.

Moreover, seeking professional advice can be particularly important when you're dealing with complex financial products or strategies. For example, if you're considering investing in alternative assets, such as real estate or private equity, or if you're interested in using advanced tax optimization techniques, working with a knowledgeable professional can help you navigate the intricacies and potential pitfalls of these approaches. They can provide expert insights, due diligence, and ongoing support to help you make informed decisions and manage your investments effectively.

It's important to note that not all financial professionals are created equal, and it's crucial to choose an advisor who is qualified, reputable, and aligned with your interests. Look for professionals who hold relevant certifications, such as the Certified Financial Planner (CFP) or Chartered Financial Analyst (CFA) designations, and who have a proven track record of success in helping clients achieve their financial goals. Consider factors such as their experience, expertise, communication style, and fee structure when evaluating potential advisors.

When working with a financial professional, it's essential to establish clear expectations and maintain open communication. Be honest about your financial situation, goals, and concerns, and ask questions to ensure that you fully understand their recommendations and the reasoning behind them. Remember that while an advisor can provide valuable guidance, ultimately, the final decisions about your investments and financial future rest with you.

In conclusion, seeking professional advice when necessary is a smart and proactive step in implementing your investment plan. Whether you're facing a major financial decision, feeling uncertain about your investment strategy, or dealing with complex financial products, working with a qualified and trusted advisor can provide the expertise, support, and peace of mind you need to make informed choices and stay on track towards your long-term financial goals.

Summary: Turning Your Investment Plan into Action

Implementing your investment plan is a crucial step in turning your financial goals into reality. By carefully selecting the right investment platform and brokerage, conducting thorough research and due diligence, regularly monitoring your investments, and seeking professional advice when necessary, you can navigate the complex world of investing with confidence and purpose.

Remember that investing is not a one-time event but an ongoing journey that requires discipline, patience, and adaptability. As you put your plan into action, stay focused on your long-term objectives and avoid getting swayed by short-term market fluctuations or emotions. Trust in the power of time and compounding, and remain committed to your strategy even in the face of challenges or setbacks.

Implementing your investment plan is not about achieving perfection but about making progress towards your financial goals. Celebrate your successes, learn from your mistakes, and maintain a growth mindset as you continue to expand your knowledge and refine your approach. By taking control of your financial future and actively managing your investments, you are empowering yourself to create the life you envision and secure a brighter tomorrow.

As you embark on this exciting journey, remember that investing is not just about numbers and returns but about the impact it can have on your life and the lives of those around you. By making informed decisions, taking calculated risks, and staying true to your values and goals, you can harness the power of investing to achieve financial freedom, support your loved ones, and make a positive difference in the world.

So, take a deep breath, trust in the groundwork you've laid, and take that first step towards implementing your investment plan. The road ahead may be uncertain, but with knowledge, discipline, and a steadfast commitment to your goals, you have the power to shape your financial destiny and create a legacy that will endure for generations to come.

Section 7: Tax Considerations and Investment Accounts

Picture this: you've been diligently investing your hard-earned money, watching your portfolio grow, and feeling confident about your financial future. But then, tax season rolls around, and suddenly, you're faced with a daunting realization—you need to pay taxes on your investment gains. This eye-opening moment highlights the crucial role that tax considerations play in your overall investment strategy.

In the world of investing, it's not just about how much you earn but also about how much you get to keep. Taxes can take a significant bite out of your investment returns, making it essential to understand the tax implications of your investment decisions. By being strategic about the types of investment accounts you use and the way you manage your investments, you can potentially minimize your tax liabilities and keep more of your money working for you.

In this section, we'll dive into the complex world of taxes and investment accounts, demystifying the jargon and providing you with practical insights to help you navigate this critical aspect of your financial journey. We'll explore the different types of investment accounts, such as taxable accounts and tax-advantaged retirement accounts, and discuss their unique characteristics and benefits. You'll learn how to make informed decisions about where to allocate your investments based on your tax situation and financial goals.

Moreover, we'll delve into tax-efficient investing strategies that can help you minimize the impact of taxes on your investment returns. From understanding the difference between short-term and long-term capital gains to considering tax-loss harvesting and asset location, we'll provide you with valuable tools and techniques to optimize your investment portfolio from a tax perspective.

By the end of this section, you'll have a clearer understanding of how taxes and investment accounts interplay, empowering you to make smarter, more tax-efficient investment choices. Whether you're just starting your investment journey or looking to refine your existing strategy, the knowledge you gain here will be invaluable in helping you keep more of your hard-earned money and accelerating your progress towards your financial goals. So, let's dive in and explore the world of tax considerations and investment accounts together!

Subsection 7.1: Taxable Investment Accounts

When it comes to investing, one of the most common types of accounts you'll encounter is the taxable investment account. These accounts, also known as brokerage accounts or non-registered accounts, allow you to invest in a wide range of financial instruments, such as stocks, bonds, mutual funds, and exchange-traded funds (ETFs). While taxable investment accounts offer flexibility and easy access to your funds, it's crucial to understand their tax implications to make informed decisions about your investments.

One of the key characteristics of taxable investment accounts is that any income or gains generated within the account are subject to taxation in the year they are realized. This means that if you sell an investment for a profit, you'll need to report the capital gain on your tax return and pay taxes accordingly. The tax rate applied to your capital gains depends on how long you held the investment before selling it. Short-term capital gains, which are gains from investments held for one year or less, are taxed at your ordinary income tax rate. Long-term capital gains, on the other hand, are gains from investments held for more than one year and are typically taxed at a lower rate, depending on your income level.

In addition to capital gains, taxable investment accounts are also subject to taxes on other types of investment income, such as dividends and interest. Dividends, which are payments made by companies to their shareholders, are often taxed at a lower rate than ordinary income, provided they meet certain qualifications. Interest income, such as the interest earned on bonds or cash holdings, is generally taxed at your ordinary income tax rate.

It's important to note that the tax treatment of investments within a taxable account can vary depending on the specific type of investment. For example, certain investments, such as municipal bonds, may be exempt from federal income taxes, while others, like real estate investment trusts (REITs), may have unique tax considerations. Understanding the tax implications of each investment type is crucial for making informed decisions and optimizing your tax strategy.

One potential advantage of taxable investment accounts is the ability to offset capital gains with capital losses. If you sell an investment for a loss, you can use that loss to offset capital gains from other investments, effectively reducing your overall tax liability. This strategy, known as tax-loss harvesting, can be a powerful tool for minimizing the impact of taxes on your investment returns.

When managing your taxable investment account, it's essential to keep accurate records of your transactions, including the purchase and sale dates, prices, and any dividend or interest income received. These records will be necessary when filing your tax returns and can help you make informed decisions about when to buy or sell investments based on their tax implications.

In summary, taxable investment accounts are a common and flexible option for investing, but it's crucial to understand their tax treatment to make the most of your investment strategy. By being aware of the tax implications of different types of investments, utilizing strategies like tax-loss harvesting, and keeping accurate records, you can navigate the world of taxable investing with greater confidence and potentially minimize the impact of taxes on your investment returns.

Subsection 7.2: Tax-Advantaged Retirement Accounts: IRAs and 401(k)s

Saving for retirement is one of the most important financial goals you'll ever pursue, and fortunately, there are powerful tools available to help you achieve it. Enter tax-advantaged retirement accounts, such as Individual Retirement Accounts (IRAs) and 401(k)s. These investment vehicles offer unique benefits that can supercharge your retirement savings and provide significant tax advantages along the way.

Let's start with IRAs, which come in two main flavors: Traditional and Roth. With a Traditional IRA, your contributions are tax-deductible, meaning you can lower your taxable income in the year you make the contribution. Your investments grow tax-deferred, and you pay taxes on withdrawals in retirement. On the other hand, Roth IRA contributions are made with after-tax dollars, but your investments grow tax-free, and you can enjoy tax-free withdrawals in retirement, provided you meet certain requirements.

The beauty of IRAs lies in their flexibility and control. You can open an IRA at various financial institutions, such as banks, brokerages, or robo-advisors, and you have a wide range of investment options to choose from, including stocks, bonds, mutual funds, and ETFs. You can tailor your investment strategy to your specific goals and risk tolerance, and you have the freedom to change your investments as your needs evolve.

Now, let's turn our attention to 401(k)s, which are employer-sponsored retirement plans. If your employer offers a 401(k), you can contribute a portion of your paycheck directly into the plan, often with the added benefit of an employer match. Like Traditional IRAs, your 401(k) contributions are made with pre-tax dollars, lowering your current taxable income. Your investments grow tax-deferred, and you pay taxes on withdrawals in retirement.

One of the standout features of 401(k)s is the potential for higher contribution limits compared to IRAs. As of 2021, you can contribute up to $19,500 per year to your 401(k), with an additional $6,500 catch-up contribution allowed if you're age 50 or older. This higher limit allows you to save more for retirement and take full advantage of the tax benefits.

Another advantage of 401(k)s is the convenience factor. Since contributions are automatically deducted from your paycheck, you can easily establish a consistent savings habit without having to remember to make manual contributions. Plus, many employers offer a match on a portion of your contributions, essentially providing you with free money to boost your retirement savings.

It's worth noting that some employers also offer a Roth 401(k) option, which combines features of both Roth and Traditional accounts. With a Roth 401(k), your contributions are made with after-tax dollars, but your investments grow tax-free, and you can enjoy tax-free withdrawals in retirement, similar to a Roth IRA.

When it comes to choosing between a Traditional or Roth account, whether an IRA or 401(k), the decision largely depends on your current tax situation and future expectations. If you expect to be in a lower tax bracket in retirement, a Traditional account may be more beneficial, as you'll pay taxes at a lower rate when you withdraw funds. Conversely, if you anticipate being in a higher tax bracket in retirement, a Roth account may be more advantageous, as you'll enjoy tax-free withdrawals.

Regardless of which type of account you choose, the key is to start saving as early as possible and contribute consistently over time. By taking advantage of tax-advantaged retirement accounts like IRAs and 401(k)s, you can harness the power of compound growth, minimize your tax liabilities, and set yourself up for a more secure and comfortable retirement. Remember, the earlier you start, the more time your money has to grow, so don't delay in making retirement savings a top priority in your financial plan.

Subsection 7.3: Tax-Efficient Investing Strategies

When it comes to investing, it's not just about how much you earn but also about how much you get to keep after taxes. Implementing tax-efficient investing strategies can help you minimize your tax liabilities and maximize your investment returns over the long term. By being strategic about how you structure your portfolio and manage your investments, you can potentially save a significant amount of money on taxes and keep more of your hard-earned wealth working for you.

One key strategy for tax-efficient investing is to be mindful of asset location. This means strategically placing your investments in the most tax-advantaged accounts based on their tax treatment. For example, investments that generate high levels of taxable income, such as bonds or REITs, may be better suited for tax-deferred accounts like Traditional IRAs or 401(k)s. By doing so, you can defer paying taxes on the income until you withdraw the funds in retirement, when you may be in a lower tax bracket. On the other hand, investments that generate tax-efficient returns, such as qualified dividends or long-term capital gains, may be better held in taxable accounts, where they can benefit from lower tax rates.

Another powerful tax-efficient investing strategy is tax-loss harvesting. This involves selling investments that have declined in value to realize capital losses, which can then be used to offset capital gains from other investments or even ordinary income, up to a certain limit. By strategically realizing losses, you can potentially reduce your overall tax liability and free up more money to reinvest in your portfolio. However, it's important to be mindful of the wash-sale rule, which prohibits repurchasing substantially identical securities within 30 days before or after the sale, as this can negate the tax benefits.

Diversification is not only important for managing investment risk but also for tax efficiency. By holding a diverse mix of investments across different asset classes, sectors, and geographies, you can potentially minimize the impact of any single investment on your overall tax situation. Additionally, diversifying your portfolio with tax-efficient investments, such as index funds or ETFs that track broad market indices, can help reduce the turnover within your portfolio and minimize the realization of capital gains.

When it comes to selling investments, being strategic about the timing and method can also have significant tax implications. For example, holding investments for longer than one year before selling can qualify them for lower long-term capital gains tax rates, as opposed to short-term capital gains, which are taxed at ordinary income rates. Additionally, using specific lot identification methods, such as first-in, first-out (FIFO) or highest-in, first-out (HIFO), when selling partial positions can help optimize your tax liability based on the specific shares being sold.

Another tax-efficient investing strategy to consider is donating appreciated securities to charity. By donating investments that have increased in value directly to a charitable organization, you can potentially avoid paying capital gains taxes on the appreciation while still claiming a tax deduction for the full market value of the donated securities. This can be a win-win situation, allowing you to support causes you care about while also minimizing your tax liability.

Finally, it's important to stay informed about tax laws and regulations, as they can change over time and impact your investing strategies. Consulting with a qualified tax professional or financial advisor can help you stay up-to-date on the latest tax-efficient investing techniques and ensure that your portfolio is optimized for your specific tax situation.

In summary, implementing tax-efficient investing strategies is a crucial component of maximizing your investment returns and building long-term wealth. By being strategic about asset location, utilizing tax-loss harvesting, diversifying your portfolio, timing your sales, considering charitable donations, and staying informed about tax laws, you can potentially minimize your tax liabilities and keep more of your money working for you.

Remember, it's not just about what you earn but also about what you keep, and tax-efficient investing can help you achieve your financial goals more effectively.

Summary: Navigating Taxes and Investment Accounts for Financial Success

In this section, we've explored the crucial role that tax considerations and investment account choices play in your overall financial strategy. By understanding the tax implications of different investment vehicles and making informed decisions about where to allocate your assets, you can potentially minimize your tax liabilities and keep more of your hard-earned money working for you.

We've delved into the world of taxable investment accounts, examining how capital gains, dividends, and interest income are taxed and discussing strategies like tax-loss harvesting to optimize your tax situation. We've also highlighted the importance of keeping accurate records and staying informed about the tax treatment of different investment types.

Furthermore, we've explored the powerful tax advantages offered by retirement accounts like Traditional and Roth IRAs and 401(k)s. By understanding the differences between these accounts and leveraging their unique benefits, you can supercharge your retirement savings and potentially enjoy significant tax savings along the way.

Finally, we've discussed various tax-efficient investing strategies, such as strategic asset location, diversification, timing of sales, and charitable donations of appreciated securities. By implementing these techniques and staying informed about evolving tax laws, you can create a more tax-efficient portfolio and maximize your long-term wealth accumulation.

As you continue your financial journey, remember that tax considerations and investment account choices are not one-time decisions but rather ongoing aspects of your overall financial plan. By staying proactive, informed, and strategic, you can navigate the complex world of taxes and investment accounts with confidence and set yourself up for long-term financial success.

In the next section, we'll explore common investing mistakes and how to avoid them, further empowering you to make sound financial decisions and reach your goals with greater certainty. So, let's continue our journey towards financial mastery, armed with the knowledge and tools to create a brighter, more prosperous future.

Section 8: Avoiding Common Investing Mistakes

Picture this: you've done your research, carefully selected your investments, and feel confident about your financial future. But then, the market takes an unexpected turn, and you find yourself making hasty decisions driven by emotions rather than logic. Suddenly, your well-planned investment strategy is derailed, and you're left wondering what went wrong.

Investing can be a thrilling and rewarding journey, but it's not without its pitfalls. Even the most experienced investors can fall prey to common mistakes that can undermine their financial goals. In this section, we'll explore some of the most prevalent investing missteps and provide you with the knowledge and tools to avoid them.

From the perils of emotional investing and market timing to the dangers of chasing past performance and neglecting diversification, we'll delve into the psychological traps and behavioral biases that can lead investors astray. By recognizing these common errors and understanding how to overcome them, you'll be better equipped to make rational, informed decisions about your investments.

But avoiding mistakes isn't just about what not to do; it's also about adopting positive habits and strategies that can help you stay on track. We'll discuss the importance of maintaining a long-term perspective, setting realistic expectations, and regularly reviewing and rebalancing your portfolio. By incorporating these best practices into your investment approach, you'll be better positioned to weather market fluctuations and achieve your financial objectives.

So, whether you're a novice investor just starting out or a seasoned pro looking to refine your skills, this section is designed to help you navigate the complex world of investing with confidence and clarity. By learning to recognize and avoid common pitfalls, you'll be empowered to make smarter, more informed decisions about your money and take control of your financial destiny. Let's dive in and discover how to sidestep the most common investing mistakes and pave the way for a more secure financial future.

Subsection 8.1: Emotional Investing and Market Timing

Investing can be an emotional roller coaster, with the ups and downs of the market often mirroring the highs and lows of our own feelings. When the market is soaring, it's easy to get caught up in the excitement and feel invincible. Conversely, when the market takes a tumble, panic and fear can quickly set in, leading to impulsive decisions that can derail even the most well-crafted investment strategy.

One of the most common mistakes investors make is letting their emotions dictate their investment choices. This can manifest in various ways, such as selling off investments in a panic when the market dips or chasing after the latest hot stock based on a fear of missing out (FOMO). Emotional investing can lead to a vicious cycle of buying high and selling low, the exact opposite of what a successful investor should aim for.

Another related pitfall is attempting to time the market, which involves trying to predict when the market will rise or fall and making investment decisions accordingly. While it may be tempting to try to outsmart the market and capitalize on short-term fluctuations, the reality is that even the most experienced investors and financial experts struggle to consistently and accurately predict market movements.

Numerous studies have shown that attempting to time the market often leads to subpar investment returns compared to a simple buy-and-hold strategy. In fact, a study by Dalbar, a financial research firm, found that over a 20-year period ending in 2020, the average investor underperformed the S&P 500 by a staggering 4.2% per year, largely due to attempts at market timing and emotional decision-making.

So, how can investors avoid falling prey to emotional investing and market timing? The key is to develop a rational, disciplined approach to investing that takes emotion out of the equation. This involves creating a well-diversified portfolio aligned with your long-term financial goals and risk tolerance, and sticking to it through market ups and downs.

It also means resisting the urge to constantly monitor your investments or react to short-term market fluctuations. Instead, focus on the big picture and trust in the power of time in the market, rather than trying to time the market. By staying the course and maintaining a long-term perspective, you'll be better positioned to weather market volatility and achieve your financial objectives.

Of course, this is easier said than done, especially when emotions are running high. That's why it's essential to have a solid investment plan in place before emotions take over. By setting clear goals, establishing a diversified portfolio, and automating your investments through tools like dollar-cost averaging, you can minimize the impact of emotional decision-making and stay on track.

Ultimately, successful investing is about controlling what you can, which is your own behavior and reactions to market events. By recognizing the dangers of emotional investing and market timing, and taking proactive steps to avoid these pitfalls, you can position yourself for long-term financial success and peace of mind.

Subsection 8.2: Chasing Past Performance and Trends

In the world of investing, it's natural to be drawn to assets or strategies that have recently performed well or are currently trending. After all, who wouldn't want to jump on the bandwagon of a seemingly surefire way to make money? However, this tendency to chase past performance and trends can be a dangerous trap that often leads to suboptimal investment outcomes.

One of the most common manifestations of this pitfall is the "hot hand fallacy," which refers to the belief that an investment that has performed well in the recent past is likely to continue doing so in the future. Investors may flock to a particular stock, fund, or asset class based solely on its recent track record, without considering the underlying fundamentals or the potential for mean reversion.

The problem with this approach is that past performance is not necessarily indicative of future results. Just because an investment has had a good run doesn't mean it will continue to outperform indefinitely. In fact, research has shown that asset classes and investment strategies that have outperformed in the recent past often underperform in the subsequent period, a phenomenon known as "reversion to the mean."

Another related issue is the tendency to chase investment trends or "hot" sectors, such as technology or cryptocurrency. While these areas may experience periods of rapid growth and excitement, they can also be subject to excessive hype, overvaluation, and eventual correction. Investors who jump on the bandwagon too late may find themselves buying at the peak and suffering significant losses when the trend inevitably cools off.

The psychological factors behind this behavior are understandable. The fear of missing out (FOMO) can be a powerful motivator, as can the desire to follow the crowd and feel like part of a winning team. However, these emotions can cloud judgment and lead to impulsive decisions that deviate from a well-planned investment strategy.

So, how can investors avoid falling into the trap of chasing past performance and trends? The key is to maintain a disciplined, long-term approach to investing that is grounded in fundamental analysis and risk management. This means looking beyond short-term fluctuations and focusing on the underlying value and growth potential of individual investments.

It also means having a well-diversified portfolio that is not overly concentrated in any one asset class, sector, or geographic region. By spreading investments across a range of uncorrelated assets, investors can mitigate the impact of any one investment's underperformance and smooth out overall returns.

Another important strategy is to resist the urge to constantly tinker with one's portfolio based on short-term market movements or news events. While it may be tempting to try to capitalize on the latest trend or "hot tip," this approach often leads to excessive trading, higher costs, and subpar returns. Instead, investors should stick to a disciplined rebalancing strategy that maintains their desired asset allocation over time.

Finally, it's essential to have realistic expectations about investment returns and to avoid chasing unrealistic or unsustainable performance. While it's natural to want to maximize returns, it's important to remember that investing is a long-term game that requires patience, discipline, and a willingness to ride out short-term volatility.

By avoiding the pitfalls of chasing past performance and trends, and instead focusing on a fundamentally sound, diversified investment strategy, investors can position themselves for long-term success and financial security. While it may not always be the most exciting approach, slow and steady often wins the race when it comes to building wealth over time.

Subsection 8.3: Failing to Diversify and Overconcentration

One of the most fundamental principles of investing is diversification, which involves spreading your investments across a range of asset classes, sectors, and geographic regions to mitigate risk. However, many investors make the mistake of failing to adequately diversify their portfolios, instead concentrating their holdings in a small number of investments or sectors. This overconcentration can leave them vulnerable to significant losses if those particular investments or sectors experience a downturn.

The allure of overconcentration often stems from a belief in one's ability to pick winners or a desire to capitalize on a particular trend or opportunity. For example, an investor may have a strong conviction about a particular stock or sector and decide to allocate a large portion of their portfolio to that investment. While this approach can lead to outsized returns if the investment performs well, it also comes with a high level of risk.

The dangers of overconcentration are well-documented. Consider the dot-com bubble of the late 1990s, when many investors piled into technology stocks, believing that the sector could only go up. When the bubble eventually burst, those who had concentrated their portfolios in tech stocks suffered significant losses. More recently, the COVID-19 pandemic highlighted the risks of overconcentration in sectors such as hospitality and travel, which were hit particularly hard by the economic fallout.

Diversification, on the other hand, helps to mitigate these risks by ensuring that no single investment or sector has an outsized impact on the overall portfolio. By spreading investments across a range of assets, investors can reduce their exposure to any one particular risk factor and smooth out overall returns over time.

One way to think about diversification is through the lens of the old adage, "Don't put all your eggs in one basket." Just as it would be risky to carry all of your eggs in a single basket that could easily be dropped or crushed, it's risky to concentrate all of your investments in a single stock, sector, or asset class that could be impacted by unforeseen events or market shifts.

So, how can investors ensure that they are adequately diversified? One approach is to use a combination of asset allocation and individual security selection to build a well-rounded portfolio. This might involve investing in a mix of stocks, bonds, and other assets, as well as diversifying within each asset class by investing in a range of sectors, geographies, and individual securities.

Another strategy is to use investment vehicles such as mutual funds or exchange-traded funds (ETFs) that provide instant diversification by holding a basket of securities across different asset classes and sectors. These funds can be a simple and cost-effective way for investors to achieve diversification without having to manage a large number of individual holdings.

It's important to note that diversification does not guarantee profits or protect against losses in a declining market. However, it does help to manage risk and reduce the impact of any one investment's performance on the overall portfolio.

In addition to diversifying across asset classes and sectors, investors should also consider diversifying across time horizons. This means holding a mix of short-term, medium-term, and long-term investments to balance the potential for growth with the need for stability and liquidity.

Ultimately, the key to avoiding the pitfalls of overconcentration and inadequate diversification is to have a well-thought-out investment plan that takes into account your financial goals, risk tolerance, and time horizon. By sticking to a disciplined, diversified approach and resisting the temptation to chase short-term gains or concentrate bets, investors can position themselves for long-term success and financial security.

Subsection 8.4: Neglecting Fees and Expenses

When it comes to investing, it's easy to focus solely on potential returns and overlook the impact of fees and expenses. However, neglecting these costs can have a significant detrimental effect on your investment outcomes over the long term. In fact, even seemingly small differences in fees can compound over time, eating away at your returns and hindering your ability to reach your financial goals.

One of the most common types of fees investors face are expense ratios, which are charged by mutual funds and exchange-traded funds (ETFs) to cover the costs of managing and operating the fund. These fees are expressed as a percentage of your investment and can range from a few basis points (0.01%) to over 2% annually. While a 1% difference in fees may not seem like much in the short term, over a 20 or 30-year investment horizon, it can add up to tens of thousands of dollars in lost returns.

To illustrate this point, let's consider a hypothetical example. Suppose you invest $10,000 in a mutual fund with an annual expense ratio of 1%, and another $10,000 in a similar fund with an expense ratio of 0.25%. Assuming both funds earn an average annual return of 7% before fees, after 30 years, the fund with the 1% expense ratio would have grown to approximately $57,435, while the fund with the 0.25% expense ratio would have grown to around $70,964. That's a difference of over $13,529, simply due to the impact of fees.

But expense ratios aren't the only fees investors need to be aware of. Other common costs include transaction fees, such as commissions and trading fees, which can add up quickly if you're frequently buying and selling investments. There are also account maintenance fees, which some brokerages charge on a monthly or annual basis, and redemption fees, which some mutual funds charge when you sell your shares within a certain timeframe.

To minimize the impact of fees on your investment returns, it's essential to be proactive and informed. When selecting investments, look for low-cost options such as index funds and ETFs, which tend to have lower expense ratios than actively managed funds. Be sure to read the fine print and understand all the fees associated with an investment before committing your money.

It's also important to consider the value you're getting in exchange for the fees you pay. In some cases, paying a higher fee may be justified if the investment offers unique benefits or has a track record of outperformance. However, it's crucial to critically evaluate these claims and ensure that the potential benefits outweigh the costs.

Another strategy to minimize fees is to be mindful of your trading frequency. Frequent buying and selling not only incurs transaction costs but can also lead to behavioral pitfalls such as trying to time the market. By adopting a long-term, buy-and-hold approach and avoiding unnecessary trades, you can keep your costs down and improve your overall returns.

Finally, it's worth periodically reviewing your investment accounts and evaluating the fees you're paying. As your portfolio grows and your needs change, you may find that certain fees that once seemed reasonable are no longer justified. Don't be afraid to shop around and compare costs between different brokerages and investment providers to ensure you're getting the best value for your money.

In summary, neglecting fees and expenses is a common pitfall that can have a significant negative impact on your investment returns over the long run. By being proactive, informed, and strategic in your investment choices, you can minimize these costs and keep more of your hard-earned money working for you. Remember, every dollar you save in fees is a dollar that can continue to grow and compound over time, bringing you one step closer to achieving your financial goals.

Summary: Navigating the Pitfalls for Long-Term Investing Success

Throughout this section, we've explored some of the most common mistakes investors make and the strategies to avoid them. From the perils of emotional investing and market timing to the dangers of chasing past performance and neglecting diversification, these pitfalls can derail even the most well-intentioned investment plans.

However, by recognizing these common traps and implementing the strategies discussed, you can position yourself for long-term investing success. Remember to maintain a disciplined, rational approach to investing that takes emotion out of the equation and focuses on the fundamentals. Resist the temptation to constantly monitor your investments or react to short-term market fluctuations, and instead trust in the power of time in the market.

Diversification remains a key principle in mitigating risk and smoothing out returns over time. By spreading your investments across a range of asset classes, sectors, and geographies, you can reduce your exposure to any one particular risk factor and improve your overall portfolio resilience.

Finally, don't underestimate the impact of fees and expenses on your long-term investment outcomes. By being proactive, informed, and strategic in your investment choices, you can minimize these costs and keep more of your money working for you.

As you continue your investing journey, keep these lessons in mind and stay committed to your long-term financial goals. By avoiding common mistakes and staying the course, you'll be well on your way to achieving the financial security and freedom you desire. Remember, successful investing is not about timing the market, but about time in the market, patience, and discipline. With the knowledge gained from this section, you're now equipped to navigate the pitfalls and make informed, confident decisions about your financial future.

Chapter Summary: Investing Wisely for a Secure Financial Future

Investing is a crucial component of building long-term wealth and securing your financial future. By understanding the various investment options available, such as stocks, bonds, mutual funds, ETFs, real estate, and alternative investments, you can make informed decisions that align with your goals and risk tolerance. Building a diversified investment portfolio is key to managing risk and maximizing returns, and this can be achieved through effective asset allocation and regular rebalancing.

Adopting the right investing strategy, whether it be active or passive, value or growth-oriented, or focused on income generation, depends on your individual circumstances and preferences. Navigating market cycles and economic conditions requires patience, discipline, and a long-term perspective. By staying informed, conducting thorough research, and seeking professional advice when necessary, you can make sound investment decisions and avoid common pitfalls.

Remember, investing is not a one-time event but a lifelong journey. As you implement your investment plan, be sure to consider tax implications, choose the appropriate investment accounts, and monitor your progress regularly. By taking control of your investments and staying committed to your financial goals, you can build a solid foundation for a prosperous future and enjoy the rewards of your hard work and diligence.

Chapter 8: Retirement Planning: Securing Your Financial Future

Imagine yourself in your golden years, free from the daily grind of work and filled with the excitement of pursuing your passions and spending time with loved ones. This idyllic vision of retirement is what many of us aspire to, but it doesn't happen by chance. Securing a comfortable and fulfilling retirement requires careful planning and strategic decision-making throughout your working life.

Retirement planning is not just for the wealthy or those nearing the end of their careers. It's a crucial aspect of personal finance that everyone should prioritize, regardless of age or income level. By starting early and consistently working towards your retirement goals, you can build a solid foundation for your financial future and enjoy the peace of mind that comes with knowing you're on track to achieve your dreams.

In this chapter, we'll dive deep into the world of retirement planning, exploring the key concepts, strategies, and tools you need to know to create a roadmap to a secure and enjoyable retirement. We'll discuss the importance of setting clear retirement goals, understanding the various retirement savings vehicles available, and developing an investment strategy that aligns with your risk tolerance and time horizon.

But retirement planning isn't just about numbers and spreadsheets. It's also about envisioning the lifestyle you want to lead in your post-work years and taking steps to make that vision a reality. We'll explore the non-financial aspects of retirement planning, such as considering your housing options, planning for healthcare needs, and finding purpose and fulfillment in your daily life.

Whether you're just starting your career or already counting down the years to retirement, this chapter will provide you with the knowledge and inspiration you need to take control of your financial future and create the retirement of your dreams. So let's get started on this exciting journey together, and discover how you can secure a comfortable and rewarding retirement through smart planning and strategic decision-making.

Section 1: The Importance of Retirement Planning

Imagine yourself in your golden years, free from the daily grind of work and finally able to pursue your lifelong dreams. Perhaps you envision traveling the world, spending quality time with loved ones, or dedicating yourself to a beloved hobby. Whatever your aspirations may be, one thing is certain: a comfortable and fulfilling retirement requires careful planning and preparation.

Far too often, people put off thinking about retirement until it's too late, assuming that they'll have plenty of time to sort out their finances later in life. However, the reality is that the earlier you start planning for retirement, the more likely you are to achieve your goals and enjoy a worry-free future.

In this section, we'll explore the critical importance of retirement planning and why it should be a top priority for everyone, regardless of age or income level. We'll examine the changing landscape of retirement, the risks of delaying planning, and the numerous benefits of starting early. By the end of this section, you'll have a clear understanding of why retirement planning is not just a smart financial move, but a necessary step in securing your long-term happiness and well-being.

Subsection 1.1: The Changing Landscape of Retirement

Gone are the days when retirement was synonymous with a gold watch, a guaranteed pension, and a leisurely lifestyle. In recent decades, the retirement landscape has undergone a dramatic transformation, shifting the responsibility of planning and saving for retirement squarely onto the shoulders of individuals.

One of the most significant changes has been the decline of traditional defined-benefit pension plans. In the past, many employers offered these plans, which promised a fixed monthly income throughout retirement based on factors such as salary and years of service. However, as companies sought to reduce costs and limit their long-term liabilities, defined-benefit plans have become increasingly rare, replaced by defined-contribution plans like 401(k)s.

With defined-contribution plans, the onus is on employees to make investment decisions and bear the risks associated with market fluctuations. This shift has placed a greater responsibility on individuals to actively participate in their retirement planning, as the amount they save and the performance of their investments directly impact their retirement income.

Moreover, the rise of the gig economy and freelance work has further complicated the retirement landscape. Without the traditional benefits and stability of full-time employment, many individuals find themselves navigating the challenges of saving for retirement on their own, without the guidance or support of an employer-sponsored plan.

Compounding these challenges is the fact that people are living longer than ever before. While increased longevity is undoubtedly a positive development, it also means that individuals must plan for a potentially longer retirement period, requiring more significant savings and careful financial management to ensure their resources last a lifetime.

Furthermore, the uncertainty surrounding Social Security and the increasing cost of healthcare in retirement add additional layers of complexity to the retirement planning process. With the long-term sustainability of Social Security in question and healthcare costs continuing to rise, individuals must take a proactive approach to ensure they have sufficient funds to cover these expenses in their golden years.

In light of these changes, it has become increasingly clear that the traditional notion of retirement as a time of complete leisure and freedom from financial concerns is no longer a reality for most people. Instead, retirement planning has become a lifelong process that requires ongoing effort, education, and adaptation to navigate the evolving landscape successfully.

By understanding these shifts and taking an active role in their retirement planning, individuals can better position themselves to overcome the challenges posed by the changing retirement landscape. Through diligent saving, informed investment decisions, and a commitment to ongoing learning and adjustment, they can work towards building a secure and fulfilling retirement, even in the face of uncertainty.

Subsection 1.2: The Risks of Delaying Retirement Planning

Procrastination is a common human tendency, and when it comes to retirement planning, many people fall into the trap of thinking, "I'll start saving later" or "I have plenty of time." However, delaying retirement planning can have serious consequences that can jeopardize your financial future and limit your options in your golden years.

One of the most significant risks of postponing retirement planning is missing out on the power of compound interest. When you save and invest money over a long period, your wealth grows exponentially as the returns on your investments begin to generate their own returns. The earlier you start saving, the more time your money has to grow, and the less you'll need to save each month to reach your goals. Conversely, delaying retirement planning means you'll have to save more money each month to catch up, which can be challenging, especially as you approach retirement age.

Another risk of delaying retirement planning is that you may not have enough time to recover from financial setbacks. Life is unpredictable, and unexpected events such as job loss, health issues, or market downturns can derail your financial plans. If you haven't started saving early, you may not have the financial cushion to weather these storms and stay on track for retirement. The earlier you start planning, the more time you have to adapt to changing circumstances and make necessary adjustments to your strategy.

Delaying retirement planning can also limit your investment options and potential returns. When you're young, you can afford to take on more investment risk because you have time to recover from market fluctuations. As you get closer to retirement, however, you may need to shift your portfolio to more conservative investments to protect your savings. If you wait too long to start investing, you may miss out on the potential for higher returns and have to settle for lower-yield options that may not provide enough income in retirement.

Furthermore, postponing retirement planning can lead to increased financial stress and anxiety as you approach retirement age. Without a clear plan in place, you may worry about whether you'll have enough money to support your desired lifestyle in retirement or if you'll have to work longer than planned. This stress can take a toll on your mental and physical health, affecting your overall well-being and quality of life.

Delaying retirement planning can also impact your ability to take advantage of certain tax benefits and employer-sponsored retirement plans. For example, if you wait too long to start contributing to a 401(k) or IRA, you may miss out on valuable employer matching contributions or tax deductions that can help you save more money for retirement. The earlier you start participating in these plans, the more you can benefit from their features and grow your retirement savings.

In addition, delaying retirement planning can limit your options for retirement income and force you to rely more heavily on Social Security benefits. While Social Security can provide a valuable source of income in retirement, it was never intended to be the sole source of support. By starting to plan early, you can explore various retirement income streams, such as investments, rental properties, or part-time work, that can supplement your Social Security benefits and provide a more comfortable and secure retirement.

In conclusion, the risks of delaying retirement planning are significant and can have long-lasting consequences for your financial future. By starting to plan early, you can harness the power of compound interest, create a financial cushion to weather unexpected events, maximize your investment options, reduce financial stress, take advantage of tax benefits and employer-sponsored plans, and explore diverse retirement income streams. Don't let procrastination jeopardize your golden years – start planning for retirement today and take control of your financial destiny.

Subsection 1.3: The Benefits of Starting Early

When it comes to retirement planning, the old adage "the early bird catches the worm" couldn't be more apt. Starting to plan and save for retirement early in your career can have a profound impact on your financial future, offering numerous advantages that can make the difference between a comfortable retirement and one fraught with financial stress.

One of the most significant benefits of starting early is the power of compound interest. Compound interest is often referred to as the eighth wonder of the world, and for good reason. When you save and invest money over a long period, your wealth grows exponentially as the returns on your investments begin to generate their own returns. The earlier you start saving, the more time your money has to grow, and the less you'll need to save each month to reach your goals.

To illustrate the power of compound interest, let's consider an example. Imagine two individuals, Sarah and David, both age 25. Sarah starts saving $200 per month for retirement, while David decides to wait until age 35 to begin saving. Assuming an annual return of 7% and retirement at age 65, Sarah will have accumulated approximately $479,126 by the time she retires. In contrast, David, who started saving the same amount but ten years later, will have only around $226,706 at retirement. This significant difference demonstrates the tremendous advantage of starting early and allowing compound interest to work its magic over time.

In addition to harnessing the power of compound interest, starting retirement planning early gives you more time to develop good financial habits and make informed decisions about your future. When you begin thinking about retirement at a young age, you have the opportunity to educate yourself about personal finance, explore different investment options, and create a long-term plan that aligns with your goals and values. By starting early, you can avoid the stress and pressure of trying to play catch-up later in life when you may have less flexibility and fewer resources.

Moreover, starting retirement planning early allows you to take advantage of tax benefits and employer-sponsored retirement plans that can help you save more money in the long run. For example, contributing to a 401(k) or IRA early in your career can provide valuable tax deductions and potentially earn you employer matching contributions, essentially giving you free money to invest in your future. The earlier you start participating in these plans, the more you can benefit from their features and grow your retirement savings over time.

Another advantage of starting retirement planning early is that it gives you more flexibility and options as you approach retirement age. When you have a longer time horizon, you can afford to take on more investment risk and potentially earn higher returns, as you have time to weather market fluctuations and recover from any short-term losses. As you get closer to retirement, you may need to adjust your portfolio to be more conservative, but starting early gives you the freedom to adapt your strategy as your circumstances and goals change.

Furthermore, starting early can help you build a larger financial cushion to protect against unexpected events and setbacks. Life is unpredictable, and unexpected expenses such as medical emergencies, job loss, or market downturns can derail even the best-laid plans. By starting to save and invest early, you give yourself more time to accumulate a financial safety net that can help you weather these storms and stay on track for retirement.

Finally, starting retirement planning early can provide immense psychological benefits and peace of mind. Knowing that you're taking proactive steps to secure your financial future can reduce stress, increase confidence, and give you a sense of control over your life. When you have a clear plan in place and are making progress towards your goals, you can enjoy the present moment more fully, without constantly worrying about your long-term financial security.

In conclusion, the benefits of starting retirement planning early are numerous and far-reaching. From harnessing the power of compound interest and developing good financial habits, to taking advantage of tax benefits and employer-sponsored plans, to building a financial cushion and gaining peace of mind, the advantages of starting early cannot be overstated. By taking control of your financial future today, you can set yourself up for a more secure, comfortable, and fulfilling retirement tomorrow.

Summary: Embracing the Power of Proactive Retirement Planning

In this section, we've explored the critical importance of retirement planning and why it should be a top priority for everyone, regardless of age or income level. We've seen how the retirement landscape has shifted dramatically in recent years, placing a greater responsibility on individuals to actively plan and save for their golden years. From the decline of traditional pension plans to the rise of the gig economy, the changing nature of retirement has made it more important than ever to take control of your financial future.

We've also examined the risks of delaying retirement planning, including missing out on the power of compound interest, having less time to recover from financial setbacks, and limiting your investment options and potential returns. By understanding these risks, you can be motivated to start planning early and avoid the stress and anxiety that come with postponing this crucial aspect of your financial life.

Finally, we've highlighted the numerous benefits of starting retirement planning early, such as harnessing the power of compound interest, developing good financial habits, taking advantage of tax benefits and employer-sponsored plans, and building a financial cushion to weather unexpected events. By starting early, you give yourself the gift of time – time to explore your options, make informed decisions, and course-correct as needed.

The key takeaway from this section is that retirement planning is not a one-time event, but a lifelong process that requires ongoing effort, education, and adaptation. By embracing the power of proactive retirement planning, you can take control of your financial destiny and set yourself up for a more secure, comfortable, and fulfilling retirement.

As we move forward in this book, we'll dive deeper into the various strategies and tools you can use to create a comprehensive retirement plan that aligns with your unique goals and circumstances. Whether you're just starting your career or nearing retirement age, the insights and advice in the coming chapters will empower you to make informed decisions and take meaningful steps towards a brighter financial future. So, let's continue this journey together and discover how you can transform your retirement dreams into a reality.

Section 2: Determining Your Retirement Goals

Picture this: you're sitting on a beach, sipping a cocktail, and watching the sun slowly dip into the horizon. Or maybe you're exploring a new city, immersing yourself in a foreign culture, and savoring every moment of your adventure. Whatever your ideal retirement looks like, one thing is certain – it's a time to enjoy the fruits of your labor and live life on your own terms.

But here's the thing: your retirement dreams won't just magically happen. They require careful planning, goal-setting, and a clear vision of what you want your golden years to look like. And that's precisely what this section is all about – helping you define your unique retirement objectives and lifestyle aspirations.

You see, retirement planning isn't just about crunching numbers and saving money (although those are certainly important aspects). It's also about figuring out what truly matters to you and what kind of life you want to lead when you're no longer tied to a 9-to-5 job. Do you want to travel the world? Spend more time with family and friends? Pursue a passion project or volunteer for a cause you believe in? The possibilities are endless, but it's up to you to decide what your ideal retirement looks like.

In the following subsections, we'll dive deeper into the process of envisioning your dream retirement lifestyle, estimating your retirement expenses, and setting realistic savings targets to make your goals a reality. By the end of this section, you'll have a clearer picture of what you're working towards and what steps you need to take to get there.

So, let's get started on this exciting journey of self-discovery and retirement planning. Your future self will thank you for taking the time to map out your path to a fulfilling and financially secure retirement.

Subsection 2.1: Envisioning Your Ideal Retirement Lifestyle

Close your eyes and imagine yourself in retirement. What do you see? Are you lounging on a sandy beach, listening to the gentle crash of waves? Or perhaps you're exploring a vibrant city, immersing yourself in new cultures and experiences. Maybe you're spending quality time with loved ones, pursuing a beloved hobby, or volunteering for a cause close to your heart.

Everyone's vision of the perfect retirement is unique, shaped by their individual values, passions, and aspirations. Some may dream of a life filled with adventure and travel, while others may prefer a more relaxed, low-key lifestyle. Some may envision a retirement centered around family and community, while others may seek solitude and personal growth.

The key to creating a fulfilling retirement plan is to take the time to really visualize what your ideal retirement looks like. Ask yourself questions like:

- What activities bring me joy and a sense of purpose?

- Where do I want to live? Do I want to stay in my current home, downsize, or relocate to a new area?

- Who do I want to spend my time with? Family, friends, or new acquaintances who share my interests?

- What legacy do I want to leave behind? How can I make a positive impact on the world?

Answering these questions can help you paint a vivid picture of your dream retirement lifestyle. Maybe you see yourself waking up each morning to a beautiful view, spending your days hiking, gardening, or practicing yoga. Perhaps you envision traveling the world, learning new languages, and immersing yourself in different cultures. Or maybe you picture yourself surrounded by loved ones, hosting family gatherings, and volunteering in your community.

Whatever your ideal retirement looks like, it's important to have a clear vision in mind. This vision will serve as your north star, guiding your financial planning and decision-making as you work towards making your retirement dreams a reality.

But it's not just about daydreaming – it's also about being realistic. Consider factors like your health, family obligations, and financial resources when envisioning your retirement lifestyle. While it's important to dream big, it's equally important to ensure that your vision is achievable and sustainable over the long term.

Once you have a clear picture of your ideal retirement lifestyle, you can start breaking it down into specific goals and milestones. For example, if your vision involves traveling the world, you might set a goal to visit one new country each year. If your dream is to start a small business or pursue a creative passion, you might set a goal to save a certain amount of money to fund your venture.

By setting specific, measurable goals, you can create a roadmap to turn your retirement vision into a reality. And as you work towards these goals, remember to stay flexible and open to new possibilities. Your vision of retirement may evolve over time as your priorities and circumstances change, and that's okay.

The most important thing is to keep your ideal retirement lifestyle at the forefront of your mind, using it as a source of motivation and inspiration as you navigate the financial planning process. With a clear vision and a well-crafted plan, you can create a retirement that is truly fulfilling, joyful, and uniquely yours.

Subsection 2.2: Estimating Your Retirement Expenses

Now that you have a clear vision of your ideal retirement lifestyle, it's time to get down to the nitty-gritty of estimating your retirement expenses. This is a crucial step in the retirement planning process, as it will help you determine how much money you'll need to save to make your retirement dreams a reality.

At first glance, estimating your retirement expenses may seem like a daunting task. After all, how can you predict what your costs will be 10, 20, or even 30 years down the line? But don't worry – with a few simple strategies and tools, you can create a realistic estimate of your retirement expenses and use it to guide your savings and investment decisions.

One of the most effective ways to estimate your retirement expenses is to start with your current expenses and adjust them based on how you expect your lifestyle to change in retirement. For example, if you plan to downsize your home or relocate to a less expensive area, your housing costs may decrease. On the other hand, if you plan to travel more or take up new hobbies, your discretionary expenses may increase.

To get started, take a look at your current budget and categorize your expenses into essential and discretionary categories. Essential expenses include things like housing, food, healthcare, and transportation – expenses that you'll need to cover no matter what. Discretionary expenses include things like entertainment, dining out, and travel – expenses that you have more control over and can adjust based on your retirement lifestyle and budget.

Once you have a clear picture of your current expenses, consider how they may change in retirement. Will you have a mortgage or rent payment? Will you need to budget more for healthcare costs as you age? Will you have additional expenses related to your retirement lifestyle, such as travel or hobbies?

One helpful rule of thumb is to assume that you'll need about 80% of your pre-retirement income to maintain your standard of living in retirement. So, if you currently earn $100,000 per year, you can estimate that you'll need about $80,000 per year in retirement. However, this is just a general guideline – your actual retirement expenses will depend on your unique circumstances and goals.

Another useful tool for estimating retirement expenses is the 4% rule. This rule suggests that you can safely withdraw 4% of your retirement savings each year without running out of money, assuming a 30-year retirement. So, if you have $1 million saved for retirement, you can expect to withdraw about $40,000 per year ($1 million x 0.04).

Of course, the 4% rule is not a guarantee – your actual withdrawal rate will depend on factors like your investment returns, inflation, and life expectancy. But it can be a helpful starting point for estimating your retirement income needs.

When estimating your retirement expenses, it's also important to consider the impact of inflation. Over time, the cost of goods and services tends to rise, which means that your retirement savings will need to keep pace with inflation to maintain your purchasing power. One way to account for inflation in your retirement planning is to assume an annual inflation rate of 2-3% and adjust your savings and withdrawal rates accordingly.

Finally, don't forget to factor in any additional sources of retirement income, such as Social Security benefits, pensions, or rental income. These income streams can help offset your expenses and reduce the amount you need to save on your own.

Estimating your retirement expenses may seem like a daunting task, but with a little bit of planning and some helpful tools and strategies, you can create a realistic estimate that will guide your retirement savings and investment decisions. By taking the time to understand your current expenses, anticipate how they may change in retirement, and factor in additional sources of income, you can create a retirement budget that will help you achieve your goals and live the life you've always dreamed of.

Subsection 2.3: Setting Realistic Retirement Savings Targets

Now that you have a clear vision of your ideal retirement lifestyle and a solid understanding of your estimated retirement expenses, it's time to set realistic savings targets to help you achieve your goals. This process involves taking a close look at your current financial situation, determining how much you need to save, and creating a plan to reach your targets.

One of the first steps in setting retirement savings targets is to assess your current savings and investments. Take stock of all your accounts, including employer-sponsored retirement plans, individual retirement accounts (IRAs), savings accounts, and investment portfolios. This will give you a clear picture of your starting point and help you determine how much more you need to save to reach your goals.

Next, consider the age at which you plan to retire and the number of years you expect to spend in retirement. These factors will have a significant impact on how much you need to save. Generally, the earlier you plan to retire and the longer you expect to live in retirement, the more you'll need to save to ensure a comfortable lifestyle.

To calculate your retirement savings targets, you can use the following formula:

$$\text{Retirement Savings Target} = \frac{\text{Annual Retirement Expense} \times 25}{(1 + \text{Expected Annual Return})^{\text{Years Until Retirement}}}$$

For example, let's say you've determined that you'll need $60,000 per year in retirement, and you plan to retire in 20 years. Assuming an expected annual return of 7% on your investments, your retirement savings target would be:

$$\text{Retirement Savings Target} = \frac{\$60,000 \times 25}{(1 + 0.07)^{20}} \approx \$387,600$$

This means you'd need to have approximately $387,600 saved right now, assuming a 7% annual return over the next 20 years, to support your desired retirement lifestyle of $60,000 per year for 25 years.

Keep in mind that this is just a rough estimate, and your actual savings needs may vary based on factors such as inflation, market performance, and changes in your personal circumstances. It's important to regularly review and adjust your savings targets to ensure you're on track to meet your goals.

To help you stay on track, consider breaking your retirement savings targets down into smaller, more manageable milestones. For example, you might aim to save a certain percentage of your income each year or set a goal to have a specific amount saved by a certain age. This can make the process feel less overwhelming and help you stay motivated as you work towards your ultimate target.

Another important aspect of setting realistic retirement savings targets is to create a budget that prioritizes saving and investing. Look for opportunities to reduce expenses and increase your contributions to retirement accounts. Consider automating your savings so that a portion of your income is automatically transferred to your retirement accounts each month. This can help you stay disciplined and make steady progress towards your goals.

Finally, don't be discouraged if your current savings fall short of your targets. It's never too late to start saving for retirement, and even small contributions can add up over time. Focus on making steady progress and adjusting your plan as needed to ensure you're on track to achieve your retirement dreams.

In conclusion, setting realistic retirement savings targets is a crucial step in creating a comprehensive retirement plan. By assessing your current financial situation, calculating your savings needs, and breaking your targets down into manageable milestones, you can create a roadmap to help you achieve the retirement lifestyle you've always dreamed of. With dedication, discipline, and a well-crafted plan, you can take control of your financial future and enjoy a comfortable, fulfilling retirement.

Summary: Charting Your Path to a Fulfilling Retirement

Determining your retirement goals is a crucial step in creating a comprehensive and effective retirement plan. By envisioning your ideal retirement lifestyle, estimating your expenses, and setting realistic savings targets, you lay the foundation for a fulfilling and financially secure future.

Visualizing your dream retirement allows you to identify what truly matters to you and what kind of life you want to lead when you're no longer tied to a 9-to-5 job. Whether it's traveling the world, pursuing a passion project, or spending more time with loved ones, having a clear picture of your aspirations will guide your financial planning and decision-making.

Estimating your retirement expenses is equally important, as it helps you understand how much money you'll need to save to support your desired lifestyle. By analyzing your current expenses, anticipating how they may change in retirement, and accounting for factors like inflation and additional income sources, you can create a realistic retirement budget.

With your vision and estimated expenses in mind, you can then set realistic retirement savings targets. By assessing your current financial situation, calculating your savings needs, and breaking your targets down into manageable milestones, you create a roadmap to help you achieve your retirement dreams.

Remember, retirement planning is not a one-time event, but an ongoing process. As your life circumstances and priorities evolve, so too should your retirement goals and plans. Regularly reviewing and adjusting your targets, budget, and investment strategies will ensure that you stay on track and adapt to changes along the way.

Ultimately, the key to a successful retirement lies in taking control of your financial future. By proactively defining your retirement objectives, creating a comprehensive plan, and staying committed to your goals, you empower yourself to live the retirement lifestyle you've always envisioned. So, dream big, plan wisely, and look forward to a retirement filled with joy, purpose, and financial security.

Section 3: Retirement Savings Vehicles

Imagine a future where you can spend your days pursuing your passions, traveling to exotic locations, or simply enjoying a comfortable life with your loved ones. This dream is within reach, but it requires careful planning and smart decisions about how you save and invest your money today. With so many options available, it can be overwhelming to navigate the landscape of retirement savings vehicles. In this section, we'll explore the various tools at your disposal, from employer-sponsored plans to individual retirement accounts, and help you understand how each one can contribute to a secure financial future.

Picture yourself as the architect of your retirement, laying the foundation brick by brick. Just as a skilled architect carefully selects the right materials to create a strong and lasting structure, you must choose the retirement savings vehicles that best fit your unique needs and goals. Whether you're just starting your career or nearing the end of it, there are options available to help you build a robust retirement portfolio.

As we delve into the world of 401(k)s, pensions, IRAs, and more, keep in mind that knowledge is power. By understanding the features, benefits, and limitations of each savings vehicle, you'll be empowered to make informed decisions and take control of your financial destiny. So, let's embark on this journey together, exploring the tools that can help you turn your retirement dreams into a reality.

Subsection 3.1: Employer-Sponsored Retirement Plans: 401(k)s and Pensions

For many people, the journey towards a secure retirement begins with their employer. Employer-sponsored retirement plans, such as 401(k)s and pensions, offer a powerful way to save for the future while enjoying unique benefits and incentives. These plans are designed to help you build wealth over time, harnessing the power of compound interest and regular contributions to create a substantial nest egg.

One of the most common types of employer-sponsored retirement plans is the 401(k). Named after the section of the tax code that governs them, 401(k)s allow you to contribute a portion of your paycheck before taxes are taken out. This means that you can lower your taxable income while saving for retirement, providing an immediate tax benefit. Many employers also offer matching contributions, effectively giving you free money to invest in your future.

For example, let's say your employer matches 50% of your contributions up to 6% of your salary. If you earn $50,000 per year and contribute 6% ($3,000), your employer will add an additional $1,500 to your account. That's an instant 50% return on your investment, even before considering any potential market gains. Over time, these matching contributions can add up to a significant sum, supercharging your retirement savings.

Another type of employer-sponsored plan is the traditional pension, also known as a defined benefit plan. With a pension, your employer promises to pay you a specific monthly benefit in retirement, based on factors such as your salary and years of service. While pensions are becoming less common, they can still provide a valuable source of guaranteed income in retirement, helping to ensure that you have a stable foundation to build upon.

However, it's important to understand that employer-sponsored plans come with certain rules and restrictions. For example, 401(k)s often have a limited selection of investment options, and you may face penalties if you withdraw funds before age 59 1/2. Additionally, if you leave your job, you'll need to decide what to do with your 401(k) balance, such as rolling it over into an Individual Retirement Account (IRA) or leaving it with your former employer.

Despite these limitations, employer-sponsored retirement plans remain a cornerstone of many people's retirement savings strategy. By taking advantage of these plans and maximizing your contributions, you can take a significant step towards securing your financial future. And as we'll explore in the following subsections, there are many other tools and strategies you can use to complement your employer-sponsored savings and build a comprehensive retirement portfolio.

Subsection 3.2: Individual Retirement Accounts (IRAs): Traditional and Roth

While employer-sponsored retirement plans can provide a solid foundation for your savings, Individual Retirement Accounts (IRAs) offer another powerful tool to help you build wealth for the future. IRAs are personal savings accounts that come with unique tax advantages, allowing you to save and invest money independently from your employer. There are two main types of IRAs: Traditional and Roth, each with its own set of benefits and considerations.

Traditional IRAs have been around since the 1970s and offer a straightforward way to save for retirement. With a Traditional IRA, you can contribute pre-tax dollars, effectively lowering your taxable income for the year. For example, if you earn $50,000 and contribute $5,000 to a Traditional IRA, you'll only pay taxes on $45,000 of income. This immediate tax benefit can be especially valuable if you're in a high tax bracket or expect to be in a lower bracket in retirement.

However, it's important to note that Traditional IRA contributions are tax-deferred, not tax-free. When you withdraw money from your Traditional IRA in retirement, you'll pay taxes on the distributions at your ordinary income tax rate. Additionally, you must start taking required minimum distributions (RMDs) from your Traditional IRA once you reach age 72, ensuring that you (and the IRS) eventually receive the tax revenue.

On the other hand, Roth IRAs, introduced in the late 1990s, offer a different approach to retirement savings. With a Roth IRA, you contribute after-tax dollars, meaning you won't receive an immediate tax deduction. However, the real magic of Roth IRAs happens in retirement. When you withdraw money from your Roth IRA, you can do so tax-free, provided you've held the account for at least five years and are over age 59 1/2.

This tax-free growth potential can be incredibly powerful, especially if you expect to be in a higher tax bracket in retirement or believe that tax rates will increase in the future. By paying taxes upfront, you can lock in your current tax rate and enjoy the benefits of compounded growth without the burden of future taxes.

Another advantage of Roth IRAs is that they don't have RMDs. This means you can let your money continue to grow tax-free for as long as you like, making Roth IRAs an attractive option for those who want to leave a financial legacy to their heirs. In fact, Roth IRAs can be an effective estate planning tool, allowing you to pass on tax-free wealth to the next generation.

It's worth noting that both Traditional and Roth IRAs have contribution limits and income restrictions. As of 2021, the maximum annual contribution for both types of IRAs is $6,000 ($7,000 if you're age 50 or older). However, the ability to contribute to a Roth IRA phases out at higher income levels, while Traditional IRA contributions may not be tax-deductible if you or your spouse are covered by an employer-sponsored plan and your income exceeds certain thresholds.

Ultimately, the choice between a Traditional and Roth IRA depends on your individual financial situation and long-term goals. If you expect to be in a lower tax bracket in retirement and want an immediate tax break, a Traditional IRA may be the better choice. On the other hand, if you anticipate being in a higher tax bracket later in life or want the flexibility of tax-free withdrawals, a Roth IRA could be the way to go.

In some cases, it may even make sense to contribute to both types of IRAs, diversifying your tax benefits and giving yourself more flexibility in retirement. By understanding the unique advantages of Traditional and Roth IRAs, you can make informed decisions about how to best save and invest for your future, taking control of your financial destiny one contribution at a time.

Subsection 3.3: Annuities and Guaranteed Income Streams

In the quest for a secure retirement, many people seek sources of guaranteed income that can provide a reliable stream of funds throughout their golden years. One financial tool that has gained popularity in recent years is the annuity. Annuities are contracts between an individual and an insurance company, designed to provide a steady income stream in exchange for a lump sum payment or series of payments.

The concept of annuities dates back to ancient Rome, where citizens would make a one-time payment to the government in exchange for a lifetime of annual payments. Today, annuities come in various forms, each with its own set of features and benefits. The most common types of annuities are fixed, variable, and indexed.

Fixed annuities offer a guaranteed interest rate and a fixed stream of payments, providing a predictable income source that can help mitigate the risk of outliving one's savings. With a fixed annuity, the insurance company assumes the investment risk, ensuring that the annuitant receives the promised payments regardless of market conditions.

On the other hand, variable annuities allow investors to choose from a range of investment options, such as mutual funds, with the potential for higher returns. However, this potential for growth comes with increased risk, as the value of the annuity and the income payments can fluctuate based on the performance of the underlying investments.

Indexed annuities offer a middle ground between fixed and variable annuities, providing the opportunity for growth based on the performance of a specified market index, such as the S&P 500, while also offering a guaranteed minimum return. This combination of potential growth and downside protection can be appealing to those who want some exposure to the market without the full risk of a variable annuity.

When considering an annuity as part of a retirement income strategy, it's essential to understand the various payout options available. The most common payout options include lifetime payments, which provide a guaranteed income stream for the duration of the annuitant's life, and period certain payments, which offer a fixed income stream for a specified number of years.

Joint and survivor annuities are another popular option for married couples, as they provide payments for the lifetime of both spouses, with the payments continuing for the surviving spouse after the first spouse's death. This feature can provide peace of mind and financial security for couples who want to ensure that their partner is taken care of in the event of their passing.

While annuities can offer a valuable source of guaranteed income in retirement, they are not without their drawbacks. One potential disadvantage is the lack of liquidity, as funds invested in an annuity may be subject to surrender charges if withdrawn before a specified period. Additionally, some annuities come with high fees and commissions, which can eat into the overall return.

Another consideration is the creditworthiness of the insurance company offering the annuity. As with any financial product, it's crucial to research and choose a reputable, financially stable company to ensure that the promised payments will be made.

Despite these potential drawbacks, annuities can play a valuable role in a comprehensive retirement income plan. By providing a guaranteed income stream, annuities can help retirees manage the risk of outliving their savings and maintain a comfortable standard of living throughout their retirement years.

When incorporating an annuity into a retirement plan, it's essential to consider factors such as one's age, health, and overall financial situation. Working with a qualified financial professional can help individuals determine whether an annuity is appropriate for their unique needs and goals, and if so, which type of annuity and payout option best fits their circumstances.

In conclusion, annuities offer a unique opportunity for retirees to secure a guaranteed income stream in retirement, providing a measure of financial security and peace of mind. While they are not a one-size-fits-all solution, annuities can be a valuable component of a well-rounded retirement income strategy when carefully selected and integrated with other savings and investment vehicles. By understanding the features, benefits, and limitations of annuities, individuals can make informed decisions about how best to incorporate these financial tools into their plans for a comfortable and secure retirement.

Subsection 3.4: Health Savings Accounts (HSAs) for Healthcare Expenses

As you navigate the landscape of retirement savings vehicles, it's crucial to consider not only your future income needs but also the potential healthcare expenses you may face. With the rising cost of medical care and the uncertainty of health in later years, preparing for these expenses is an essential part of a comprehensive retirement strategy. One powerful tool that can help you save for retirement healthcare costs is a Health Savings Account (HSA).

An HSA is a unique savings account designed specifically for individuals with high-deductible health plans (HDHPs). These accounts offer a triple tax advantage: contributions are tax-deductible, the money grows tax-free, and withdrawals for qualified medical expenses are also tax-free. This combination of tax benefits makes HSAs a highly attractive option for those looking to save for both current and future healthcare costs.

To be eligible for an HSA, you must be enrolled in an HDHP, which is a health insurance plan with a higher deductible than traditional plans. The idea behind HDHPs is that by taking on a higher deductible, you'll have lower monthly premiums, allowing you to allocate more money towards your HSA. In 2021, the minimum deductible for an HDHP is $1,400 for an individual and $2,800 for a family.

One of the most significant advantages of an HSA is that the funds roll over from year to year, unlike Flexible Spending Accounts (FSAs) which typically have a "use it or lose it" rule. This means that you can accumulate a substantial balance in your HSA over time, investing the money and allowing it to grow tax-free until you need it for medical expenses.

In fact, many financial experts recommend maximizing your HSA contributions each year and treating the account as a long-term investment vehicle for retirement. By contributing the maximum amount allowed and investing the funds wisely, you can build a significant nest egg to cover healthcare costs in your golden years.

As of 2021, the maximum annual contribution for an HSA is $3,600 for an individual and $7,200 for a family. If you're age 55 or older, you can make an additional "catch-up" contribution of $1,000 per year. These contribution limits are adjusted annually for inflation, allowing you to save more over time.

When it comes to using your HSA funds, the list of qualified medical expenses is extensive, ranging from doctor visits and prescription medications to dental and vision care. In retirement, you can use your HSA to pay for Medicare premiums, long-term care insurance, and other healthcare expenses that may arise.

It's important to note that if you use your HSA funds for non-medical expenses before age 65, you'll face a 20% penalty in addition to regular income taxes. However, after age 65, you can withdraw money from your HSA for any purpose without penalty, although you'll still pay income taxes on non-medical withdrawals.

Another advantage of HSAs is that they are portable, meaning you can take the account with you if you change jobs or retire. This flexibility ensures that you have continued access to your savings and can use the funds when you need them most.

When choosing an HSA provider, it's essential to consider factors such as fees, investment options, and ease of use. Some HSAs offer a wide range of investment choices, including mutual funds and exchange-traded funds (ETFs), allowing you to tailor your portfolio to your risk tolerance and financial goals.

In conclusion, Health Savings Accounts (HSAs) offer a powerful way to save for retirement healthcare costs while enjoying unique tax advantages. By combining the benefits of an HDHP with the long-term growth potential of an HSA, you can take control of your future healthcare expenses and ensure a more secure retirement. As with any financial decision, it's essential to research your options carefully and consult with a qualified professional to determine if an HSA is right for your individual circumstances. By incorporating an HSA into your broader retirement savings strategy, you can take a significant step towards a healthier financial future.

Summary: Building Your Retirement Savings with the Right Tools

As we conclude this exploration of retirement savings vehicles, it's clear that there are numerous tools at your disposal to help you build a secure financial future. From employer-sponsored plans like 401(k)s and pensions to individual options such as Traditional and Roth IRAs, each vehicle offers unique benefits and considerations for your retirement savings journey.

Understanding the features, advantages, and limitations of each option is crucial in creating a well-rounded retirement savings strategy. Whether you're just starting your career or nearing retirement age, taking advantage of these savings vehicles can help you harness the power of compound growth and maximize your retirement income potential.

Remember, there is no one-size-fits-all approach to retirement savings. The key is to evaluate your individual financial situation, goals, and risk tolerance to determine which combination of savings vehicles works best for you. By diversifying your retirement savings across various tools, you can create a robust portfolio that is resilient to market fluctuations and provides the flexibility you need to adapt to changing circumstances.

As you move forward on your retirement savings journey, keep in mind the importance of starting early, contributing consistently, and staying informed about your options. By taking proactive steps to save and invest for your future, you are empowering yourself to achieve the retirement lifestyle you envision.

In the following sections, we will delve deeper into strategies for maximizing your retirement savings, navigating investment choices, and creating a comprehensive retirement income plan. Armed with the knowledge of these powerful savings vehicles and the skills to use them effectively, you are well on your way to building a strong foundation for a financially secure and fulfilling retirement.

Section 4: Maximizing Your Retirement Savings

Picture yourself in your golden years, enjoying the fruits of your labor and living the retirement lifestyle you've always dreamed of. Whether it's traveling the world, pursuing your hobbies, or simply spending quality time with your loved ones, a comfortable retirement is a goal shared by many.

However, achieving this goal requires more than just wishful thinking; it demands a proactive approach to maximizing your retirement savings.

In this section, we'll explore a range of strategies designed to help you optimize your retirement savings and investments. From taking full advantage of employer-sponsored plans to increasing your contributions over time, these techniques can make a significant impact on your financial future. We'll also discuss the importance of balancing your retirement savings with other financial priorities and provide guidance on how to navigate these competing demands.

But why is maximizing your retirement savings so crucial? The answer lies in the power of compound growth. By consistently saving and investing a portion of your income over the long term, you allow your money to work harder for you. Each dollar saved today has the potential to grow exponentially over the decades leading up to your retirement, providing you with a larger nest egg to support your desired lifestyle.

Moreover, in an era where traditional pension plans are becoming increasingly rare, the responsibility for securing a comfortable retirement falls squarely on the shoulders of individuals. By taking charge of your retirement savings and implementing effective strategies, you can build a strong foundation for your financial future and reduce your reliance on uncertain sources of income.

Throughout this section, we'll provide actionable advice and real-world examples to help you make the most of your retirement savings opportunities. Whether you're just starting your career or nearing the end of your working years, it's never too early or too late to optimize your approach. So, let's dive in and explore how you can supercharge your retirement savings and pave the way for a fulfilling and financially secure retirement.

Subsection 4.1: Taking Advantage of Employer Matching Contributions

One of the most powerful ways to supercharge your retirement savings is by taking full advantage of employer matching contributions in your workplace retirement plan, such as a 401(k) or 403(b). Many employers offer to match a portion of the contributions you make to your retirement account, essentially providing you with free money to bolster your savings. However, failing to contribute enough to receive the full employer match means leaving valuable funds on the table.

Imagine you earn an annual salary of $60,000, and your employer offers a 50% match on your contributions up to 6% of your salary. If you contribute 6% of your salary ($3,600) to your 401(k), your employer will add another $1,800 to your account. That's an instant 50% return on your investment, even before considering any potential market gains. Over time, these matching contributions can significantly enhance your retirement nest egg.

To illustrate the long-term impact of employer matching, let's consider two scenarios. In the first scenario, an employee consistently contributes enough to receive the full employer match throughout their career. In the second scenario, the employee fails to take advantage of the match. Assuming a 30-year career, a 7% annual return, and a 50% employer match on contributions up to 6% of a $60,000 salary, the difference in retirement savings is staggering:

$$\text{Scenario 1: Full Match} = \$5{,}400 \times [(1 + 0.07)^{30} - 1] \div 0.07 \approx \$510{,}088$$

$$\text{Scenario 2: No Match} = \$0$$

By simply contributing enough to receive the full employer match, the employee in Scenario 1 ends up with about $510,000 more in the retirement savings compared to the employee in Scenario 2.

To ensure you're maximizing your employer match, follow these steps:

1. Familiarize yourself with your employer's matching policy,

including the match percentage and any vesting requirements.
2. Calculate the minimum contribution needed to receive the full match based on your salary.
3. Adjust your contribution rate to meet or exceed the minimum required for the full match.
4. Review your contributions annually and increase them as your salary grows or as you're able to save more.

Remember, employer matching contributions are a valuable benefit that can significantly boost your retirement savings over time. By taking advantage of this opportunity and consistently contributing enough to receive the full match, you'll be well on your way to building a robust retirement nest egg.

Subsection 4.2: Increasing Your Savings Rate Over Time

As you progress through your career and your income grows, it's essential to avoid the temptation of lifestyle inflation. While it's natural to want to enjoy the fruits of your labor, increasing your spending in lockstep with your income can hinder your ability to save for retirement. Instead, consider gradually increasing your retirement contributions over time, allocating a portion of each raise or bonus to your savings.

The power of incremental increases in your savings rate cannot be overstated. By consistently boosting your contributions, even by small amounts, you can significantly enhance your retirement nest egg over the long term. This approach allows you to strike a balance between enjoying your present lifestyle and securing your financial future.

To illustrate the impact of gradually increasing your savings rate, let's consider an example. Imagine you start contributing 6% of your $50,000 salary to your 401(k) at age 25. If you continue contributing at this rate, assuming a 7% annual return, you would have approximately $598,905 by age 65. However, if you increase your contribution rate by just 1% every year until you reach a 15% savings rate, your retirement savings would grow to over $1.231 million by age 65. That's a staggering difference of more than $632,000, simply by gradually increasing your savings rate over time.

To put this incremental approach into practice, consider the following strategies:

1. Automate your contribution increases: Many retirement plans offer an auto-escalation feature, which automatically increases your contribution rate by a set percentage each year. By opting into this feature, you can ensure that your savings rate grows consistently over time without requiring manual adjustments.

2. Allocate a portion of each raise: When you receive a raise, consider allocating a significant portion of the increase to your retirement savings. For example, if you receive a 5% raise, you could increase your contribution rate by 2-3%, while still enjoying a slight bump in your take-home pay.

3. Reassess your budget regularly: As your income grows, take the time to review your budget and identify areas where you can redirect funds towards your retirement savings. By continuously optimizing your spending and prioritizing your long-term financial goals, you can find opportunities to boost your savings rate without compromising your quality of life.

4. Set milestone targets: Establish specific savings rate milestones to work towards over time. For example, aim to reach a 10% savings rate by age 30, 15% by age 40, and 20% by age 50. Having clear targets can help you stay motivated and on track as you gradually increase your contributions.

Remember, the key is to start early and remain consistent in your efforts to increase your savings rate. By making incremental improvements and staying committed to your long-term financial goals, you can harness the power of compound growth and build a substantial retirement nest egg over the course of your career. Every additional dollar saved today can make a significant difference in the lifestyle you'll be able to enjoy in your golden years.

Subsection 4.3: Catch-Up Contributions for Older Investors

As you approach retirement age, you may find yourself with more disposable income and a desire to supercharge your savings. Fortunately, the IRS recognizes this and offers a valuable opportunity for older investors to boost their retirement contributions through catch-up contributions. If you're aged 50 or above, you can take advantage of these higher contribution limits to make up for any savings shortfalls in earlier years and strengthen your retirement nest egg.

Catch-up contributions are additional amounts that older investors can contribute to their retirement accounts beyond the standard annual limits. For example, in 2021, the regular contribution limit for a 401(k) plan is $19,500, but those aged 50 and above can make an additional catch-up contribution of $6,500, bringing their total contribution limit to $26,000. Similarly, IRA catch-up contributions allow older investors to save an extra $1,000 per year, on top of the standard $6,000 limit.

To illustrate the power of catch-up contributions, consider the following scenario: Imagine two investors, both aged 50, with retirement savings of $500,000 each. Investor A continues contributing the standard $19,500 per year to their 401(k), while Investor B takes advantage of catch-up contributions and saves an additional $6,500 annually. Assuming an annual return of 7% and a retirement age of 65, the difference in their retirement savings is significant:

Investor A: Standard Contributions = $1,869,532

Investor B: Catch-up Contributions = $2,032,870

By utilizing catch-up contributions, Investor B ends up with $163,338 more in their retirement account, simply by saving an extra $6,500 per year for 15 years.

To make the most of catch-up contributions, consider the following strategies:

1. Maximize your contributions: If financially feasible, aim to contribute the full catch-up amount each year to your 401(k), IRA, or other eligible retirement accounts. Even if you can't reach the maximum, every additional dollar saved can make a difference in the long run.

2. Prioritize your accounts: If you have multiple retirement accounts, prioritize maximizing catch-up contributions in the accounts with the most favorable tax treatment or employer matching contributions. This may include your 401(k), followed by a Roth IRA or traditional IRA.

3. Reassess your budget: Review your current expenses and look for opportunities to redirect funds towards your catch-up contributions. Consider reducing discretionary spending or finding ways to increase your income to accommodate the additional savings.

4. Use windfalls wisely: If you receive a windfall, such as a bonus, inheritance, or tax refund, consider allocating a portion of it towards your catch-up contributions. These one-time influxes of cash can provide a significant boost to your retirement savings.

5. Stay invested: Remember that catch-up contributions are most effective when invested in a well-diversified portfolio aligned with your risk tolerance and retirement goals. Avoid letting the additional funds sit idle in low-yield accounts, and instead put them to work in the market.

By seizing the opportunity to make catch-up contributions, older investors can take a proactive step towards securing a more comfortable retirement. Even if you haven't been able to save as much as you would have liked in earlier years, catch-up contributions provide a valuable chance to close the gap and bolster your retirement readiness. Remember, it's never too late to start prioritizing your financial future, and catch-up contributions are a powerful tool to help you get there.

Subsection 4.4: Balancing Retirement Savings with Other Financial Priorities

As you navigate your financial journey, it's crucial to recognize that retirement savings, while undeniably important, are just one piece of the larger puzzle. Throughout your life, you'll encounter a multitude of competing financial priorities that demand your attention and resources. From buying a home and starting a family to paying off student loans and managing unexpected expenses, these goals can often seem at odds with your retirement savings efforts. However, by striking a thoughtful balance and employing smart strategies, you can successfully manage your retirement savings alongside your other financial responsibilities.

One of the first steps in achieving this balance is to create a comprehensive financial plan that takes into account both your short-term and long-term objectives. This plan should include a clear picture of your current financial situation, including your income, expenses, debts, and assets. By having a thorough understanding of your financial landscape, you can make informed decisions about how to allocate your resources and prioritize your goals.

When it comes to balancing retirement savings with other financial priorities, it's essential to adopt a holistic approach. Rather than viewing your goals as isolated silos, consider how they interact and impact one another. For example, paying off high-interest debt, such as credit card balances, can indirectly benefit your retirement savings by freeing up more of your income to contribute to your nest egg. Similarly, building an emergency fund can provide a financial safety net, reducing the likelihood that you'll need to tap into your retirement savings in the face of unexpected expenses.

Another key aspect of balancing competing financial priorities is to prioritize your goals based on their urgency and long-term impact. While it's natural to feel pulled in multiple directions, it's important to recognize that some goals may take precedence over others. For instance, if you have limited funds available, contributing to your employer-sponsored retirement plan to take advantage of matching contributions should generally take priority over saving for a luxury vacation. By carefully evaluating your goals and making informed trade-offs, you can ensure that your financial resources are allocated in a way that aligns with your values and long-term financial well-being.

One effective strategy for managing retirement savings alongside other financial priorities is to employ a "pay yourself first" approach. This involves automatically directing a portion of your income into your retirement accounts before allocating funds to other expenses or goals. By treating your retirement savings as a non-negotiable "expense," you can ensure that you consistently make progress towards your long-term financial security, even as you navigate competing short-term priorities.

It's also important to regularly review and adjust your financial plan as your circumstances and goals evolve over time. As you progress through different stages of life, your priorities and financial responsibilities will likely shift. For example, once you've paid off your student loans or achieved a major milestone like buying a home, you may have more capacity to increase your retirement contributions. By remaining flexible and adaptable, you can ensure that your financial plan continues to serve your needs and support your long-term retirement savings goals.

Ultimately, balancing retirement savings with other financial priorities requires a combination of careful planning, disciplined execution, and ongoing monitoring. By taking a proactive and holistic approach to your financial life, you can successfully navigate competing demands and work towards a secure and fulfilling financial future. Remember, while retirement savings are a critical component of your overall financial well-being, they should not come at the expense of your present-day financial health and happiness. By striking a thoughtful balance and employing smart strategies, you can enjoy the peace of mind that comes with knowing you're making progress towards all of your important financial goals.

Summary: Unlocking Your Retirement Potential

Throughout this section, we've explored a range of powerful strategies designed to help you maximize your retirement savings and secure a comfortable financial future. From taking full advantage of employer matching contributions to gradually increasing your savings rate over time, these techniques can have a profound impact on your ability to build a robust retirement nest egg.

We've seen how even small changes, such as consistently contributing enough to receive the full employer match or making incremental increases to your savings rate, can result in substantial differences in your retirement savings over the long term. By harnessing the power of compound growth and making smart financial decisions, you can unlock the full potential of your retirement savings and pave the way for a fulfilling and financially secure retirement.

Moreover, we've discussed the importance of seizing opportunities like catch-up contributions for older investors, which allow those aged 50 and above to supercharge their retirement savings and make up for any shortfalls in earlier years. By taking proactive steps to boost your contributions and optimize your investment strategies, you can significantly enhance your retirement readiness and enjoy greater peace of mind as you approach your golden years.

However, maximizing your retirement savings doesn't exist in a vacuum. We've also explored the critical concept of balancing your retirement savings with other competing financial priorities, such as paying off debt, building an emergency fund, and achieving short-term goals. By adopting a holistic approach to your financial life and making informed trade-offs, you can successfully navigate these competing demands and ensure that your retirement savings remain a top priority.

As you move forward on your retirement savings journey, remember that the key to success lies in consistent effort, disciplined execution, and a willingness to adapt as your circumstances change. By staying focused on your long-term goals, regularly reviewing your progress, and making adjustments as needed, you can create a powerful momentum that will carry you towards a brighter financial future.

In the next section, we'll dive into the world of retirement investing, exploring how to construct a well-diversified portfolio that aligns with your risk tolerance and retirement objectives. Armed with the knowledge and strategies gained from maximizing your retirement savings, you'll be well-positioned to make informed investment decisions and continue building a strong foundation for your golden years. So, let's embrace the exciting possibilities that lie ahead and continue our journey towards retirement success.

Section 5: Investing for Retirement

Picture yourself on the cusp of retirement, eagerly anticipating the freedom to pursue your passions and enjoy the fruits of your labor. But have you taken the necessary steps to ensure that your golden years are financially secure? Investing for retirement is a crucial aspect of your financial journey, and it requires careful planning and strategic decision-making.

Many people find the world of investing intimidating, with its complex jargon and countless options. However, constructing an appropriate retirement investment portfolio is not as daunting as it may seem. By understanding a few key principles and strategies, you can create a portfolio that aligns with your goals, risk tolerance, and timeline.

In this section, we will demystify the process of investing for retirement and provide you with the knowledge and tools you need to make informed decisions. We'll explore the importance of asset allocation, which involves dividing your investments among different asset classes such as stocks, bonds, and cash. You'll learn how to adjust your risk tolerance as retirement approaches, ensuring that your portfolio reflects your changing needs and objectives.

Moreover, we'll delve into the power of diversification and rebalancing strategies, which can help mitigate risk and optimize your returns over the long term. We'll also introduce you to target-date funds, a simple yet effective approach to retirement investing that automatically adjusts your asset allocation as you near your target retirement date.

Whether you're just starting your career or are well on your way to retirement, the insights and guidance provided in this section will empower you to take control of your financial future. By investing wisely and consistently, you can build a nest egg that will support the retirement lifestyle you've always dreamed of. So, let's dive in and discover how to construct an appropriate retirement investment portfolio that will serve you well for years to come.

Subsection 5.1: Asset Allocation in Retirement Portfolios

As you embark on your retirement investing journey, one of the most crucial decisions you'll make is how to allocate your assets. Asset allocation refers to the strategic distribution of your investment portfolio across various asset classes, such as stocks, bonds, and cash. The goal is to strike a balance between risk and return, ensuring that your portfolio is well-positioned to weather market fluctuations while still generating the growth necessary to fund your retirement dreams.

The role of asset allocation in retirement investing cannot be overstated. It serves as the foundation upon which your entire investment strategy is built. By carefully considering your risk tolerance, time horizon, and financial goals, you can create an asset allocation that aligns with your unique needs and aspirations.

One of the key benefits of a well-designed asset allocation is diversification. By spreading your investments across different asset classes, you can potentially reduce the overall risk of your portfolio. For example, if the stock market experiences a downturn, having a portion of your assets invested in bonds or cash can help cushion the blow. Conversely, when stocks are performing well, your equity investments can provide the growth potential needed to outpace inflation and build your wealth over time.

When determining your asset allocation, it's essential to consider your risk tolerance. Are you comfortable with the idea of short-term market fluctuations in exchange for the potential of higher long-term returns? Or do you prefer a more conservative approach that prioritizes stability and preservation of capital? Your risk tolerance will greatly influence the proportion of stocks, bonds, and other assets in your portfolio.

Another factor to consider is your time horizon. As you near retirement, you may want to gradually shift your asset allocation towards a more conservative mix. This typically involves reducing your exposure to stocks and increasing your allocation to bonds and cash. The rationale behind this approach is that as you have less time to recover from potential market downturns, preserving your wealth becomes increasingly important.

However, it's crucial to remember that retirement investing is not a one-size-fits-all endeavor. What works for one person may not be suitable for another. That's why it's essential to work with a financial advisor who can help you develop a personalized asset allocation strategy that takes into account your unique circumstances and goals.

In addition to the traditional asset classes of stocks, bonds, and cash, there are also alternative investments to consider, such as real estate, commodities, and private equity. While these investments can offer diversification benefits and potentially higher returns, they also come with their own set of risks and complexities. It's important to thoroughly research and understand these alternative investments before incorporating them into your retirement portfolio.

Ultimately, the key to successful asset allocation in retirement investing is regular monitoring and rebalancing. As market conditions change and your personal circumstances evolve, it's essential to review your portfolio periodically and make adjustments as needed. This helps ensure that your asset allocation remains aligned with your goals and risk tolerance over time.

In the following subsections, we'll delve deeper into the nuances of asset allocation, exploring strategies for adjusting your risk tolerance as retirement approaches, the power of diversification and rebalancing, and the role of target-date funds in simplifying the investment process. By mastering these concepts, you'll be well-equipped to construct a retirement portfolio that works hard for you, providing the financial security and peace of mind you deserve in your golden years.

Subsection 5.2: Adjusting Risk Tolerance as Retirement Approaches

As you navigate the path towards retirement, it's crucial to recognize that your investment strategy should evolve alongside your changing circumstances. One of the most significant adjustments you'll need to make is in your risk tolerance, which refers to your ability and willingness to withstand potential losses in pursuit of higher returns.

When you're young and have a longer time horizon until retirement, you can afford to take on more risk in your investment portfolio. This is because you have the luxury of time on your side, allowing you to weather short-term market fluctuations and benefit from the long-term growth potential of higher-risk assets like stocks. However, as retirement approaches, it becomes increasingly important to reevaluate your risk tolerance and make necessary adjustments to your portfolio composition.

The primary reason for adjusting your risk tolerance as retirement nears is to protect the wealth you've accumulated over the years. As you have less time to recover from potential market downturns, preserving your capital becomes a top priority. A significant market decline in the years leading up to or during the early stages of retirement can have a profound impact on your financial security, potentially derailing your retirement plans.

To mitigate this risk, it's generally recommended to gradually shift your asset allocation towards a more conservative mix as you approach retirement. This typically involves reducing your exposure to stocks and increasing your allocation to less volatile assets like bonds and cash. By doing so, you can help safeguard your portfolio against market turbulence and ensure that you have a stable foundation for generating retirement income.

However, it's important to strike a balance between risk reduction and growth potential. While it's prudent to dial down your risk exposure, completely eliminating stocks from your portfolio may not be the best approach. Stocks can still play a valuable role in providing the growth necessary to outpace inflation and maintain your purchasing power throughout retirement. The key is to find a balance that aligns with your personal risk tolerance and retirement goals.

One strategy to consider is the "glide path" approach, which involves gradually reducing your stock allocation as you near retirement and continuing to do so in the early years of retirement. For example, you might start with a portfolio that is 70% stocks and 30% bonds when you're 10-15 years away from retirement. As you get closer to retirement, you could incrementally shift your allocation to a more conservative mix, such as 60% stocks and 40% bonds, and eventually to a 50/50 split or even more conservative allocation in retirement.

It's worth noting that there is no one-size-fits-all approach to adjusting risk tolerance. The appropriate asset allocation for you will depend on a variety of factors, including your specific retirement goals, risk profile, and overall financial situation. Some individuals may be comfortable with a higher level of risk, while others may prefer a more conservative approach. It's essential to work with a financial advisor who can help you develop a personalized retirement investment strategy that takes into account your unique circumstances.

In addition to adjusting your asset allocation, there are other strategies you can employ to manage risk as retirement approaches. One such strategy is diversification, which involves spreading your investments across a range of asset classes, sectors, and geographies. By diversifying your portfolio, you can potentially reduce the impact of any single investment or market segment on your overall returns, thereby lowering your portfolio's overall risk profile.

Another important consideration is the role of rebalancing. As market conditions change and your investments grow at different rates, your portfolio's asset allocation can drift away from your target mix. Regular rebalancing helps ensure that your portfolio stays aligned with your desired risk level and investment strategy. This involves selling assets that have become overweighted and buying assets that have become underweighted, thereby bringing your portfolio back to its intended allocation.

As you approach retirement, it's also crucial to have a clear understanding of your retirement income needs and how your investment portfolio will support those needs. This involves estimating your expected expenses in retirement, considering factors such as healthcare costs, lifestyle choices, and any planned travel or major purchases. By having a well-defined retirement income plan, you can make informed decisions about your risk tolerance and portfolio composition, ensuring that your investments are working in harmony with your overall retirement strategy.

In conclusion, adjusting your risk tolerance as retirement approaches is a critical component of a successful retirement investment plan. By gradually shifting your portfolio towards a more conservative mix, employing diversification and rebalancing strategies, and aligning your investments with your retirement income needs, you can help protect the wealth you've worked so hard to build and ensure a financially secure retirement. Remember, the key is to find a balance that allows you to sleep well at night, knowing that your investments are well-positioned to support the retirement lifestyle you've envisioned.

Subsection 5.3: Diversification and Rebalancing Strategies

In the world of investing, the age-old adage "don't put all your eggs in one basket" holds true, especially when it comes to retirement planning. Diversification and rebalancing are two powerful strategies that can help you navigate the complexities of the financial markets and build a robust retirement portfolio.

Diversification is the practice of spreading your investments across various asset classes, sectors, and geographies to minimize risk and maximize potential returns. By allocating your funds to a diverse range of investments, you can potentially offset losses in one area with gains in another, thereby reducing the overall volatility of your portfolio.

Think of diversification as a buffet of investments, each with its own unique flavor and characteristics. Just as you wouldn't fill your plate with only one type of food, you shouldn't concentrate your entire portfolio in a single asset class or sector. By sampling a variety of investments, you can create a well-balanced portfolio that can withstand the ups and downs of the market.

One way to achieve diversification is through asset allocation, which involves dividing your portfolio among different asset classes such as stocks, bonds, and cash. Each asset class has its own risk and return profile, and by combining them in a way that aligns with your goals and risk tolerance, you can create a portfolio that is tailored to your specific needs.

For example, stocks have historically provided higher returns over the long term but come with greater short-term volatility. Bonds, on the other hand, tend to be less volatile but offer lower returns. By including both stocks and bonds in your portfolio, you can potentially benefit from the growth potential of stocks while the stability of bonds helps smooth out the ride.

However, diversification doesn't stop at asset allocation. Within each asset class, you can further diversify by investing in a range of sectors, industries, and geographies. For instance, instead of investing in a single company's stock, you could invest in a mutual fund or exchange-traded fund (ETF) that holds a basket of stocks from various companies and sectors. This helps spread your risk and reduces your exposure to company-specific events that could negatively impact your portfolio.

International diversification is another important consideration, especially in today's globalized economy. By investing a portion of your portfolio in international markets, you can potentially benefit from the growth opportunities in other countries while reducing your reliance on the performance of any single economy.

While diversification helps manage risk, it's important to remember that it does not guarantee a profit or protect against loss. Market conditions can still affect your portfolio, and some asset classes may underperform others over certain periods. This is where rebalancing comes into play.

Rebalancing is the process of periodically adjusting your portfolio to maintain your desired asset allocation. Over time, the performance of different investments can cause your portfolio to drift away from its original target allocation. For example, if stocks outperform bonds, your portfolio may become overweighted in stocks, exposing you to more risk than you had initially intended.

By regularly rebalancing your portfolio, you can bring your investments back in line with your target allocation, ensuring that your portfolio remains aligned with your risk tolerance and investment strategy. Rebalancing involves selling assets that have become overweighted and buying assets that have become underweighted, thereby restoring balance to your portfolio.

There are different approaches to rebalancing, such as time-based rebalancing (e.g., annually or quarterly) or threshold-based rebalancing (e.g., when an asset class deviates by a certain percentage from its target allocation). The appropriate rebalancing strategy for you will depend on your specific circumstances and preferences, and it's essential to work with a financial advisor to develop a plan that meets your needs.

Rebalancing can be emotionally challenging, as it often involves selling assets that have performed well and buying assets that have underperformed. However, it's important to remember that rebalancing is a disciplined approach to investing that can help you stay on track towards your long-term goals, rather than chasing short-term market trends.

In addition to diversification and rebalancing, there are other strategies you can employ to further optimize your retirement portfolio. One such strategy is dollar-cost averaging, which involves investing a fixed amount of money at regular intervals, regardless of market conditions. By investing consistently over time, you can potentially smooth out the impact of market volatility and avoid the temptation to time the market.

Another strategy is tax-efficient investing, which involves considering the tax implications of your investment decisions. For example, holding investments in tax-advantaged accounts such as 401(k)s or IRAs can help defer or minimize taxes, allowing your money to grow more efficiently over time. Additionally, being mindful of the tax consequences of selling investments can help you make more informed decisions and potentially reduce your tax burden in retirement.

In conclusion, diversification and rebalancing are essential strategies for building a strong and resilient retirement portfolio. By spreading your investments across various asset classes, sectors, and geographies, and regularly adjusting your portfolio to maintain your desired allocation, you can potentially manage risk, maximize returns, and stay on track towards your retirement goals. Remember, investing for retirement is a long-term journey, and by employing these strategies consistently over time, you can create a portfolio that works hard for you, providing the financial security and peace of mind you deserve in your golden years.

Subsection 5.4: The Role of Target-Date Funds

Investing for retirement can be a daunting task, especially for those who lack the time, knowledge, or inclination to actively manage their portfolios. Enter target-date funds, a type of mutual fund that has gained popularity in recent years as a simple and effective solution for retirement investing.

Target-date funds, also known as lifecycle funds, are designed to simplify the investment process by automatically adjusting the asset allocation of your portfolio as you approach your target retirement date. The concept behind these funds is straightforward: as you get closer to retirement, the fund gradually shifts its holdings from riskier, growth-oriented investments like stocks to more conservative, income-generating investments like bonds.

The beauty of target-date funds lies in their simplicity. When you invest in a target-date fund, you typically choose a fund with a target year that aligns with your expected retirement date. For example, if you plan to retire in 2050, you might invest in a "2050 Fund." The fund manager then takes care of the rest, making the necessary adjustments to the fund's asset allocation over time.

One of the primary advantages of target-date funds is that they offer a "set it and forget it" approach to retirement investing. You don't need to worry about rebalancing your portfolio or making complex investment decisions. The fund does the heavy lifting for you, ensuring that your asset allocation remains appropriate for your age and risk tolerance.

Another benefit of target-date funds is that they provide instant diversification. These funds typically invest in a broad range of asset classes, including domestic and international stocks, bonds, and sometimes even alternative investments like real estate or commodities. By spreading your money across multiple investments, target-date funds can help reduce the overall risk of your portfolio.

However, it's important to understand that not all target-date funds are created equal. Each fund family has its own "glide path," which refers to the way the fund's asset allocation changes over time. Some funds may have a more aggressive glide path, maintaining a higher proportion of stocks even as you near retirement, while others may take a more conservative approach.

When considering a target-date fund, it's crucial to review the fund's glide path and ensure that it aligns with your personal risk tolerance and retirement goals. It's also important to pay attention to the fund's fees, as high expenses can eat into your returns over time.

While target-date funds can be an excellent choice for many investors, they may not be suitable for everyone. If you have a more complex financial situation, such as multiple sources of retirement income or specific tax considerations, you may benefit from a more personalized investment approach.

Additionally, some investors may prefer to have more control over their investment decisions. If you enjoy actively managing your portfolio and making tactical adjustments based on market conditions, a target-date fund may not provide the level of flexibility you desire.

Despite these limitations, target-date funds remain a popular and effective tool for retirement investing. They offer a simple, accessible way for investors to build a well-diversified portfolio that automatically adjusts over time. By taking the guesswork out of asset allocation and rebalancing, target-date funds can help investors stay on track towards their retirement goals.

In conclusion, target-date funds play a valuable role in the world of retirement investing. They provide a streamlined, hands-off approach to building a diversified portfolio that evolves with you as you near retirement. While they may not be the perfect solution for every investor, target-date funds offer a compelling option for those seeking simplicity and ease in their retirement planning. As with any investment decision, it's essential to carefully consider your unique circumstances and goals before choosing a target-date fund, and to regularly review your portfolio to ensure it remains aligned with your needs over time.

Summary: Investing Wisely for a Secure Retirement

Investing for retirement is a crucial aspect of securing your financial future. By understanding the key principles of asset allocation, risk tolerance, diversification, and rebalancing, you can construct an investment portfolio that aligns with your goals and helps you navigate the complexities of the financial markets.

As you approach retirement, it's essential to adjust your risk tolerance and portfolio composition to protect the wealth you've accumulated over the years. Gradually shifting towards a more conservative mix of investments can help safeguard your portfolio against market volatility while still allowing for growth potential.

Diversification and rebalancing are powerful tools in your retirement investing arsenal. By spreading your investments across various asset classes, sectors, and geographies, you can potentially reduce risk and maximize returns. Regular rebalancing ensures that your portfolio stays aligned with your target allocation, keeping you on track towards your retirement objectives.

For those seeking a simpler approach to retirement investing, target-date funds offer a convenient and effective solution. These funds automatically adjust their asset allocation as you near your target retirement date, providing a diversified and age-appropriate investment mix.

Ultimately, the key to successful retirement investing lies in developing a well-thought-out plan, staying disciplined, and making informed decisions based on your unique circumstances and goals. By taking control of your financial future and investing wisely, you can build a retirement portfolio that provides the security, growth, and peace of mind you deserve in your golden years.

As you move forward on your retirement investing journey, remember that the knowledge and strategies gained in this section are just the beginning. Continue to educate yourself, stay informed about market trends and economic conditions, and seek guidance from trusted financial professionals when needed. By remaining proactive and engaged in your retirement planning, you can confidently navigate the path towards a fulfilling and financially secure retirement.

Section 6: Retirement Income Planning

Picture this: you've spent decades diligently saving and investing for retirement, eagerly anticipating the day when you can bid farewell to the daily grind and embark on a new chapter of life. But as that milestone approaches, a critical question looms: how will you transform your hard-earned nest egg into a reliable stream of income that will sustain you throughout your golden years? Enter retirement income planning, a crucial aspect of securing your financial future.

In this section, we'll dive deep into the strategies and considerations for generating and managing income in retirement. From understanding safe withdrawal rates to creating a diversified income stream, we'll explore the key principles that will help you navigate the complexities of retirement income planning. You'll learn about the role of Social Security benefits, the impact of taxes on your retirement income, and how to optimize your withdrawals to ensure a comfortable and worry-free retirement lifestyle.

But retirement income planning isn't just about crunching numbers and following formulas. It's about crafting a personalized strategy that aligns with your unique goals, risk tolerance, and lifestyle aspirations. Whether you envision a retirement filled with travel and adventure or a more laid-back lifestyle focused on family and hobbies, having a well-thought-out income plan is essential to turning those dreams into reality.

So, if you're ready to take control of your retirement income and build a solid foundation for your financial future, let's dive in. In the coming subsections, we'll arm you with the knowledge, tools, and confidence you need to create a retirement income plan that will provide you with the security and peace of mind you deserve. Get ready to embark on a journey towards a fulfilling and financially stable retirement.

Subsection 6.1: The 4% Rule and Safe Withdrawal Rates

When it comes to retirement income planning, one of the most critical questions is, "How much can I safely withdraw from my retirement savings each year without running out of money?" This is where the concept of safe withdrawal rates comes into play, and the 4% rule has become a popular rule of thumb in the financial planning community.

The 4% rule, first introduced by financial advisor William Bengen in 1994, suggests that retirees can safely withdraw 4% of their initial retirement portfolio balance each year, adjusted for inflation, without running out of money over a 30-year retirement period. For example, if you have a $1 million retirement portfolio, the 4% rule would suggest that you can withdraw $40,000 in the first year of retirement. In subsequent years, you would adjust this amount for inflation to maintain your purchasing power.

Bengen's research was based on historical data from 1926 to 1976, which included periods of market volatility, recessions, and high inflation. He found that a 4% withdrawal rate, combined with a portfolio of 50% stocks and 50% bonds, would have survived even the worst 30-year period in his study.

However, it's essential to understand that the 4% rule is a general guideline, not a guarantee. The rule has its limitations and critiques, particularly in the current low-interest-rate environment and with longer life expectancies. Some experts argue that a lower withdrawal rate, such as 3% or 3.5%, may be more appropriate for today's retirees to minimize the risk of outliving their savings.

It's also crucial to consider your personal circumstances when determining your safe withdrawal rate. Factors such as your age, health, lifestyle, and risk tolerance can all impact how much you can comfortably withdraw from your retirement savings each year. For example, if you retire early or expect to have a longer retirement period, you may need to adjust your withdrawal rate accordingly.

To calculate your personal safe withdrawal rate, you can use the following formula:

$$\text{Safe Withdrawal Rate} = \frac{\text{Annual Retirement Expenses - Other Income Sources}}{\text{Retirement Portfolio Balance}}$$

For instance, if your annual retirement expenses are $60,000, you expect to receive $20,000 from Social Security and pensions, and your retirement portfolio balance is $1 million, your safe withdrawal rate would be:

$$\text{Safe Withdrawal Rate} = \frac{\$60,000 - \$20,000}{\$1,000,000} = 0.04 \text{ or } 4\%$$

Keep in mind that this calculation is a starting point, and you may need to adjust your withdrawal rate based on market conditions and your personal circumstances over time.

In summary, the 4% rule and safe withdrawal rates are essential concepts in retirement income planning. While the 4% rule provides a helpful guideline, it's crucial to consider your unique situation and work with a financial advisor to develop a personalized withdrawal strategy that balances your income needs with the long-term sustainability of your retirement savings.

Subsection 6.2: Creating a Retirement Income Stream

After years of diligent saving and investing, the time has come to turn your retirement nest egg into a reliable income stream that will support you throughout your golden years. Creating a retirement income stream involves carefully managing your assets and implementing strategies to ensure a steady flow of funds while minimizing the risk of outliving your savings.

One popular approach to generating retirement income is the "bucket strategy." This method involves dividing your retirement assets into three to four "buckets," each with a specific purpose and time horizon. The first bucket, often referred to as the "cash bucket," holds enough money to cover your living expenses for the first one to three years of retirement. This bucket is typically invested in low-risk, liquid assets such as cash, money market funds, or short-term bonds, ensuring easy access to funds for immediate needs.

The second bucket, known as the "income bucket," is designed to generate a steady stream of income for the next five to ten years. This bucket may include investments such as dividend-paying stocks, bonds, or annuities that provide regular payouts. The goal is to create a predictable income stream that can help cover your ongoing expenses while allowing some growth potential to keep pace with inflation.

The third bucket, often called the "growth bucket," is invested in a diversified mix of assets with a longer time horizon, typically ten years or more. This bucket aims to provide long-term growth potential to replenish the other buckets and maintain the overall sustainability of your retirement income. Assets in this bucket may include a mix of stocks, mutual funds, exchange-traded funds (ETFs), and real estate investment trusts (REITs) that align with your risk tolerance and investment goals.

By segmenting your retirement assets into these distinct buckets, you can create a more structured and manageable approach to generating income. As you draw from the cash bucket for your immediate needs, you can periodically refill it with funds from the income and growth buckets, maintaining a steady flow of income throughout retirement.

Another important consideration when creating a retirement income stream is the order in which you withdraw from your various retirement accounts. Generally, it's recommended to withdraw from taxable accounts first, followed by tax-deferred accounts (such as traditional IRAs and 401(k)s), and finally, tax-free accounts like Roth IRAs. This sequence allows you to benefit from the tax-deferred growth in your retirement accounts for as long as possible while minimizing your annual tax burden.

In addition to the bucket strategy and withdrawal sequence, there are several other methods for converting your retirement savings into income, such as:

1. Systematic withdrawals: This approach involves withdrawing a

fixed percentage or dollar amount from your retirement portfolio each year, adjusting for inflation over time. The 4% rule, discussed in the previous subsection, is an example of a systematic withdrawal strategy.

2. Annuities: Annuities are insurance products that can provide a guaranteed income stream for a specified period or for the remainder of your life. There are various types of annuities, such as fixed, variable, and indexed, each with its own features and benefits. While annuities can offer a sense of security, they may come with higher fees and less flexibility compared to other income strategies.

3. Dividend-paying investments: Building a portfolio of dividend-paying stocks, bonds, or mutual funds can provide a regular income stream while potentially offering some growth to keep pace with inflation. However, it's essential to carefully select investments and diversify your portfolio to manage risk.

4. Rental income: For retirees who own rental properties, the income generated from these investments can be a valuable source of retirement income. However, being a landlord comes with its own set of responsibilities and challenges, such as property maintenance, tenant management, and potential vacancies.

5. Part-time work or consulting: Some retirees may choose to continue working part-time or offer their expertise as consultants in their former fields. This can provide a supplemental income stream while allowing for greater flexibility and work-life balance in retirement.

Creating a retirement income stream requires careful planning, ongoing management, and the flexibility to adapt to changing circumstances. It's essential to regularly review your income strategy, assess your spending and lifestyle needs, and make adjustments as necessary to ensure the long-term sustainability of your retirement income. Working with a financial advisor can help you develop a personalized income plan that aligns with your unique goals and circumstances, providing the guidance and support you need to navigate the complexities of retirement income planning.

Subsection 6.3: The Role of Social Security Benefits

For many retirees, Social Security benefits form a crucial component of their retirement income. These benefits, earned through years of paying into the Social Security system during your working life, can provide a reliable foundation for your retirement income strategy. However, navigating the complexities of Social Security can be challenging, and understanding how these benefits work is essential to maximizing their potential and integrating them into your overall retirement income plan.

At its core, Social Security is a social insurance program designed to provide a basic level of income for retirees, as well as disability and survivor benefits for eligible individuals and their families. The amount of your Social Security benefit is based on your earnings history, with higher lifetime earnings generally translating to higher benefits in retirement.

One of the most critical decisions you'll face when it comes to Social Security is when to start claiming your benefits. While you can begin receiving benefits as early as age 62, doing so will result in a permanently reduced monthly payment. On the other hand, delaying your benefits past your full retirement age (which varies based on your birth year) will result in a higher monthly payment, thanks to delayed retirement credits.

For example, if your full retirement age is 67 and you start claiming benefits at 62, your monthly payment will be reduced by about 30%. Conversely, if you wait until age 70 to start claiming, your monthly benefit will be about 24% higher than it would be at your full retirement age.

Deciding when to claim Social Security benefits is a highly personal choice that depends on factors such as your health, life expectancy, other sources of retirement income, and your overall financial goals. Some retirees may benefit from claiming early if they need the income right away or have health concerns that may limit their lifespan. Others may find that delaying benefits is a smart move, particularly if they have other sources of income to rely on in the meantime and want to maximize their monthly payments later in retirement.

In addition to timing your benefits, it's important to understand how Social Security fits into your overall retirement income strategy. While Social Security can provide a valuable base of income, it's rarely sufficient to fund a comfortable retirement on its own. As a result, you'll likely need to supplement your Social Security benefits with other sources of income, such as pension payments, retirement account withdrawals, and investment income.

One strategy to consider is the "Social Security bridge," which involves using other sources of income to delay claiming Social Security benefits until a later age. For example, if you retire at 65 but want to wait until 70 to start claiming Social Security, you could rely on withdrawals from your 401(k) or IRA to bridge the gap and provide income in the meantime. This approach can help you maximize your Social Security benefits while still ensuring a steady stream of income throughout retirement.

It's also worth noting that Social Security benefits are subject to taxes, depending on your overall income level. If your combined income (which includes your adjusted gross income, nontaxable interest, and half of your Social Security benefits) exceeds certain thresholds, you may owe taxes on up to 85% of your benefits. This is an important consideration when planning your retirement income strategy, as taxes can take a significant bite out of your overall income.

To navigate the complexities of Social Security and make informed decisions about claiming your benefits, it's often helpful to work with a financial advisor who specializes in retirement income planning. They can help you understand your options, assess your unique financial situation, and develop a claiming strategy that aligns with your overall retirement income goals.

In summary, Social Security benefits play a vital role in many retirees' income strategies, providing a reliable foundation of income that can be supplemented with other sources. Understanding how these benefits work, when to claim them, and how they fit into your overall financial picture is crucial to making the most of this valuable resource and ensuring a secure, comfortable retirement.

Subsection 6.4: Managing Taxes in Retirement

As you transition into retirement, tax planning becomes an integral part of managing your finances. While you may have less income in retirement, that doesn't necessarily mean you'll have a lower tax bill. In fact, without proper planning, taxes can take a significant bite out of your retirement savings. However, by understanding the tax implications of your retirement income sources and implementing smart tax minimization strategies, you can keep more of your hard-earned money and enjoy a more financially secure retirement.

One of the first steps in managing taxes in retirement is to understand how your various income sources are taxed. For example, withdrawals from traditional IRAs and 401(k)s are generally taxed as ordinary income, while Roth IRA withdrawals are tax-free if you meet certain criteria. Social Security benefits may also be taxable, depending on your overall income level. Pension payments, rental income, and investment income each have their own tax treatment, which can impact your overall tax liability.

To minimize your tax burden in retirement, consider implementing the following strategies:

1. Diversify your retirement accounts: By having a mix of taxable, tax-deferred, and tax-free accounts (such as Roth IRAs), you can create a more tax-efficient withdrawal strategy. For example, you might withdraw from taxable accounts first, followed by tax-deferred accounts, and finally, tax-free accounts to minimize your annual tax liability.
2. Consider Roth conversions: If you have significant assets in traditional IRAs or 401(k)s, converting a portion of these funds to a Roth IRA can help reduce your future tax burden. While

you'll owe taxes on the converted amount in the year of the conversion, future withdrawals from the Roth IRA will be tax-free. This strategy can be particularly beneficial if you expect to be in a higher tax bracket in retirement.

3. Take advantage of tax deductions: Even in retirement, there may be deductions you can claim to reduce your taxable income. For example, if you have significant medical expenses, you may be able to deduct the portion that exceeds 7.5% of your adjusted gross income. Charitable contributions and certain business expenses (if you have self-employment income) may also be deductible.

4. Manage your required minimum distributions (RMDs): Once you reach age 72 (or 70½ if you reached that age before January 1, 2020), you must start taking RMDs from your traditional IRAs and 401(k)s. Failing to take your RMD or taking less than the required amount can result in a hefty 50% penalty. To minimize the tax impact of RMDs, consider strategies such as charitable giving through qualified charitable distributions (QCDs) or reinvesting the after-tax portion of your RMD in a taxable account.

5. Consider tax-efficient investing: When it comes to your taxable investment accounts, choosing investments that generate less taxable income can help reduce your overall tax bill. For example, long-term capital gains and qualified dividends are taxed at a lower rate than ordinary income. Municipal bonds, which are issued by state and local governments, may offer tax-free interest at the federal level (and sometimes at the state level, too).

6. Plan your state residency: If you're considering relocating in retirement, be aware that state tax laws vary widely. Some states have no income tax, while others tax retirement income differently than the federal government. Researching the tax implications of your potential retirement destinations can help you make a more informed decision and potentially save on taxes.

7. Work with a tax professional: Navigating the complex world of taxes in retirement can be overwhelming. Working with a

qualified tax professional who specializes in retirement planning can help you develop a personalized tax strategy that minimizes your tax liability and ensures you're taking advantage of all available deductions and credits.

Remember, tax planning in retirement is an ongoing process. As tax laws change and your financial situation evolves, it's essential to review and adjust your strategies regularly. By staying proactive and informed, you can make the most of your retirement income and enjoy the financial freedom you've worked so hard to achieve.

Summary: Crafting Your Retirement Income Strategy

Retirement income planning is a critical aspect of ensuring a comfortable and financially secure future. By understanding the various strategies and considerations involved in generating and managing income in retirement, you can create a personalized plan that aligns with your unique goals and circumstances.

The 4% rule and safe withdrawal rates provide a helpful starting point for determining how much you can comfortably withdraw from your retirement savings each year. However, it's essential to consider your individual situation and work with a financial advisor to develop a withdrawal strategy that balances your income needs with the long-term sustainability of your assets.

Creating a diversified retirement income stream, such as through the bucket strategy or a combination of investments, annuities, and other income sources, can help you maintain a steady flow of funds while minimizing the risk of outliving your savings. By carefully managing your assets and implementing tax-efficient withdrawal strategies, you can optimize your retirement income and make the most of your hard-earned nest egg.

Social Security benefits play a vital role in many retirees' income plans, providing a reliable foundation that can be supplemented with other income sources. Understanding how these benefits work, when to claim them, and how they integrate with your overall financial picture is crucial to maximizing their potential and ensuring a secure retirement.

Finally, managing taxes in retirement is an ongoing process that requires proactive planning and strategic decision-making. By diversifying your retirement accounts, considering Roth conversions, and working with a tax professional, you can minimize your tax liability and keep more of your money working for you in retirement.

As you embark on this new chapter of life, remember that retirement income planning is not a one-time event, but rather a continuous journey of adaptation and growth. By staying informed, proactive, and open to new strategies and opportunities, you can navigate the challenges and rewards of retirement with confidence and peace of mind. With a well-crafted retirement income plan in place, you can enjoy the financial freedom and security you've worked so hard to achieve, and truly make the most of your golden years.

Section 7: Retirement Lifestyle Considerations

Imagine waking up each morning with a sense of freedom and excitement, knowing that the day ahead is yours to shape as you please. This is the essence of retirement – a time when you can finally pursue your passions, spend quality time with loved ones, and enjoy the fruits of your lifelong labor. However, creating a fulfilling retirement lifestyle involves more than just financial planning. It requires a holistic approach that encompasses various non-financial aspects, such as housing, healthcare, personal growth, and leisure activities.

In this section, we will explore the key lifestyle considerations that can make your retirement years truly golden. From choosing the ideal living arrangement to staying engaged and purposeful, we'll provide insights and guidance to help you navigate this exciting new chapter of your life. Whether you envision yourself downsizing to a cozy cottage, embarking on world travels, or dedicating time to volunteer work, the choices you make will shape the quality of your retirement experience.

As we delve into these non-financial aspects of retirement planning, remember that the ultimate goal is to create a lifestyle that aligns with your values, interests, and aspirations. By taking a proactive approach and considering these factors early on, you can lay the foundation for a retirement that is not only financially secure but also emotionally fulfilling and personally meaningful. So, let's embark on this journey together and discover how to make your retirement years the best years of your life.

Subsection 7.1: Housing and Living Arrangements

As you enter retirement, one of the most significant decisions you'll face is where and how to live. Your housing and living arrangements can greatly impact your quality of life, financial well-being, and overall happiness in your golden years. It's essential to consider your unique needs, preferences, and budget when exploring the various options available to you.

One popular choice among retirees is downsizing. After years of maintaining a large family home, many find that a smaller, more manageable space is both practical and liberating. Downsizing can help you reduce expenses, simplify your lifestyle, and free up equity for other retirement goals. Whether you opt for a cozy apartment, a compact house, or a senior living community, downsizing can offer a sense of freedom and a fresh start.

Another option to consider is aging in place. If you have a strong emotional attachment to your current home or neighborhood, you may prefer to stay put. However, it's crucial to assess whether your home is suitable for your changing needs as you age. You may need to make modifications, such as installing grab bars, widening doorways, or adding ramps, to ensure your safety and comfort. Additionally, consider the ongoing maintenance and upkeep costs associated with remaining in your home.

For those seeking a more carefree lifestyle, senior living communities can be an attractive choice. These communities offer a range of housing options, from independent living apartments to assisted living facilities, catering to various levels of care and support. They often provide amenities such as housekeeping, dining services, transportation, and social activities, fostering a sense of community and convenience. However, it's important to carefully research and compare different communities to find one that aligns with your values, interests, and budget.

Some retirees may also consider relocating to a new city or state. Factors such as cost of living, climate, proximity to family and friends, and access to healthcare and recreational activities can influence this decision. Relocating can offer a fresh perspective, new experiences, and potentially lower living expenses. However, it's essential to thoroughly research potential destinations, considering both the financial and emotional implications of a move.

Ultimately, the key to finding the ideal housing and living arrangement in retirement is to assess your unique needs and priorities. Take the time to explore your options, crunch the numbers, and have honest conversations with your loved ones. By carefully considering your lifestyle preferences, financial situation, and long-term goals, you can make an informed decision that sets the stage for a fulfilling and comfortable retirement.

Subsection 7.2: Healthcare and Long-Term Care Planning

As you enter your retirement years, one of the most critical aspects of your overall planning is ensuring that you have adequate healthcare coverage and a solid strategy for potential long-term care needs. While it's not pleasant to think about the possibility of declining health or needing assistance with daily activities, failing to plan for these eventualities can have severe financial and emotional consequences.

Healthcare costs have been rising steadily over the years, and they show no signs of slowing down. Even with Medicare coverage, retirees can face significant out-of-pocket expenses for premiums, deductibles, copayments, and uncovered services. It's essential to understand the various parts of Medicare, including Part A (hospital insurance), Part B (medical insurance), Part C (Medicare Advantage plans), and Part D (prescription drug coverage). You may also want to consider purchasing supplemental insurance, such as a Medigap policy, to help cover the gaps in Medicare coverage.

In addition to ongoing healthcare expenses, it's crucial to plan for the possibility of needing long-term care. Long-term care refers to a range of services and support that help individuals with chronic illnesses, disabilities, or cognitive impairments perform activities of daily living, such as bathing, dressing, and eating. These services can be provided in various settings, including at home, in assisted living facilities, or in nursing homes.

The costs of long-term care can be staggering, with the median annual cost of a private room in a nursing home exceeding $100,000 in many parts of the United States. Unfortunately, Medicare does not cover most long-term care expenses, leaving retirees to find alternative ways to pay for these services. Some options to consider include long-term care insurance, self-funding through savings and investments, or relying on Medicaid if you exhaust your personal resources.

When planning for healthcare and long-term care needs, it's essential to start early and be proactive. Consider the following steps:

1. Educate yourself about Medicare and its various parts, as well as the costs associated with each.
2. Research and compare supplemental insurance options, such as Medigap policies or Medicare Advantage plans, to determine which best fits your needs and budget.
3. Investigate long-term care insurance options, including traditional policies, hybrid policies that combine life insurance with long-term care benefits, and state partnership programs that offer asset protection.
4. Assess your personal risk factors for needing long-term care, such as family history, chronic health conditions, and lifestyle choices, and factor these into your planning.
5. Have open and honest conversations with your family members

about your preferences for care and how you plan to pay for it, to ensure everyone is on the same page.

6. Consider working with a financial advisor who specializes in retirement planning and can help you develop a comprehensive strategy for managing healthcare and long-term care costs.

By taking a proactive approach to healthcare and long-term care planning, you can help protect your financial security and ensure that you have access to the care you need in your retirement years. While it may not be the most pleasant topic to think about, having a solid plan in place can provide peace of mind and allow you to focus on enjoying your well-earned retirement lifestyle.

Subsection 7.3: Staying Engaged and Purposeful in Retirement

Retirement is not the end of the road, but rather the beginning of a new chapter filled with endless opportunities for personal growth, fulfillment, and joy. While the freedom from the daily grind of work can be exhilarating, it's essential to find ways to stay engaged and maintain a sense of purpose in this new phase of life. Without the structure and routine of a job, some retirees may find themselves feeling lost, bored, or even depressed. However, by actively seeking out meaningful activities and pursuits, you can ensure that your retirement years are not only enjoyable but also deeply satisfying.

One of the keys to staying engaged in retirement is to explore your passions and interests. Take some time to reflect on the hobbies, skills, or causes that have always piqued your curiosity but perhaps took a backseat during your working years. Whether it's learning a new language, taking up painting, or volunteering for a local charity, pursuing your passions can provide a sense of excitement and purpose. Engaging in activities that challenge you mentally, physically, or creatively can help keep your mind sharp, your body active, and your spirit invigorated.

Another way to find fulfillment in retirement is to connect with others and build meaningful social relationships. Loneliness and isolation can be significant challenges for retirees, especially if they've relied heavily on workplace interactions for social connection. Seek out opportunities to meet new people who share your interests, such as joining a club, attending community events, or taking classes. Nurturing existing relationships with family and friends is equally important. Make an effort to stay in touch, plan regular get-togethers, and offer support and companionship to loved ones.

Volunteering is another excellent way to stay engaged and make a positive impact in your community. Giving back not only benefits others but also provides a sense of purpose and fulfillment. Consider sharing your skills, knowledge, and experience with organizations that align with your values and interests. Whether it's mentoring young people, assisting at a local food bank, or participating in environmental conservation efforts, volunteering can be a deeply rewarding way to spend your time and make a difference in the world.

For some retirees, staying engaged may involve pursuing new educational opportunities or even embarking on a second career. The concept of "encore careers" has gained popularity in recent years, with many retirees choosing to start new ventures or pursue work that aligns with their passions and values. This could involve starting a small business, consulting in your area of expertise, or turning a hobby into a profitable endeavor. Pursuing new learning opportunities, such as taking courses at a local college or university, can also provide intellectual stimulation and a sense of personal growth.

Ultimately, the key to staying engaged and purposeful in retirement is to be proactive and intentional about how you spend your time. Rather than viewing retirement as a time to simply relax and wind down, approach it as an opportunity to explore new horizons, pursue your passions, and make meaningful contributions to the world around you. By staying curious, connected, and committed to personal growth, you can ensure that your retirement years are not only enjoyable but also deeply fulfilling.

Subsection 7.4: Traveling and Leisure in Retirement

Retirement opens up a world of possibilities for travel and leisure, allowing you to explore new destinations, immerse yourself in different cultures, and pursue the hobbies and activities that bring you joy. With more free time and potentially fewer responsibilities, retirement can be the perfect opportunity to embark on the adventures you've always dreamed of.

One of the most exciting aspects of retirement travel is the freedom to plan trips on your own schedule, without the constraints of limited vacation days or work obligations. Whether you prefer short weekend getaways or extended international journeys, you have the flexibility to craft your travel experiences to suit your preferences and interests.

To make the most of your travel opportunities in retirement, consider creating a bucket list of destinations and experiences you'd like to prioritize. This could include visiting iconic landmarks, exploring natural wonders, or immersing yourself in the local culture of a far-off land. By setting clear travel goals and aspirations, you can ensure that you make the most of your retirement years and create lasting memories.

When planning your retirement travels, it's essential to consider your budget and find ways to stretch your funds without compromising on the quality of your experiences. One strategy is to take advantage of off-peak travel seasons, when prices for flights, accommodations, and activities may be lower. You can also explore alternative lodging options, such as vacation rentals or home exchanges, which can offer more space and amenities at a lower cost compared to traditional hotels.

Another way to make travel more affordable in retirement is to leverage travel rewards programs, such as credit card points or airline miles. By strategically using these programs and accumulating rewards over time, you can potentially offset the cost of flights, hotels, or other travel expenses, allowing you to travel more frequently or indulge in higher-end experiences.

In addition to traditional leisure travel, retirement can also be an ideal time to pursue educational or volunteer travel opportunities. Many organizations offer specialized travel programs for retirees, such as cultural immersion trips, language learning excursions, or volunteer projects in communities around the world. These experiences can provide a sense of purpose and fulfillment, allowing you to give back while exploring new places and expanding your horizons.

Beyond travel, retirement is also an opportunity to dive deeper into the leisure activities and hobbies that bring you joy and fulfillment. Whether it's golf, gardening, painting, or playing music, having more free time allows you to dedicate yourself to these pursuits and develop your skills and passions. Consider joining local clubs or groups related to your interests, as this can provide a sense of community and shared experience, as well as opportunities for socializing and making new friends.

Retirement can also be a great time to explore new hobbies and activities that you may not have had time for during your working years. This could include learning a new language, taking up a musical instrument, or exploring a new form of artistic expression. By staying open to new experiences and embracing a spirit of lifelong learning, you can ensure that your retirement years are filled with growth, discovery, and personal fulfillment.

Ultimately, the key to enjoying travel and leisure in retirement is to be intentional about how you spend your time and resources. By setting clear goals, creating a budget, and staying open to new experiences, you can make the most of this exciting chapter in your life and create lasting memories that bring you joy and satisfaction. Whether it's exploring far-off lands, pursuing your passions, or simply savoring the freedom to do what you love, retirement can be a time of incredible richness and fulfillment.

Summary: Embracing a Fulfilling Retirement Lifestyle

As we conclude this section on retirement lifestyle considerations, it's clear that creating a fulfilling retirement goes beyond just financial planning.

It's about embracing a holistic approach that encompasses the various non-financial aspects of your life, from housing and healthcare to personal growth and leisure activities.

Throughout this section, we've explored the importance of making informed decisions about your living arrangements, whether it's downsizing, aging in place, or opting for a senior living community. We've also discussed the critical role of healthcare and long-term care planning in protecting your well-being and financial security in retirement.

Moreover, we've emphasized the value of staying engaged and purposeful in retirement, whether through pursuing your passions, volunteering, or building meaningful social connections. By actively seeking out activities that bring you joy and fulfillment, you can ensure that your retirement years are rich with personal growth and satisfaction.

Finally, we've highlighted the exciting opportunities for travel and leisure in retirement, from exploring new destinations to diving deeper into your favorite hobbies. By being intentional about how you spend your time and resources, you can create lasting memories and find true enjoyment in this new chapter of your life.

As you move forward in your retirement planning journey, remember that the ultimate goal is to create a lifestyle that aligns with your unique values, interests, and aspirations. By taking a proactive and holistic approach to retirement planning, you can lay the foundation for a retirement that is not only financially secure but also emotionally fulfilling and personally meaningful.

So, embrace this opportunity to design a retirement lifestyle that brings you joy, purpose, and satisfaction. With careful consideration and planning, you can make your retirement years the best years of your life, filled with endless possibilities for growth, adventure, and happiness.

Section 8: Seeking Professional Advice

Navigating the complex world of personal finance can be overwhelming, especially when it comes to securing your financial future. While this book aims to provide you with a solid foundation and practical strategies for retirement planning, there may be times when seeking professional advice is not only beneficial but necessary. Just as you would consult a doctor for medical concerns or a lawyer for legal matters, working with a qualified financial professional can offer valuable guidance and support tailored to your unique circumstances.

Many people hesitate to seek professional advice, often due to concerns about cost, trust, or the belief that they can handle everything on their own. However, the right financial advisor can save you time, help you avoid costly mistakes, and provide objective insights to optimize your retirement plan. They can assist you in making informed decisions, adapting to life changes, and staying on track to achieve your long-term goals.

In this section, we will explore the importance of seeking professional advice and how to find the right financial advisor for your needs. We'll discuss the different types of financial professionals, the services they offer, and the key qualities to look for in a trusted advisor. Additionally, we'll provide guidance on preparing for retirement planning consultations and the importance of ongoing plan reviews and adjustments.

By understanding when and how to seek professional advice, you can take a proactive approach to your retirement planning and benefit from the expertise of experienced financial professionals. With the right support and guidance, you can navigate the challenges and opportunities of retirement with greater confidence and peace of mind.

Subsection 8.1: Identifying the Right Financial Advisor

When it comes to selecting a financial advisor, it's crucial to find someone who is not only qualified but also trustworthy and compatible with your unique needs and goals. The right financial advisor can make a significant difference in your retirement planning journey, providing valuable guidance, support, and expertise to help you navigate the complexities of personal finance.

To begin your search, start by assessing your own needs and preferences. Consider factors such as your current financial situation, long-term goals, risk tolerance, and communication style. Having a clear understanding of what you're looking for in an advisor will help you narrow down your options and find the best fit.

One of the first things to look for in a financial advisor is proper credentials and qualifications. Look for professionals who hold recognized certifications such as Certified Financial Planner (CFP), Chartered Financial Analyst (CFA), or Certified Public Accountant (CPA). These designations indicate that the advisor has met rigorous education, experience, and ethical requirements in their field.

In addition to credentials, consider the advisor's experience and area of expertise. Ideally, you want to work with someone who has a proven track record of helping clients with similar needs and goals to yours. Don't hesitate to ask for references or case studies that demonstrate their ability to deliver results.

Another important factor to consider is the advisor's compensation structure. Some advisors charge a flat fee for their services, while others earn commissions based on the products they sell or a percentage of assets under management. Fee-only advisors are often preferred, as they have fewer potential conflicts of interest and are more likely to provide unbiased advice.

When evaluating potential advisors, pay attention to their communication style and approach to client relationships. You want to work with someone who takes the time to understand your unique circumstances, listens to your concerns, and explains complex concepts in a way that you can easily understand. Look for advisors who are responsive, proactive, and committed to your success.

Finally, trust your instincts and choose an advisor who you feel comfortable with on a personal level. Retirement planning is a long-term partnership, and it's essential to have open, honest communication and a strong working relationship with your advisor. Schedule an initial consultation to get a sense of their personality, values, and approach to financial planning.

By taking the time to identify the right financial advisor for your needs, you can ensure that you have a trusted partner on your side as you work towards a secure and fulfilling retirement. Remember, the right advisor is not just a financial expert, but also a coach, mentor, and advocate for your success.

Subsection 8.2: Preparing for Retirement Planning Consultations

Preparing for retirement planning consultations is a crucial step in ensuring that you make the most of your time with a financial advisor. By gathering the necessary information and formulating relevant questions in advance, you can have more productive and meaningful discussions about your retirement goals and strategies.

Before your consultation, take the time to assess your current financial situation and future aspirations. Gather important documents such as recent statements from your bank accounts, investment portfolios, retirement plans, and insurance policies. Having a clear picture of your assets, liabilities, income, and expenses will provide a solid foundation for your discussions with the advisor.

In addition to financial documents, consider your personal goals and expectations for retirement. Think about the lifestyle you envision, the activities you want to pursue, and the legacy you wish to leave behind. Reflect on your risk tolerance, investment preferences, and any specific concerns or challenges you face in your financial life. Having a well-defined set of goals and priorities will help guide your conversations and ensure that the advisor's recommendations align with your values and aspirations.

To make the most of your consultation, prepare a list of questions that address your key concerns and knowledge gaps. Consider asking about the advisor's experience, investment philosophy, and approach to retirement planning. Inquire about their strategies for managing risk, optimizing tax efficiency, and generating reliable income streams in retirement. Don't hesitate to ask for clarification on any concepts or recommendations that you don't fully understand.

Other important questions to ask may include:

- What services do you offer, and how can you help me achieve my retirement goals?

- How do you tailor your advice to my unique circumstances and risk tolerance?

- What are the potential challenges and opportunities in my current retirement plan?

- How can I optimize my savings and investments to maximize growth and minimize taxes?

- What strategies do you recommend for generating income in retirement?

- How can I ensure that my retirement plan remains flexible and adaptable to changing circumstances?

- What steps can I take to protect my assets and ensure a lasting legacy for my loved ones?

Remember, a retirement planning consultation is a two-way conversation. While the advisor brings expertise and guidance to the table, you are the ultimate decision-maker in your financial life. Don't be afraid to ask questions, challenge assumptions, and express your preferences and concerns. The more openly and honestly you communicate with your advisor, the better they can understand your needs and provide personalized recommendations.

Finally, approach your retirement planning consultations with an open mind and a willingness to learn. While you may have preconceived notions about certain strategies or products, be receptive to new ideas and perspectives. A skilled financial advisor can offer valuable insights and help you explore options that you may not have considered before.

By thoroughly preparing for your retirement planning consultations, you can foster a productive and collaborative relationship with your financial advisor. With the right information, questions, and mindset, you can work together to develop a comprehensive and personalized retirement plan that helps you achieve your goals and secure your financial future.

Subsection 8.3: Ongoing Retirement Plan Reviews and Adjustments

Retirement planning is not a one-time event, but rather an ongoing process that requires regular reviews and adjustments. Just as your life and circumstances change over time, so too should your retirement plan adapt to ensure that it remains aligned with your goals, risk tolerance, and financial realities. Regularly reviewing and updating your plan with the guidance of a professional advisor is crucial for staying on track and making informed decisions throughout your retirement journey.

One of the primary reasons for ongoing plan reviews is to account for changes in your personal life that may impact your retirement goals or strategies. Major life events such as marriage, divorce, the birth of a child, or the loss of a loved one can significantly alter your financial priorities and needs. Similarly, changes in your health, career, or living situation may require adjustments to your retirement plan to ensure that it remains feasible and relevant.

Another important aspect of ongoing plan reviews is monitoring the performance of your investments and making necessary adjustments to your portfolio. Over time, market conditions, economic factors, and individual investment returns can cause your asset allocation to drift away from your intended targets. By regularly reviewing your investment mix with your advisor, you can ensure that your portfolio remains properly diversified and aligned with your risk tolerance and long-term objectives. Rebalancing your investments periodically can help maintain the appropriate level of risk and potentially enhance your returns over the long run.

In addition to personal and investment-related factors, ongoing plan reviews also allow you to stay informed about changes in laws, regulations, and financial products that may impact your retirement strategies. Tax laws, pension rules, and government benefits programs can undergo significant changes over time, and it's essential to understand how these updates may affect your retirement income and distribution plans. Your financial advisor can help you navigate these changes and make necessary adjustments to optimize your plan within the current legal and financial landscape.

Regular plan reviews also provide an opportunity to assess your progress towards your retirement goals and make course corrections if needed. By comparing your current savings and investment balances to your projected retirement income needs, you can determine whether you are on track or if additional steps are required to close any gaps. Your advisor can help you explore strategies such as increasing your savings rate, adjusting your investment mix, or considering alternative income sources to ensure that you remain on a sustainable path towards a secure retirement.

When conducting plan reviews, it's important to approach the process with an open and collaborative mindset. Be prepared to share any changes in your personal or financial circumstances with your advisor, and be receptive to their insights and recommendations. Remember that your advisor is there to provide objective guidance and support, and their expertise can be invaluable in helping you make informed decisions and navigate the complexities of retirement planning.

The frequency of plan reviews may vary depending on your individual needs and circumstances, but it's generally recommended to meet with your advisor at least annually or whenever significant life changes occur. These regular check-ins provide an opportunity to assess your progress, discuss any concerns or challenges, and make proactive adjustments to keep your retirement plan on track.

In conclusion, ongoing retirement plan reviews and adjustments are essential for ensuring that your plan remains dynamic, flexible, and responsive to your changing needs and circumstances. By working closely with a trusted financial advisor and regularly assessing your progress, you can make informed decisions, adapt to new realities, and maintain a clear path towards a secure and fulfilling retirement. Embrace the process of ongoing review and adjustment as a vital part of your retirement planning journey, and you'll be well-positioned to achieve your goals and enjoy the retirement lifestyle you envision.

Summary: Partnering with a Trusted Advisor for Retirement Success

Seeking professional advice is a crucial component of a comprehensive retirement planning strategy. By partnering with a qualified and trusted financial advisor, you gain access to valuable expertise, objective guidance, and personalized recommendations that can help you navigate the complexities of retirement planning with greater confidence and clarity.

Throughout this section, we've explored the importance of identifying the right financial advisor for your needs, preparing for productive retirement planning consultations, and engaging in ongoing plan reviews and adjustments. By taking a proactive and collaborative approach to working with a professional advisor, you can ensure that your retirement plan remains aligned with your goals, adapts to changing circumstances, and maximizes your chances of achieving a secure and fulfilling retirement.

Remember, the right financial advisor is not just a source of technical expertise, but also a partner in your journey towards retirement success. By fostering open communication, trust, and a shared commitment to your financial well-being, you can build a lasting relationship that supports your goals and empowers you to make informed decisions at every stage of your retirement planning process.

As you move forward in your retirement planning journey, embrace the value of professional guidance and make seeking advice an integral part of your strategy. With the right advisor by your side, you'll be well-equipped to overcome challenges, seize opportunities, and create the retirement lifestyle you've always envisioned. The path to retirement success is rarely a solo journey, but with the support and expertise of a trusted financial advisor, you can navigate the road ahead with greater clarity, confidence, and peace of mind.

Chapter Summary: Securing Your Financial Future Through Retirement Planning

Retirement planning is a crucial aspect of your overall financial journey, and taking proactive steps to secure your financial future is essential for a comfortable and fulfilling retirement. By understanding the importance of retirement planning, setting clear goals, and implementing effective strategies, you can navigate the challenges and opportunities that come with this significant life transition.

Throughout this chapter, we have explored the various facets of retirement planning, from determining your unique retirement objectives to maximizing your savings and investments. We have discussed the different retirement savings vehicles available, such as employer-sponsored plans, IRAs, and annuities, and provided guidance on how to optimize your contributions and investment choices.

Moreover, we have emphasized the importance of creating a comprehensive retirement income plan, considering factors such as safe withdrawal rates, Social Security benefits, and tax management. By diversifying your income sources and adapting your strategies as you approach retirement, you can ensure a stable and lasting financial foundation.

Beyond the financial aspects, we have also addressed the lifestyle considerations that come with retirement, such as housing, healthcare, and staying engaged and purposeful. By taking a holistic approach to retirement planning and seeking professional advice when needed, you can make informed decisions and enjoy a fulfilling retirement that aligns with your values and aspirations.

Remember, retirement planning is an ongoing process that requires regular review and adjustment as your circumstances and goals evolve. By staying proactive, informed, and committed to your financial well-being, you can look forward to a secure and rewarding retirement.

As you continue your financial journey, keep the lessons and strategies from this chapter in mind, and take confident steps towards securing your financial future. With careful planning and dedication, you can turn your retirement dreams into a reality and enjoy the fruits of your lifelong efforts.